Creating a Business Plan

FOR

DUMMIES

A Wiley Brand

Creating a Business Plan

FOR DUMMIES®

A Wiley Brand

by Veechi Curtis

FOR DUMMIES®
A Wiley Brand

Creating a Business Plan For Dummies®

Published by
Wiley Publishing Australia Pty Ltd
42 McDougall Street
Milton, Qld 4064
www.dummies.com

Copyright © 2014 Wiley Publishing Australia Pty Ltd

The moral rights of the author have been asserted.

National Library of Australia
Cataloguing-in-Publication data:

Autho:	Curtis, Veechi
Title:	Creating a Business Plan For Dummies / Veechi Curtis
ISBN:	9781118641224 (pbk.)
	9781118641255 (ebook)
Notes:	Includes index
Subjects:	Business planning
Dewey Number:	658.4012

Cover image: © iStockphoto.com/alphaspirit

Typeset by diacriTech, Chennai, India

10 9 8 7 6 5 4 3 2 1

Contents at a Glance

Introduction 1

Part I: Getting Started 7

Chapter 1: Letting Your Plan Take Flight 9
Chapter 2: Figuring Out What's So Special about You (and Your Business) 27
Chapter 3: Sizing up the Competition 39

Part II: Doing the Groundwork 57

Chapter 4: Budgeting for Start-Up Expenses 59
Chapter 5: Figuring out Prices and Predicting Sales 77
Chapter 6: Calculating Costs and Gross Profit 97
Chapter 7: Planning for Expenses 119

Part III: Checking Your Idea Makes Financial Sense... 145

Chapter 8: Assembling Your Profit & Loss Projection....................................147
Chapter 9: Calculating Your Break-Even Point 169
Chapter 10: Creating Cashflows and Building Budgets 179

Part IV: Transforming Your Idea into Reality 199

Chapter 11: Separating Yourself from Your Business.....................................201
Chapter 12: Developing a Strong Marketing Plan 219
Chapter 13: Staying One Step Ahead..243
Chapter 14: Managing Risk 259
Chapter 15: Pulling Together Your Written Plan 275

Part V: The Part of Tens 295

Chapter 16: Ten Tips for Using Excel in Your Business Plan............................297
Chapter 17: Ten Ideas for a Well-Presented Plan 309
Chapter 18: Ten Questions to Ask before You're Done 319
Appendix: Sample Business Plan 327

Index 349

Table of Contents

Introduction 1

About This Book 2
Foolish Assumptions 2
Icons Used in This Book 3
Beyond the Book 4
Where to Go from Here 4

Part I: Getting Started 7

Chapter 1: Letting Your Plan Take Flight 9

Getting Your Feet Wet and Having Fun 10
    Deciding who this plan is for 10
    Choosing your dance partners 11
    Looking at different online planning tools 12
Scoping the Nature of Your Plan 14
    Structuring your plan 14
    Setting aside enough time 15
    Deciding how far into the future you want to go 18
Understanding Why Your Plan Needs Constant Love and Attention 18
    Going for rhythm with financial planning 19
    Keeping everything on track with your marketing cycle 21
Conjuring Up a One-Page Business Plan 22
Scoring Your Business out of 10 25

Chapter 2: Figuring Out What's So Special about You (and Your Business) 27

Understanding Strategic Advantage 28
    Looking at examples of strategic advantage 28
    Focusing on real-life examples 30
Understanding How Risk Relates to Gain 31
Justifying Why You Can Succeed 32
    Uncovering your inner mojo 32
    Asking three key questions for each of your advantages 33
    Rating how you score 34
Developing Your Strategic Advantage Statement 35
    Drafting your statement 35
    Growing your advantages over time 36
    Making sure a demand really exists 37
Looking Around for More Ideas 37

Chapter 3: Sizing up the Competition **39**

Why Analysing Competitors Is a Big Deal 40
Figuring Out Who Your Competitors Really Are 41
Organising competitors into groups 41
Homing in on head-to-head competitors 42
Thinking about future competitors 43
Engaging in Cloak-and-Dagger Tactics 45
Doing a competitor profile 45
Mirror, mirror on the wall 46
Choosing your competitive strategy 48
Matching your competitive strategy to your
strategic advantage 50
Summarising Your Competitive Strategy 50
Joining the dots 50
Measuring up the risks 52
Preparing an Elevator Speech 52
Saying what you do in 30 seconds or less 53
What to avoid with your elevator speech 53
Practice makes perfect 54

Part II: Doing the Groundwork **57**

Chapter 4: Budgeting for Start-Up Expenses **59**

Creating a Start-Up Budget 60
Purchasing materials and inventory 60
Listing your start-up expenses 61
Including expenses paid for out of personal funds 63
Adding enough to live on 63
Separating Start-Up Expenses from Operating Expenses 64
Dealing with initial start-up expenses 65
Putting theory into practice 65
Assessing How Much You Really Need 68
Calculating Likely Loan Repayments 69
Estimating loan repayment schedules 70
Calculating interest 72
Thinking about whether you can really service this loan 72
Understanding Different Finance Options 73
Getting into bed with the bank 73
Offering up collateral 74
Seeking equity partners 75
Borrowing from family 76

Chapter 5: Figuring out Prices and Predicting Sales.............. 77

Choosing a Pricing Strategy 78
  Setting prices based on costs...78
  Setting prices based on competitors 78
  Setting prices based on perceived value 79
Building a Hybrid-Pricing Plan..80
  Offering a premium product or service 80
  Cutting back the frills 81
  Getting creative with packages 82
  Charging different prices for the same thing.................................83
Forming Your Final Plan of Attack...84
Monitoring and Changing Your Price 85
Building Your Sales Forecast...86
  Calculating hours in a working week..86
  Increasing sales with extra labour..88
  Predicting sales for a new business 89
  Predicting sales for an established business 91
Creating Your Month-by-Month Forecast 92

Chapter 6: Calculating Costs and Gross Profit 97

Calculating the Cost of Each Sale 97
  Identifying your variable costs 98
  Costing your service..99
  Costing items that you buy and sell 100
  Adding import costs...101
  Creating product costings for manufacturers.............................102
Understanding Gross Profit...104
  Calculating gross profit 104
  Figuring gross profit margins 105
  Looking at margins over time...106
Analysing Margins for Your Own Business...106
  Calculating margins when you charge by the hour......................107
  Calculating margins when you sell products 108
  Calculating margins if you do big projects 109
Building Your Gross Profit Projection...109
  If you have a service business with no employees and
    no variable costs 110
  If you have a service business and you use employee or
    subcontract labour 110
  If you buy and sell a small number of products..........................112
  If you sell many different products or your variable costs
    are a percentage of sales...114

Chapter 7: Planning for Expenses **119**

Concentrating on Expenses...120
  Separating start-up expenses and variable costs from
    ongoing expenses...120
  Thinking of what expenses to include....................................121
  Building a 12-month projection...124
Finetuning Your Worksheet..127
  Recognising relationships..127
  Allowing for irregular payments 128
  Playing with the 10 per cent rule...128
Staying Real with Benchmarks..128
  Locating benchmarks for your business 129
  Using benchmarks as part of your plan..................................130
Thinking about Taxes and Loan Repayments.......................................133
  Allowing for personal and company tax..................................134
  Understanding where other taxes fit in..................................134
  Dealing with loan repayments and interest.............................135
Factoring Personal Expenses into the Equation..................................135
  Identifying income..136
  Figuring how much you need to live 137
  Setting goals and budgets..142
  Recognising why personal and business budgets connect..........143
  Seeing where you can scrimp and save 144

Part III: Checking Your Idea Makes Financial Sense .. 145

Chapter 8: Assembling Your Profit & Loss Projection **147**

Understanding More About Spreadsheets 148
  Naming worksheets within a single workbook 148
  Linking one worksheet to another...150
  Using names to identify important cells 151
Building Your Profit & Loss Projection 153
  Step one: Insert your projected sales forecasts....................153
  Step two: Bring across variable costs 154
  Step three: Add your expenses budget....................................155
  Step four: Look at the bottom line 158
  Step five: Think about tax 158
  Checking you've got it right..159
Analysing Net Profit..160
  Calculating net profit margins...160
  Assessing whether your net profit is reasonable, or not............160
  Thinking ahead further than 12 months 161
  Looking at your rate of return..162
Measuring Risk and Your Comfort Factor 163

Chapter 9: Calculating Your Break-Even Point 169
Identifying Your Tipping Point 169
Calculating business break-even 170
Factoring personal expenses into the equation 171
Calculating break-even for your business 172
Changing Your Break-Even Point 174
Looking at Things from a Cash Perspective 176

Chapter 10: Creating Cashflows and Building Budgets 179
Understanding Why Cash Is Different from Profit 180
Five reasons your projections may look rosy, but
cash could be tight 180
Five reasons your projections may look grim, but
cash could be flowing 181
Summarising what's Different about a Cashflow Report 182
Looking at Cash Coming In 184
Calculating cash collected versus sales made 184
Thinking about loans and other sources of funds 185
Thinking about Cash Flowing Out 186
Allowing for the purchase of new equipment (or other
start-up items) 186
Looking at payment for stock versus cost of sales 187
Deciding where to show tax payments 188
Factoring in loan repayments 189
Predicting the Bottom Line 190
Setting up a worksheet in Excel 190
Making a pre-emptive strike 191
Calculating sustainable growth 192
Building Your First Budget 193
Allocating budgets in detail 194
Comparing budgets against actuals 195
Creating Balance Sheet Projections 196

Part IV: Transforming Your Idea into Reality 199

Chapter 11: Separating Yourself from Your Business 201
Deciding What Path You Want to Take 202
Doing the thing you love to do 202
Getting help and delegating what you can 204
Building a business that's separate from you 205
Creating a way of doing business 206
Wearing Different Hats 207

Building a Business with a Life of its Own.................................208
    Defining your difference...209
    Documenting and building systems 210
    Setting goals for you and your business......................212
    Planning for a graceful exit 213
Appreciating the Limitations of Your Business 213
Planning for People 215
    Planning for help...215
    Deciding whether to make someone an employee, or not 216
    Calculating the costs of labour 217

Chapter 12: Developing a Strong Marketing Plan **219**
Laying Down the Elements of Your Plan...............................220
    Writing an eloquent introduction 220
    Building a brand that people want 222
Defining Your Target Market...223
    Analysing your customers 224
    Thinking creatively about channels 226
    Researching the market 226
Summarising Your Competitor Analysis 227
Setting Sales Targets 227
    Slicing goals into bite-sized chunks..........................228
    Expressing goals in other ways..................................228
    Getting SMART: Five essential ingredients for
        any goal 229
Creating Strategies to Support Your Targets.......................230
    Making a list of your top ten......................................230
    Creating websites and marketing materials 232
    Planning an advertising strategy 234
    Reaching out to the public 235
    Working your networks...236
Planning For Customer Service 238
Keeping Yourself Honest..239
    Comparing dollar targets against actuals.................240
    Tracking referral sources...241
    Analysing online success 241
    Measuring overall conversion rates..........................242

Chapter 13: Staying One Step Ahead **243**
Taking an Eagle-Eye View..244
    Looking at what's happening in your industry 244
    Responding to industry trends 247
Rating Your Capabilities 248
    Putting yourself through the griller...........................248
    Prioritising where you need to do better 249

Identifying Opportunities and Threats 251
Doing a SWOT Analysis... 253
    Putting theory into practice 253
    Translating your SWOT analysis into action............................ 255
Creating a Plan for Change 256

Chapter 14: Managing Risk............................... 259

Mitigating Financial Risk.. 260
    Maintaining profitability 260
    Guarding against bad debts... 261
    Managing cashflow 262
    Staying on top of stock levels... 263
Protecting Your Intellectual Property 264
    Safeguarding your name, brand and designs 264
    Making sure you're not on someone else's patch..................... 266
    Restricting employees with a view to when they move on 266
Limiting Your Liability... 267
    Choosing a business structure.. 267
    Signing up for insurance 268
Staying on the Right Side of the Law... 270
    Keeping your products safe... 270
    Complying with employment legislation 270
    Ensuring a safe workplace 271
    Understanding planning regulations 272
Deciding What Goes in the Plan... 273

Chapter 15: Pulling Together Your Written Plan................. 275

Reviewing the Overall Structure... 276
Introducing Yourself and Your Business.. 279
    Developing a mission statement.. 279
    Crafting a company description.. 281
    Talking about your values.. 282
Plunging into the Financials 283
    Presenting your key reports.. 283
    Pleading for finance 284
    Adding extra information.. 285
Completing the Rest of Your Plan.. 287
    Selling yourself and your team.. 288
    Providing a quick summary of operations 288
    Introducing the killer marketing plan.. 289
    Explaining how you plan to manage change and risk................ 290
Setting Milestones for Every Step of the Way 290
    Translating your plan into clear goals 291
    Creating a calendar.. 292

Part V: The Part of Tens 295

Chapter 16: Ten Tips for Using Excel in Your Business Plan 297
Get Things to Add Up Automatically 298
Learn to Drag and Copy...299
Format Cells so They Make Sense 300
Freeze Rows and Columns...301
Apply Conditional Highlights 302
Hide Stuff You Don't Need 303
Link One Worksheet to Another 303
Don't Type Values into Formulas..................................304
Spell Out Your Logic..305
Create Graphs and Charts...306

Chapter 17: Ten Ideas for a Well-Presented Plan. 309
Do a Cover Sheet 309
Create a Table of Contents 310
Get Your Financials to Fit...310
Copy Charts into Word 313
Use a Single Font, Keep Text in Black 314
Include a Picture or Two..314
Save Your Plan as a PDF...315
Consider Interactive Elements....................................315
Run a Spell Check 315
Check Language for Simplicity....................................316

Chapter 18: Ten Questions to Ask before You're Done 319
Can You Summarise Your Business in 30 Seconds or Less?................319
Does Your Plan Truly Evaluate Competitors?.........................320
Have You Double-Checked Your Numbers?.............................321
Do Your Numbers Match Your Goals?.................................321
Does Your Plan Play to Your Strengths? 322
Have You Cast Your Net as Wide as Possible? 323
Have You Made Any Assumptions You Can't Justify?....................323
What Do Others Think?...324
Do You Have a Plan for Getting Out?................................324
Is Your Plan Inspirational?..325

Appendix: Sample Business Plan 327

Index 349

Introduction

I grew up in Scotland, where the winters can be wild, wet and cold. My father was a self-employed landscape gardener and each year, as the days grew shorter, he would start hatching entrepreneurial plots to see the family through the scant earnings of the winter months. Handmade garden furniture, barrels from the local brewery scrubbed back and filled with violets, gold-leaf mirror restoration and beach-scavenged scallop shells were but a few of the ill-fated ventures that would transform our Victorian flat into a hive of industry for a few fleeting months of each year.

I started my first business at the age of 26 and have been in business ever since, oscillating in a manner not unlike my father's between the more stable income of business consulting and the somewhat precarious existence of writing and publishing.

Yet when working on this book, I realised something quite fundamental. While I've been steadily successful for more than 20 years, all too often the sensible-cardigan-wearing-accountant side of me wins out against the risk-taking-creative-why-don't-we-try-this side of me. Possibly due to the rather feast-and-famine finances of my childhood, I typically spend more time analysing profit margins than I do thinking of creative new products; I focus more on managing risk than being a trendsetter. If you've been in business before, I'm sure you too have experienced this natural tension between your entrepreneurial side and the inner voice of 'reason'.

One challenge for me in writing this book has been to find ways to encourage dreams to flourish while simultaneously exploring the somewhat sobering process of writing a business plan. I'm writing this introduction having just finished the last chapter of this book and, happily, I think that the process has worked on me. I'm itching with impatience to begin my next business venture, and feel utterly optimistic about its prospects. (I remain my father's daughter, after all.)

I hope you have a similar experience with this book, and that I share enough inspiration for your inner entrepreneur to thrive while at the same time providing unshakeable feet-on-the-ground practicality.

About This Book

I like to think that this book is a bit different from other business planning books, not least because this book is part of the *For Dummies* series. Dummies books aren't about thinking that you're a 'dummy' — far from it. What the *For Dummies* series is all about is balancing heavyweight topics with a lightweight mindset, and sharing a 'can-do' attitude that encourages anyone — no matter how young or old, how inexperienced or how veteran — to give the subject at hand a go.

I like to think that the *Dummies* way of thinking has helped me to bring a fresh approach to the subject of business planning. I've tried not to get bogged down in the same old stodgy discussions of mission statements, values and organisational charts; instead, I've focused more on working with others, being creative and thinking of your business as something that's unique and separate from yourself.

You may be surprised by the fact that I devote six whole chapters to the topic of finance (you'll only find one finance chapter in most business planning books). I'm a real advocate of the importance of financial planning and, in this book, I try to break the topic down into bite-sized chunks that anyone can understand, even if they haven't done any bookkeeping or accounting before.

I also understand that most people who've worked in business end up with knowledge that's patchy. You may know heaps about marketing but nothing about finance, or vice versa. The beauty of *Dummies* books is that you can just leap in, find the chunk of information that addresses your query, and start reading from there.

One more thing. Throughout this book you'll see *sidebars* — text that sits in a separate box with grey shading. Think of sidebars as the nut topping on your ice-cream: Nice to have, but not essential. Feel free to skip these bits.

Foolish Assumptions

When writing this book, I make no assumptions about your prior experience. Maybe you've been in business all your life or maybe you've never been in business before. It could be that you're a tech geek or it's possible that you hate computers. Maybe you love numbers or — much more likely — you may have a somewhat queasy feeling when it comes to maths.

I also make no assumptions about the age of your business, and realise that for many people reading this book, your business is still a seedling waiting to be watered. (For this reason, I include practical advice such as how to budget for personal expenses while you're building your business, and why things such as your relationships and family situation are all part of the picture.)

Last, I don't try to guess where you live in the world. After all, the principles of business planning are universal, whether you're in the snowdrifts of Alaska, the stone country of Australia or the kilt-swaying highlands of Scotland.

Icons Used in This Book

Want to get the killer edge? Then look for this handy icon.

This icon highlights free resources, worksheets, templates and checklists you can find online at www.dummies.com/go/creatingbusinessplan.

This icon alerts you to international differences. I'm not talking about language, colour or creed here, but more mundane matters such as tax rules or government contacts.

Tie a knot in that elephant's trunk, pin an eggtimer to your shirt but, whatever you do, don't forget the pointers next to this icon.

This icon points to ways to give your business plan that extra spark.

Real-life stories from others who've been there and done that.

A pitfall for the unwary. Read these warnings carefully.

Beyond the Book

I've created a whole heap of Excel and Word templates to make it easier for you to create your first plan. The Excel templates provide a great starting point for most of the financial projections, while the Word templates help you structure the narrative parts of your plan. You can find all of these templates at www.dummies.com/go/creatingbusinessplan.

On this webpage you can also find links to a few extra articles. In one article, I write about the psychology of sales projections, and in another I talk about managing expenses when cash gets tight. A third article talks about the psychology of goals and the art of setting goals that motivate you (and others) to carry out your plan.

At www.dummies.com/extras/creatingbusinessplan you can also find a bonus Part of Tens list, with ten tips for checking that your business plan idea is strong enough to fly. I also provide a neat video at www.dummies.com/go/creatingbusinessplan that corresponds to the Excel tips in Chapter 16, where you can not only watch a demonstration of each one of these tips but also have the joy of listening to my reassuring voice as the soundtrack. Almost as good — probably even better — than having me in the room beside you.

Speaking of which, I really like to think of my books as a conversation with readers, rather than a one-way monologue. If you have any comments, questions or feedback, I'd love to hear from you. Please feel free to email me at veechi@veechicurtis.com.au or go to Facebook and search for **Veechi Curtis**.

Where to Go from Here

Creating a Business Plan For Dummies is no page-turning thriller (probably a good thing given the subject matter) and doesn't require you to start at the beginning and follow through to the end. Instead, feel free to jump in and start reading from whatever section is most relevant to you:

✔ New to business and you've never created a business plan before? I suggest you read Chapters 1, 2 and 3 before doing much else. Chapter 1 provides a road map for creating your plan, and Chapters 2 and 3 help you to consolidate your business concept. From here, you're probably best to read the chapters in the order that I present them, because these chapters follow the same sequence as the topics within a business plan.

✔ If business strategy is more your concern, Chapters 2, 3, 11, 13 and 14 are the place to be.

✔ Are financial projections a source of woe? Chapters 4 to 10 are here to help.

✔ For advice on creating a plan that can't fail to impress prospective lenders or investors, Chapters 14 and 15 explain how to pull your plan together, Chapter 17 provides tips on getting your plan to look good, and Chapter 18 offers a handy checklist to make sure you don't forget a thing.

Part I
Getting Started

getting started
with

creating
a business
plan

In this part ...

- ✔ Explore the whole idea of business planning, discover how you can prepare your plan in small chunks of time over a period of weeks or even months, and assess the potential of your business idea using a simple scorecard.

- ✔ Figure out what your business does best and identify where the strategic advantage of your business really lies.

- ✔ Explore the delicate relationship between risk and gain, and understand why the craziest ideas often have the most potential.

- ✔ Go underground to research your competitors, creating a full dossier on each one, and position your business against competitors to develop a winning competitive strategy.

- ✔ Never gaze awkwardly at your feet again — prepare the killer elevator speech instead.

Chapter 1

Letting Your Plan Take Flight

. . . .

In This Chapter

▶ Getting started without another moment's hesitation

▶ Thinking about the structure of your plan and how long it's going to take

▶ Eating, drinking, sleeping and planning — all part of everyday life

▶ Summarising everything on a single page

▶ Rating yourself and your business idea with a quick and easy quiz

. . . .

You probably already know that if you spend time working *on* your business — rather than just working *in* your business — you have a heaps better chance of higher sales, more profit and a generally easier existence.

One of the main reasons people don't get around to creating a business plan is that they think they don't have enough time. Pish tosh. You don't need to spend weeks creating an impressive 30-page document. Instead, what you need to do is change your way of thinking. Rather than making a daily To Do List of all the people you have to call, brew yourself a cup of tea and have a think about your pricing strategies. Rather than fretting about all the jobs that need doing, spend a couple of hours researching your competitors.

Some of the most important elements of a business plan can be done while you're in the shower, on the beach or driving in the car. Attitude is everything. To create a great business plan, all you need is a willingness to be objective about your strategy, the discipline to analyse your financials (even if you're not naturally good with numbers) and the ability to think of your business as something that's separate from you.

So no more excuses, no skipping to another chapter, no closing this book with a sigh. It's time to start planning, and there's no time like the present.

Getting Your Feet Wet and Having Fun

In *Creating a Business Plan For Dummies*, I place less emphasis on the importance of creating a written plan and more on why planning is best viewed as an all-year-round activity. The neat thing about this way of thinking is that you can start with your plan at any time, even if you know you have only one hour free this week and you're flying to Europe for a skiing holiday the next.

Planning can be a heap of fun once you get started. Some of my best business ideas have come to me while lying in the hammock at our holiday house, digging up weeds in the garden or having a quiet coffee down at the village.

Deciding who this plan is for

You, of course. Your plan is an ongoing process, not a massive document that you create every year or so. Feel free to pick a structure, time and format that works well for you.

Occasionally, other people may want to have a stickybeak at your plan, usually prospective investors or lenders. On these occasions, you probably want to create a formal plan using a fairly traditional format, and focus more on the presentation and readability of your plan.

One thing to bear in mind, however: Regardless of who is likely to read your plan, I strongly suggest that when it comes to the financials — sales targets, income projections, profit projections and so on — you be consistent. Don't have one version of financials for your own purposes, and another spruced-up version for the bank.

One of my first jobs after I graduated was as a warehouse manager for a small but growing company. Money was always tight and we were forever presenting new plans and Cashflow Projections to prospective lenders. Part of my job was to 'massage' the figures to show that while cash was desperate in the coming six months or so (and hence loan funds were required), things would soon turn the corner and, within a couple of years, we would be awash with funds. I discovered how easy it was to manipulate figures (a topic I explore further in Chapter 8 when I look at scenario analysis). By adding 10 per cent to sales, trimming expenses by the same amount, and maybe increasing the gross profit a little, I could transform dire predictions into something that looked amazing. Trouble is, these figures were pure fiction. The manipulated scenarios inevitably created a false sense of security, and led to some pretty poor long-term decision-making.

The moral of the tale? Don't get hoodwinked into 'selling' your plan and exaggerating your likely success. Stay as realistic as possible. This tactic will help you gain respect from any likely investors and keep you grounded as to what lies ahead.

Choosing your dance partners

As a business owner, you need to have a good understanding of your financials, a solid commitment to marketing, a razor-sharp insight into your competition and a keen sense of strategy. Even if you don't have all of these skills yet, I can't think of a better way of acquiring these skills than getting involved in your own business plan. Experience is a generous teacher.

Having said this, unless you've run a business before, you'll almost certainly need a little help from outside. Good news is that all you have to do is ask. Consider the following sources:

- ✔ **Business planning courses:** In my opinion, a structured course spread over several weeks or even months is the very best possible way to accumulate basic planning skills. Not only do you have the discipline of working on your plan at least once a week, but you also usually receive expert mentoring from the teacher or teachers, as well as peer support from other people in a similar position to you.

- ✔ **Business advisory centres:** Depending on where you are in the world, business advisory centres have different names and structures. However, most state and federal governments fund some form of free advisory centres.

- ✔ **Business consultants:** While I warn against delegating the whole planning process to outsiders, expert consultants can be a great resource, especially if you retain control and ownership of your plan.

- ✔ **Your accountant:** I strongly recommend that you do your own financial projections, rather than delegating this task to a bookkeeper or accountant. (I explain just how in Chapters 4 through to 10.) However, after you have made your best attempt, consider asking your accountant to review your figures, and help you to identify anything that doesn't make sense or seems unrealistic.

- ✔ **Your lawyer:** In Chapter 14, I talk about managing risk, including protecting your name and your brand, and limiting liability through company structures. Your lawyer is an excellent source of advice for this part of the planning process.

✔ **Friends and family:** Not only is the advice of friends and family usually free, but these people also understand you like nobody else. Support and encouragement from friends and family is invaluable on those doubtful days when you think you (and your new business idea) may be crazy.

✔ **Your spouse/life partner:** Last but not least. Need I say more?

Looking at different online planning tools

In *Creating a Business Plan For Dummies*, I try to provide you with everything you need to build your plan, including a whole bunch of free templates and resources that you can download from www.dummies.com/go/creatingbusinessplan. You may be wondering how these templates compare to the many business planning templates or software applications you can find online (many of which are also free).

At a surface level, most of these templates provide you with pretty much everything you need to create a plan. However, when writing this book, I've reflected on my experience from running business plan courses. What I find is that some concepts of business planning that may take only a few sentences to summarise are really hard for those new to business to grasp.

For example, almost anyone can explain the concept of strategic advantage in a few sentences, and most business planning templates simply provide a Word template with a few blank lines in which you can write your strategic advantage. In real life, I find that these concepts usually take several sessions to gel with my students. It's for this reason that I devote two whole chapters to the concepts of strategic and competitive advantage (Chapters 2 and 3) and I recommend you read these chapters early in your business planning process, so you can be sure a solid foundation is in place when you create your plan.

However, what you may find works well is to use a business planning template in conjunction with this book. You can find a whole heap of industry-specific templates online, and you may even find topics within these templates that I don't cover in detail within this book. (Bplans, at www.bplans.com is probably the world's leader in business planning templates and software, and provides an excellent starting point.)

As well as business planning templates, you can also consider business-planning software. You can either buy software that you install on your computer (such as Business Plans Pro available from www.bplans.com or MAUS MasterPlan available from www.maus.com.au), or you can subscribe to online planning software in the cloud (such as www.liveplan.com or www.planhq.com). I prefer cloud-based software because you can pay as you go, and because the cloud makes working collaboratively with others so much easier.

The main difference between business planning templates and business planning software is the sophistication of the financials. For example, the financials in most business planning software packages (including those in the cloud) include Profit & Loss Projections, Cashflow Projections, budgets, break-even analysis, Balance Sheets and more. You usually find that all the financials interconnect so that if you change a figure in your Profit & Loss Projection, the change automatically flows through to the other financial reports.

While business planning software can be a real benefit if figures and maths don't come naturally to you, the downside can be inflexibility (for example, you may find you can't adapt the list of expenses, or that the format for sales projections is limited). Assuming you have a decent internet connection, why not weigh up the pros and cons for yourself by subscribing to a service such as www.liveplan.com for 30 days or so. Subscriptions cost approximately US$19.95 per month, and a small payment of this nature is hardly likely to break the bank.

Are you ready?

I find that if someone really wants to start their own business, wild horses can't hold them back. The idea keeps coming around and around until that person finally takes the leap and says 'I'm going to give it a go'.

So if you're champing at the bit to start your new business, I have just three questions to ask you first:

✔ Do you have experience in the kind of business you're planning to start? For example, if you're looking at buying a coffee van, have you actually spent a few days selling coffee in this way? Do you have barista or retail experience?

✔ Do you definitely have enough capital to get started? If you're not sure, do

you think you may be better saving for a while before you launch your business? (See Chapter 4 for more on budgeting for start-up expenses.)

✔ Is your partner/spouse supportive? (I remember my (now ex-) husband wanting to start up in business when our first child was just six months old. He was ready to start a new business, but I certainly wasn't.)

If your answer to any of these questions is 'no', I suggest that you try to temper your enthusiasm just a little. And if you still can't wait, then hey, I completely understand.

Scoping the Nature of Your Plan

While planning is certainly best done on an ongoing basis, the ideal approach the very first time you create a business plan is to cover all the elements of your plan — concept, strategy, financials, marketing, people and so on — within a reasonable time frame, and then collate all your workings into a single document. This approach requires a certain level of discipline, but by the time you get to the end you're going to be left with a major sense of achievement.

Structuring your plan

The best format for a business with a turnover of $100 million and 200 employees is going to be utterly different from the best format for a start-up business with no employees. For this reason, you can find as many possible formats for a business plan as recipes for bolognese sauce.

What most formats have in common, however, is certain key elements, although the sequence of these elements varies. (See the following section for how much planning time each of the elements is likely to require. I tell you where to find more detailed information on each one in the following section as well.)

Here are the key elements of a business plan:

- **An overview of the business and its strategy.** This introduction to your plan includes your mission, a brief description of your business and a strategic advantage statement.

- **A complete summary of financials.** At its simplest, the financial part of your plan may only include a Profit & Loss Projection for the next 12 months. More detailed plans include Profit & Loss Projections for 24 or 36 months ahead, plus historical Profit & Loss reports and Balance Sheets for the previous year or years. Financials often also include break-even analysis, Cashflow Projections and budgets.

- **A people plan.** Who are you, and why are you so awesome? What are your skills and the skills of those involved in your business?

- **A marketing plan.** A marketing plan is usually several pages long and includes competitor analysis, unique selling points, target market analysis, sales targets, marketing strategies and a bit more besides.

- **An analysis of industry and economic trends, as well as a summary of what you perceive to be opportunities or threats.** No business is an island, particularly in a very fast-changing world. This part of your plan looks at factors outside of your control (such as industry or economic trends), possible opportunities that your business could exploit, and threats that you need to guard against. Your risk-management plan also belongs in this section. (***Note:*** You may find that the industry analysis section sits better in the first part of your plan, immediately following your business and strategic overview, so that you provide a complete summary of your strategic platform.)

✔ **A summary of goals.** Here's where you get to share your dreams, neatly sliced and diced into monthly, six-monthly and yearly goals.

In this book, I work through the preceding six key elements in sequence. (The only exception is the mission statement, which normally goes at the beginning of a business plan but which I don't address until Chapter 15. From experience, I find it works best to delay writing a mission statement until further into the planning process.)

Setting aside enough time

Here's a bit more detail about how much time the different elements of a business plan (refer to the preceding section) typically require, and how often you need to attend to them.

Business model and strategy

How long does it take to come up with a decent business model? If you're lucky, you may be able to come up with a winning strategy over the course of a few drinks in the back of a pub. Alternatively, you may find it takes years to come up with a strong strategy that really works.

As well as coming up with a strong business strategy, the other element of developing your business model is doing a detailed analysis of your competitors. This process usually takes only a few hours, but is something that you should do every six months or so, so that you avoid being caught by surprise.

I talk about business strategy in Chapters 2, 11 and 13, and focus on competitive analysis in Chapter 3.

Financials

Creating a Profit & Loss Projection (Chapters 5 through to 8) can be pretty time-consuming the first time around, and may take several days if you're not used to working with figures or Excel. Stick with the process, though, and the next time around will only take a fraction of the time. Similarly, a Cashflow Projection (Chapter 10) can be quite technically demanding and may take many hours to pull together, especially the first time.

So how often do you need to repeat the process? I recommend you compare budgets against actual results every month when you look at your Profit & Loss report. As patterns emerge (maybe you can see that you consistently over- or under-estimate something), return to your overall Profit & Loss Projections, revise your figures, and extend these projections once more so they span a full 12 months ahead.

If your business is always tight for cash and you carry high levels of stock or customer debt, you or your finance manager may need to do Cashflow Projections all year round, updating figures on a constant basis.

I explain how to create a Profit & Loss Projection in Chapters 5 to 8, and talk about Cashflow Projections in Chapter 10. Later in this chapter (see 'Going for rhythm with financial planning') I also talk about the financial planning cycle, and about how one activity naturally flows into another.

People plan

A business isn't anything without the people who run it, and your skills, entrepreneurialism and natural abilities are as much a part of the mix as anything else, as are the skills of the people you choose to involve in your business. This part of your plan needs to outline the people element of your business: Who does what, and why they're the best choice for the job.

Even if you don't have any employees yet, you can still include details about any consultants, advisers, mentors or professionals who you plan to involve in your business. These details help to establish credibility for anybody else reading your plan, and prompt you to think further outside the business than just yourself.

Chapter 2 touches on this topic, while Chapter 11 explores the people side of your plan in more depth. (People planning doesn't necessarily take a huge amount of time at first, but is something that can be a huge time-waster if you don't get it right.)

Marketing plan

I love doing marketing plans. Thinking about sales strategies is such a creative process that it's hard not to feel a charge of energy and inspiration as you flesh out your ideas.

The first time you create a marketing plan can take anything from several hours to several days. After the first time, however, maintaining a coherent marketing plan generally only requires a half-day or so every six months.

I talk about the marketing cycle later in this chapter (see 'Keeping everything on track with your marketing cycle'), and explore marketing plans in detail in Chapter 12.

Looking into the future

In this book, I emphasise reporting for financial projections rather than reporting on actual financial results. I do this for two reasons.

First, many people reading this book are going to be working on their first business plan and won't have any results for previous months or years as yet.

Second, even if you've been trading for some time, you will always reap benefits from making financial projections and experimenting with different scenarios, such as what could happen if you increased sales by 10 per cent or decreased expenses by a similar amount.

However, if you've been trading for a while, you do need to include historical figures (Profit & Loss and Balance Sheet) for the last year or two years in your business plan. These actual results provide a great reality check for you (or anybody else) when comparing future projections against past performance.

Situational analysis

The first time you do this part of your plan, which includes both an industry analysis, as well as a SWOT (Strengths, Weaknesses, Opportunities and Threats) analysis, can take a fair chunk of time, depending on the depth in which you choose to explore this topic.

I don't usually see the need for you to update the written element of this part of your plan any more often than once a year. However, being alert to the impact of things changing around you is something you want to maintain all year round. Find ways to stay tuned to changes in your industry, possibly by attending conferences, subscribing to forum boards, researching information on industry websites or attending industry association meetings.

Planning for risk doesn't generally require significant time on an ongoing basis, but tends to demand your attention in fits and starts (for example, trademarking a logo or drawing up employee contracts may take several days to organise). However, I suggest you allow at least half a day or so each year to review your risk-management strategies.

I talk about situational and risk analysis in Chapters 13 and 14.

An action plan

The action plan is where you weave all the other elements of your plan together into a neat summary of goals and objectives, each one with a time frame. In other words, the action plan is the section that endeavours to keep you on track, hopefully providing a calendar of activities for the months to come.

An action plan usually only takes an hour or two to pull together at the end of the planning process but once done is something that you should try to keep constantly updated. I talk about creating your action plan in Chapter 15.

Deciding how far into the future you want to go

In this book, I focus on projections that cover the next 12 months (or the first 12 months from when a business starts trading). I do this largely for simplicity's sake. (The principle of creating a financial projection for 24 months is exactly the same principle as for 12 months — all you're doing is adding a few more columns.)

In practice, how far you should extend your plan into the future really depends on the nature of your business and how long it has been established. Here's what I suggest:

✔ For most new businesses, a 12-month financial projection works just fine. (Although most traditional business planning books talk about building financial projections for the next two, three or even five years ahead, I find that for new businesses, this long-term approach quickly spills into fiction territory. If you have no idea what sales you're going to make this month or next, how can you realistically predict what sales you'll make in three years' time?)

✔ For new or growing businesses where the projections show low profitability in the first 12 months because the business requires a certain sales volume before it really starts to work, I suggest you extend your projections for at least a couple of years. This is the only way you can assess the long-term viability of your concept.

✔ For an established business with three or more years of trading history, I recommend you extend your financial projections 24 months ahead.

Understanding Why Your Plan Needs Constant Love and Attention

In the preceding section, can you see that some elements of a business plan require much more regular attention than others? This is just one reason why creating a business plan once every year or two and then leaving it on a shelf to gather dust is a strategy for failure. Once you finish your first business plan, I strongly suggest that you continue to update different elements as time allows and circumstances demand.

The two elements within a business plan that require the most ongoing attention are your financial plan and your marketing plan. Each of these activities has its own planning cycle.

Going for rhythm with financial planning

Figure 1-1 shows a typical financial planning cycle, with the review of your business model at the beginning and end of each process.

Here's how you can work through the financial planning cycle:

1. **Review business model and strategy.**

   I talk about business models and strategy in Chapters 2, 3 and 11. In the context of your financial planning cycle, the idea is that if you can't get your financials to look healthy, you probably need to review the way you're doing (or planning to do) business.

2. **Review your prices, rates and sales projections.**

   Setting prices and sales targets (a topic I cover in Chapter 5) is both a financial and a marketing activity, and sales projections usually form part of your marketing plan. Some business planning books suggest you do your marketing plan before your financial projections, but I prefer to work on pricing and sales projections first.

    My argument for working on your pricing and sales projections before your marketing plan is this: If you haven't set your prices, you can't do any meaningful financial forecasts. Without financial forecasts, you don't know if your business model has any chance at all. And without having your essential idea confirmed, what is the point of doing a marketing plan? All very chicken-and-egg in its nature, but essentially you have to start somewhere.

3. **Confirm the direct costs of providing your service or making your products.**

   I talk about costing products and services in Chapter 6, and explain how to create a Gross Profit Projection for the next 12 months.

4. **Create a forecast for expenses.**

   If you're just getting started, I suggest you create a budget both for business and personal expenses (see Chapter 7). For simple cash-based businesses, this expense forecast becomes your budget for the months ahead.

5. **Create a Profit & Loss Projection for the next 12 months.**

   In Chapter 8, I explain how to create a Profit & Loss Projection, and how to forecast your net profit over the next 12 months.

6. **Work out your break-even point.**

   You can calculate your break-even point in several different ways (Chapter 9 explains just how). Understanding this information is a powerful weapon in your business artillery.

7. **Generate a Cashflow Projection.**

   Even if you're making a profit, you may find yourself short of cash. In Chapter 10, I explain how to generate a Cashflow Projection so that you can anticipate any cash shortfalls.

8. **Set sales targets and expense budgets for the 12 months ahead.**

   Committing to budgets is one of the most important elements of the financial planning cycle. In Chapter 10, I explain the subtle difference between projections and budgets.

9. **Continually review actual results against budgets, and tweak your pricing, strategy and budgets accordingly.**

   With finances, you can't 'set and forget'. Instead, the trick is to monitor your actual performance and compare this against your budgets every single month. For example, if sales fall short of targets, you need to sell more, change pricing or pull back on expenses. If sales go over targets, you probably want to look at your Cashflow Projection and check that you can finance this growth.

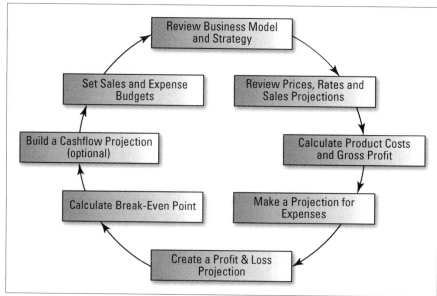

Figure 1-1:
The financial planning cycle.

Can you see how it really doesn't work to create a 12-month Profit & Loss Projection as part of your business plan and then think to yourself, Cool, that's finished for the year? I've yet to see a business where actual results are exactly the same as budgets. You will always get a difference, and you need to manage these differences on an ongoing basis.

Keeping everything on track with your marketing cycle

When you're in business, the process of marketing never stops. By marketing, I don't just mean advertising or sales strategies; rather, I mean everything from understanding competitors to analysing customers, and from reviewing pricing to ensuring excellent customer service.

The pace of change in most business environments is so fast that you can't afford to let a whole year go by without reviewing your marketing plan. In just the same way as you need to compare actuals against budgets every month for your income and expenses (refer to preceding section), you also need to review your sales targets every month against actual results. Look at the detail — even if total sales came close to budget, did the sales come from a different source than you had anticipated? What are the trends? Do you need to revise your marketing plan, or change your sales budgets (and, therefore, your expense budgets too)?

Figure 1-2 shows a typical marketing cycle (I explain each step of this cycle in detail in Chapter 12). Can you see how the fifth step of the marketing cycle (review pricing, rates and sales projections) is exactly the same as the second step of the financial cycle (shown in Figure 1-1 in the preceding section of this chapter)? That's because setting sales targets is always the point at which the sales team and the bean counters connect.

A few years ago, I worked as a consultant to a very sales-orientated business, helping to look at the finances and general profitability. One of the dynamics at play was that the company would have six-monthly sales meetings at which they'd set sales budgets for the year ahead. The vibe at these meetings was always pretty buoyant and the sales budgets reflected this. After these meetings, I'd be given these sales budgets and work with the general manager to set expense budgets accordingly. The general manager never wanted to lower sales budgets for fear her sales team would become complacent, but when working with this over-optimistic set of figures, she inevitably set her expense budgets too high. Eventually I persuaded the general manager to have two sets of sales budgets on the go at any one time. The first set was what the sales team came up with, and these budgets became their targets. The second set — which we didn't share with anyone in sales — was what we thought sales were likely to be, based on the previous year's results plus a modest 2 per cent for growth.

We then set the expense budgets accordingly. This method worked really well for the company, balancing the psychology of different individuals perfectly.

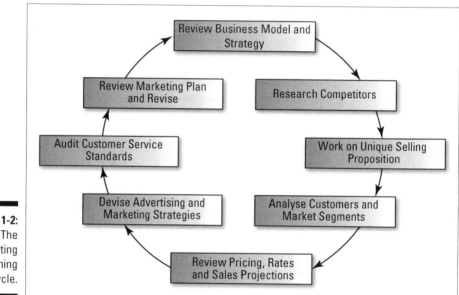

Figure 1-2:
The
marketing
planning
cycle.

Conjuring Up a One-Page Business Plan

When I was talking to my publishing manager at Wiley about writing this book, we played around with a whole heap of different possible titles. One of the ideas Clare came up with was *Creating a One-Page Business Plan For Dummies*. My response was one of immediate enthusiasm. A one-page business plan sounds so quick and easy, I thought everyone would buy a book with that title.

But then, like Pinocchio, my conscience kicked in. I knew that a one-page business plan is never enough. You simply can't fit everything you need to know on one page, and to suggest anything otherwise would just be a whopping fib. So we came up with a different — and much more realistic — title.

The one-page business plan idea sticks around, however, and at times does have a role to play. I like to think of the one-page plan as being a summary of the overall plan, a way to provide a bit of daily inspiration and keep everyone on track with overall goals. Figure 1-3 shows an example of a one-page plan (generated by MAUS MasterPlan software) and how this summary concept can work.

One-page plans are best if you create them with a specific audience in mind. I've seen one-page plans that are essentially pitches to lenders of a new idea, or one-page plans that provide performance summaries for senior management. The only time I created a one-page plan, I made a hybrid between planning elements (listing my mission and strategic advantage at the top of the document), and goal-setting (listing milestones and dates for the months ahead).

If you want to create a one-page plan for your business, I suggest you start by doing a complete plan, culminating in some kind of longer document as explained in Chapter 15. With this complete, have a think about what kind of summary you would like to see, and whether a monthly one-page plan is going to work for you.

I know a very successful CEO who expects each of his six managers to report on just eight figures every Friday. For the marketing manager, these figures include the number of hits on the website, new enquiries, the conversion rate and total marketing expenditure. For the project manager, figures include total hours worked for the current major project, total hours overtime, cost of overtime and percentage completion rate. Other managers contribute different information again. These results are all compiled onto a single dashboard that the CEO monitors continually.

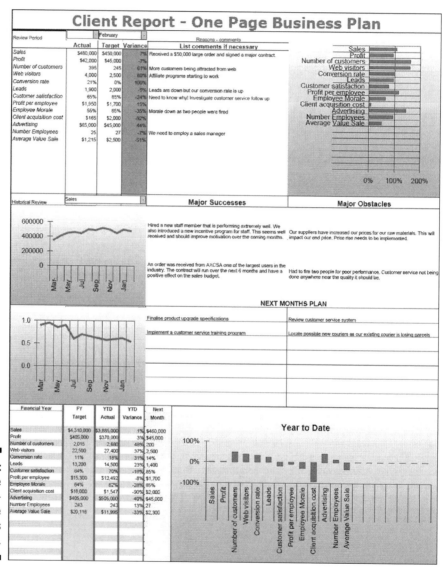

Figure 1-3:
An example
of a one-
page
business
plan.

Scoring Your Business out of 10

Are you still at the stage of thinking about your business idea and wondering if it's worth you even doing a plan? Maybe your business idea is still a glint in the eye, or maybe you've been mooching along half-heartedly with a new business for a little while now and don't know where you're headed. Just for a bit of fun (this is Chapter 1, after all), why not take a few minutes out and see how you and your business idea rate?

Use the scorecard in Table 1-1 if yours is a business that's been done before. By 'done before', I mean a business selling a service or product that many others already provide, such as a gardening business, general store, drycleaners or restaurant. Alternatively, if your business or business idea is a niche business or a new invention, use the scorecard in Table 1-2. For each question, a score of 1 is bad, and a score of 10 is good.

Wondering what a niche business is? A *niche business* is one that specialises in a small market segment. I came across a quirky example of a niche business just today. The company is called Dirty Rotten Flowers and creates unique bouquets for those who are wronged in love to send to the one who wronged them. (My favourite is probably the 'I Love You Not' bouquet, which includes a dozen twisted red carnations accompanied by a teddy bear embroidered with these very words.)

Table 1-1	Rating a Business that's Been Done Before
Ask yourself this question and then score yourself from ...	*1 to 10*
Can you think of something that will make your product or your service different from your competitors?	
Can you do something that will allow you to deliver a better product or service than your competitors?	
Are you going to be cheaper than your competitors?	
Do you love the day-to-day activity that this business demands?	
Do you know for sure that demand exists for your product or service?	
Do you (or someone in your team) have strong marketing skills?	
Are you well known locally, with a strong community network?	
Do you have enough start-up capital to give your business the best possible chance of success?	
Are you good with money, and able to understand budgets and stick to them?	
Is your vision for your business to build something that can ultimately run without your day-to-day attention?	
If you're in a relationship, does your spouse/partner support you in this venture?	

What score are you looking for? Overall, you probably want to get a score of 35 or more, although don't be dismayed if you score less than this. Chapters 2, 3, 11 and 13 provide lots of inspiration for developing your business ideas, Chapters 4 to 10 help you consolidate your financial skills, and Chapter 12 helps with the marketing side of things. You can return to this scorecard later in the planning process and see if your score improves.

Table 1-2	Rating a Niche Business or New Invention
Ask yourself this question and then score yourself from . . .	**1 to 10**
How unique is your product?	
If your idea is unique, do you have some way of safeguarding this idea from a competitor who might steal it?	
Do you know for sure that demand exists for your product or service?	
Do you have a clear strategy for launching your product or service?	
Can you do something that will allow you to deliver a better product or service than your competitors?	
Do you have enough start-up capital to give your business the best possible chance of success?	
Do you (or someone in your team) have strong marketing skills?	
Are you comfortable in the online environment (Facebook, Twitter, creating web pages and so on)?	
Is a window of opportunity emerging due to a change in the business environment, such as changing regulations, government grants or new technology?	
If you're in a relationship, does your spouse/partner support you in this venture?	

REMEMBER

Tread gently, lest you tread upon your dreams

The very nature of business planning often means taking a slightly conservative approach, dealing with facts and figures rather than dreams and inspirations. But whatever you feel when working through your plan, stay tuned to that germ of inspiration that caused you to get to this point in the first place. Building any new business is a creative process and one that requires you to believe in yourself and your own abilities.

This belief and creativity is what separates the natural entrepreneur from the nine-to-five office worker. This belief is what will ultimately lead you to business success and its many associated rewards.

Chapter 2

Figuring Out What's So Special about You (and Your Business)

In This Chapter

▶ Thinking about what edge you have over others

▶ Understanding the relationship between risk and potential gain

▶ Scoring your strategic advantage from one to ten

▶ Writing up your strategic advantage statement

▶ Rethinking whether your business idea is really strong enough to fly

*W*hat is it that makes you, or your business, so special?

Even if you have a business that's similar to thousands of others — maybe you mow lawns, have a hairdressing salon or tutor high school students — you still need to come up with an idea that makes your business different from others in some way, or that provides you with a competitive edge.

Similarly, if your business caters for a very specific niche — maybe you sell gluten-free cookies or baby clothes made from organic cotton — you still need to identify how you can service this niche in a way that others can't, or what it is about your skills or circumstances that enables you to service this niche better than others.

If your business centres on an idea that nobody has tried before, you need to address why nobody else has bothered to try this idea until now and, in the event that you're successful, what prevents others from copying your idea straightaway.

The essence of what makes your business special, or more likely to succeed than others, is called your *competitive* or *strategic advantage*. I believe that this advantage is the single most important ingredient for ongoing business success — which is why, in this chapter, I focus exclusively on this very subject.

Understanding Strategic Advantage

In the introduction for this chapter, I mention the terms *competitive advantage* and *strategic advantage*. Like many people, I tend to use these terms synonymously but, to be really precise, you could argue they relate to slightly different aspects of your business.

A *competitive advantage* is something that's different, better than or not offered by your competitors. For example, if a town has two hairdressing salons and one offers a mobile service but the other doesn't, the first salon has a competitive advantage because they're providing something their competitors aren't.

A *strategic advantage* is something that stems from capabilities within your business that are hard for others to copy. These capabilities tend to be a unique blend of assets, knowledge, people networks, skills or technology. For example, imagine the owner of the salon with the mobile haircutting service has a background in nursing, and so has a natural understanding of the needs of her many elderly housebound clients. Imagine also that the owner's husband is a mechanic, which means the vehicle used for providing the salon's mobile service is kept on the road at minimal cost. This unique blend of skills and cost efficiency forms part of this salon's strategic advantage.

Having said all this, competitive and strategic advantages tend to overlap so much that I try to avoid getting bogged down in arguing about the distinction. I use the term strategic advantage in this chapter (because, after all, a true strategic advantage should ultimately result in a competitive advantage) but if you'd rather use the term competitive advantage in your business plan, that's just fine.

Looking at examples of strategic advantage

How can your business beat the competition, and what benefits can you provide that the competition can't? Here are some ways that your business may be able to secure a strategic advantage against others in the same industry:

✔ **Added value:** Can you offer added value in comparison to your competitors? Think 24-hour delivery, locally sourced product, a mobile service, or a quality of product or service that's beyond industry norms.

- ✔ **Exclusive distribution rights:** Do you have exclusive distribution rights to a sought-after product or service?

- ✔ **First cab off the rank:** Do you have a new idea that nobody else has tried before? Or a new way of doing something that makes the product or service better, quicker or cheaper?

- ✔ **Intellectual property:** Do you have unique intellectual property (IP) that customers want and that's hard to copy? IP includes copyright, patents and trademarks. If you're just getting started with your business, your IP could be as simple as a clever business name, an eye-catching logo or a well-chosen domain name (that is, a web address).

- ✔ **Location:** If you're a retailer, do you have a great location in a central shopping area? (Location is always *the* prime strategic advantage for retailers.) Or are you the only business providing a service in a particular suburb or region? Are the demographics of your location ideally matched to your business, or are you located in a central spot for freight and transport?

- ✔ **Lower costs:** Do you have an innovative way of doing things that reduces costs, creates economies of scale or significantly improves business processes?

- ✔ **Obsession and drive:** Do you have exceptional vision or drive? Is this drive connected with a particular obsession? (For example, think of Steve Jobs and his obsession about design.)

- ✔ **Perfectly matched team:** If you're in a business partnership of some kind, do you have a unique combination of skills and do you work well together as a team? (The synergy created by two or more people who have complementary skills and who work well together can be a force to be reckoned with, and something that's hard for competition to copy.)

- ✔ **Specialist skills:** Are you a specialist who has an insight into a particular industry that nobody else is likely to have? Maybe you can see a gap in the industry that nobody else is catering for, or maybe you can see a way to do something better.

Think of a business that you know that has been really successful (maybe a local business or a friend's business, or even a big name such as The Body Shop, McDonald's or Microsoft). Go through the list of different strategic advantages and think about which of these advantages could apply to these businesses.

Focusing on real-life examples

Try to deepen your understanding of strategic advantage (refer to the preceding section) by applying the concept to a few real-life situations that are easy to imagine. Picture yourself sitting in a room with four people and each of these people sharing their idea for a new business:

- Lloyd plans to start a business mowing lawns in his local neighbourhood.

- Tess has recently qualified as an acupuncturist and plans to start up a practice specialising in children's health.

- Dave has an idea to provide a mobile home-safety service, installing devices such as gates, cupboard latches and electrical safety switches to make homes toddler-proof. His wife is in real estate and has great marketing skills.

- Leila, who is a musician, has partnered with a friend with IT skills to develop a smartphone app that simulates turntable scratch rhythms so kids can add their own backing tracks to playlists.

Referring to the strategic advantages listed in the preceding section, have a think about which of these advantages could be relevant to the example businesses. You can see how I've rated the strategic advantage potential for each of the four businesses in Table 2-1.

Table 2-1   Rating Businesses According to Potential Strategic Advantage

	Lawn Mowing	*Acupuncturist*	*Toddler Safety*	*Smartphone App*
Added value	Maybe		Yes	
Exclusive distribution				
First cab off the rank			Yes	Yes
Intellectual property				Yes
Location	Maybe	Maybe	Maybe	
Lower costs	Maybe			
Obsession and drive				Yes
Perfectly matched team		Maybe	Maybe	Maybe
Specialist skills		Yes		Yes

Of course, just because I've written 'yes' against a strategic advantage doesn't mean that this advantage necessarily exists. Rather, what I'm saying is that potential exists. For example, I've written 'yes' against 'specialist skills' for the iPhone app. However, not everyone who tries to develop an iPhone app will necessarily have good programming skills.

Have a look at Table 2-1 and see if you agree with my assessment of potential advantages. For example, can you think of ways that someone with a lawn mowing business could get an edge over competition with added value services, location or lower costs?

Understanding How Risk Relates to Gain

In most situations, the business with the highest potential strategic advantage is going to be the business that requires the most capital or involves the highest risk of failure. For example, in Table 2-1, the business with the highest number of yeses in the strategic column is the smartphone app. However, look back to the business idea itself (developing a custom-written smartphone app for a very niche market) and you can see that the idea is full of risk. Leila will have high development costs, an unknown and untested market, and a product that may not even work that well when complete.

Similarly, the toddler-safety business has the advantages of being a new idea and something that clearly adds value for customers, but involves fairly substantial risks. Because this is a new service, people aren't going to look around thinking to hire someone to make their home toddler-proof. Dave will have to spend a lot of money on marketing to make consumers aware of his services, and he may yet find that there isn't enough demand for his business idea.

In contrast, lawn mowing has few potential strategic advantages but involves the lowest risk of all. (The cost for Lloyd to set up his business could be as low as a few business cards.) Strategic advantages are hard to find for Lloyd's business because a lawn is only ever a lawn, and Lloyd is limited in what he can offer that others can't. However, I've still written 'maybe' against three possible strategic advantages for Lloyd's lawn mowing business:

✔ **Added value:** Maybe Lloyd has some specialist horticultural knowledge that could differentiate him from his competitors.

> ✔ **Location:** Maybe Lloyd would be providing the only service in his suburb, or maybe he lives in a very exclusive suburb with lots of high-income earners.
>
> ✔ **Lower costs:** Maybe Lloyd's teenage son works for him at low hourly rates, enabling Lloyd to offer very competitive prices.

Thinking of potential strategic advantages for a business or service that lots of other people provide, and where it's difficult to differentiate between your service and those of your competitors, is usually much harder. The upside of this kind of business is that the risks are usually lower; the downside is that it's always going to be tricky to charge premium rates or make above-average profits.

Justifying Why You Can Succeed

In the preceding sections in this chapter, I explore the concept of strategic advantage in relation to a range of possible businesses. I like to work with examples in this way because the different business scenarios help to highlight how this concept changes so much depending on the context.

In this section, I help you to apply the concept of strategic advantage to your business. I help you go digging to identify what it is that makes you different, and suggest you apply a strategic advantage scorecard to your business concept.

If you're struggling to come up with anything that's special about your business — maybe you haven't stumbled on that winning idea quite yet — please do persist. The process of identifying your strategic advantage is even more important for you.

Uncovering your inner mojo

One good way to broaden your sense of where your strategic advantage may lie is to look at your existing customers and their buying patterns. (Or, if you haven't started your business yet, imagine what these answers might be.) Ask yourself these questions:

✔ When customers come to me, why is that?

✔ When potential customers go to my competitors instead, why is that?

> ✔ When potential customers make an enquiry but end up not purchasing my goods or services, why is that?
>
> ✔ Are the benefits I offer (or intend to offer) to my customers unique?

The thing that I like about asking these questions is that getting the answers usually means you have to engage in some market research. This naturally crosses over with competitor analysis (which just happens to be the subject of Chapter 3).

Honest, ongoing market research that compares the benefits your business provides to customers against the benefits your competitors provide is essential to identifying and maintaining your strategic advantage.

Asking three key questions for each of your advantages

For a strategic advantage to be really worth something — in terms of the goodwill of your business or your likely financial success — this advantage has to be something that you can sustain over the long term.

I like to think that any really strong strategic advantage should have three attributes:

✔ **The advantage can't be easily copied by others.** The ideal strategic advantage is one that's really tricky for your competition to copy. Examples are a winning recipe or flavour (think Coca-Cola), a unique synergy of skills within your organisation, or expert knowledge that few others have.

✔ **The advantage is important to customers.** Think of the farmers who switched to growing organic produce in the early 1990s, before organics became more mainstream. Many of these farmers did really well because organics were so important to particular customers. (And although the advantage was relatively easy to copy, many authorities required a seven-year lead time with no chemicals before a farm could be officially certified.)

✔ **The advantage can be constantly improved.** If you can identify the thing that gives you an edge and constantly work this advantage, you have a strategic advantage that is potentially sustainable in the long term.

When Steve Jobs and Steve Wozniak started Apple, one key strategic advantage was that they were a perfectly matched team, and were passionate about design. The synergy of their skills was hard for others to copy, the beautiful design was something that customers really wanted, and Apple were in a position to continually improve and develop this advantage.

Don't fall into the trap of thinking that because you're cheaper than everyone else, this is a strategic advantage. Being cheaper than everyone else usually means one of two things: Either your business isn't as profitable as it should be, or your competitors can grab your strategic advantage at any moment just by dropping their prices too. Usually, being cheaper than others is only a strategic advantage if you have some special skills, technology or volume of production that enables you to be cheaper.

Rating how you score

This section helps you to think about your own business (or business idea) and rate how you score in potential strategic advantage.

Go to www.dummies.com/go/creatingbusinessplan and download the Strategic Advantage Scorecard (also shown in Table 2-2). Rate your own business from 1 to 10 on each of the attributes shown on the scorecard (use 1 for no real advantage, and 10 for a winner strategic advantage that anyone else will find hard to beat). In the first column, apply a rating according to the benefits this advantage brings to your business; in the second column, apply a rating according to the benefits this advantage brings to your customers.

Table 2-2	Scoring Your Business's Strategic Advantage	
Strategic Advantage	*Benefit to Business*	*Benefit to Customer*
Added value		
Exclusive distribution		
First cab off the rank		
Intellectual property		
Location		
Lower costs		
Obsession and drive		
Perfectly matched team		
Specialist skills		

You're probably wondering if a magic score exists that your business should achieve. It doesn't. But if you score 8 or more on any one count, this is a green light for you to concentrate on exploiting this advantage to the greatest extent possible. On the other hand, if you score below 3 on all counts, this indicates that unless you can come up with some new and creative ideas, your business is likely to yield similar (or even lower) returns than others working in the same industry.

Developing Your Strategic Advantage Statement

In this book, I'm pretty realistic about the written part of business plans. I know how few people actually write a 20- or 30-page business plan, despite their best intentions.

However, even if you do almost nothing else, I do recommend you formulate a statement of strategic advantage. In this statement, your purpose is to write down exactly what gives your business the edge over others.

Your strategic advantage statement is usually slightly different from your 'elevator speech' (something I talk about in Chapter 3) in that the statement may include information that you wouldn't necessarily share if 'giving the sell' about your business to a prospective customer.

Drafting your statement

Your strategic advantage statement needs only be a paragraph or two, but should include the following:

- Your company name
- How your product or service benefits your customers
- What makes your business different to your competitors, seen from the perspective of your customers
- Your strategic advantages (in other words, what knowledge, skills, synergy, team, technology or processes your business has that enables you to deliver these additional benefits to your customers)

I like to put this statement right at the beginning of any business plan because it's the knowledge of how you're different, and how you can succeed where others may fail or flounder, that needs to permeate every step of the business plan thereafter.

Figure 2-1 shows an example of an extract from Dave's business plan (making homes toddler-proof).

> *Baby Busters provides a one-stop shop to help parents create a safe home. We not only assess the home for dangers, but also provide the required products and install them properly.*
>
> *No other businesses within a 100-kilometre radius provide a similar service. We are different from competitors in that our installer (Dave) is not only a licensed carpenter, but also trained in occupational health and safety and has worked as a Risk Assessment Officer. Sandy has a marketing degree and currently works in real estate, which brings a special advantage in that she knows when people are moving into new homes and most likely to require this service.*

Figure 2-1:
An example
statement
of strategic
advantage.

In Figure 2-1, Dave and his partner, Sandy, stress how the synergy of their skills and current occupations form their main strategic advantage. Some of these skills are also selling points for their business (for example, Dave's experience with risk assessment), but some are not (knowing when people are buying new homes so you can sell your product to them may be a strategic advantage, but it's definitely not a selling point).

Growing your advantages over time

Sometimes your strategic advantage isn't something that's blindingly clear from the moment you set out in business, but instead grows over time. Your skills grow as you develop in business, and your understanding of how you're different from the competition consolidates as well.

From time to time, you can review your strategic advantage by asking yourself these questions:

✔ What am I naturally good at? (Or what is my team good at?) Where do I feel I have been particularly successful in my business?

✔ What do I offer to my customers that's either cheaper than my competitors, better value or unique in some way?

✔ Does a point exist where what I'm naturally good at connects with what I do better than my competitors? If so, how can I build and develop this?

When our local osteopath first started out in business, he didn't really have anything that separated him from the competition. The only thing that was really different about him was that he was an elite rock climber in his spare time. However, as his business grew, he became expert at treating other climbers for their injuries. His business developed, and now he treats not only climbers who live locally, but also climbers from interstate. He even does some international consultations (and yes, if you're wondering, some parts of an osteopathic consultant can be conducted via Skype!). This combination of skills — being a natural climber and a highly trained osteopath — is hard to beat, and a true strategic advantage.

Making sure a demand really exists

Earlier in this chapter, I mention that a strategic advantage only holds water if you're sure that customers really want the thing it is that you're offering (refer to the section 'Understanding How Risk Relates to Gain', for more on this). However, when reviewing the business plans of others, one common mistake that people make is they're overly optimistic about the demand or interest in their product or services. A sunhat with a solar-powered fan on top may seem a good idea, but is anyone going to be seen dead wearing such a thing?

A friend of mine had an idea to start a business selling handmade timber beds. He decided to test this idea by running a stall once a month at the local markets. The response seemed good at first, but he soon found that people were reluctant to pay the extra dollars for his products, with people comparing his prices against the mass-manufactured timber beds made from poor-quality pine and available from large discount furniture chains. His profits were also lower than expected, and the time required to liaise with customers about their individual orders was higher. The result was that he decided not to pursue this business idea, but to explore other ways of making money instead.

Looking Around for More Ideas

Keep an open mind for ways in which your business can be different, or gain an advantage. Remember to review the match of your skills and what you're good at with the thing that your customers want that's going to make you different.

The internet is a great way to look around for new ideas of doing business. If you're struggling to identify strategic advantages for your business, go online and look all around the world at similar businesses to your own.

What's their marketing strategy? Do they do anything differently with pricing? Opening hours? Added services? Is someone doing something that you could emulate?

Be prepared to revisit your ideas repeatedly and keep reshaping the concept that you have for your business until you can come up with a strong strategic advantage.

Chapter 3

Sizing up the Competition

In This Chapter

▶ Getting motivated about understanding your competition

▶ Looking at who your competitors really are

▶ Going undercover with Sherlock Holmes

▶ Doing (yet another) reality check

▶ Preparing the big sell

I'm still surprised at how often I come across people planning to start a new business, or who are in the first couple of years of business, who have yet to research who their competitors are.

Detailed competitive analysis forms a vital part of any business plan and helps you establish what it is that your business is going to do better than others. As part of this analysis, you need to organise your competitors into groups, so you differentiate between 'head-on-head' competitors and competitors who only take away business from you on an occasional basis. You also need to think about future competitors — competitors who aren't yet a big deal, but could certainly become so if circumstances change.

In this chapter, I talk about doing a thorough competitor profile for key competitors, picking apart the differences between them and yourself. I also go full circle and return to the question any business person must ask themselves repeatedly: Given what the competition are doing and how they are faring, is your business model likely to fly like an eagle or sink like a stone? Or could you risk everything, and gain little in return?

Once you've clarified where your strengths lie when compared to the competition, you're ready for the 'big sell.' At the end of this chapter I also provide some tips on selling your idea in 30 seconds — otherwise known as the 'elevator speech'.

Why Analysing Competitors Is a Big Deal

Your competition isn't just the marker of who you have to 'beat'. Your competition can be a source of inspiration or the benchmark that enables you to establish realistic expectations for your business. Your competition also provides a vital insight into where you can gain a possible edge.

Competitor analysis can also provide the reality check that prevents you from taking unnecessary risks. For example, in my local town a whole strip of cafes come and go with every change in season. If I were thinking about starting a cafe, a competitor analysis may quickly reveal that the rents in this strip are hideously high, the landlords are difficult, and nobody is making enough profits to survive, let alone thrive.

On a more positive note, interacting with competitors can also point to potential opportunities. For many people, the seed of a winning business idea is sown by not being able to receive good enough service or quite the right product. So they think, *I can do better than that*, and a new business idea or marketing strategy is born.

Getting into the detail of competitor analysis can be just as insightful. If you're going to compete head-on with another business, you want to be right across the services that business provides, and the prices it charges. Unless a massive undersupply exists, charging $20 more per hour is probably pointless if you're providing an identical service to someone who's working just next door.

Of course, price isn't the only thing that you're going to consider when comparing yourself against competitors. You also want to differentiate yourself from your competitors in ways other than price (always keep asking yourself what it is that makes *you* special) and you need to be able to convey this difference clearly in your marketing materials. Unless you know exactly what your competitors provide, you won't know how to sell your differences.

Last, and at the risk of sounding unscrupulous, researching how your competitors go about their business can often provide inspiration for stuff that you can do better. Pricing specials, weekend packages, discount offers, creative advertising or clever sales techniques are just some of the things you may decide to copy. After all, imitation is the greatest form of flattery (although your competitors may not see it that way!).

When doing your competitor analysis, don't be hesitant to compare your business against big-time competitors such as supermarket chains or large franchises. While you may find it hard to imagine how your fledgling business could ever compete, the mass-market nature of these competitors often leaves niches that are underserviced, providing opportunities for smaller players.

Figuring Out Who Your Competitors Really Are

You can't create a battle plan without knowing the enemy. In the following sections, I explore how to figure out who the enemy really is (otherwise known as your competitors, of course) and how to create a battle plan for each act of combat.

Organising competitors into groups

I like to organise competitors into three broad groups, and I suggest you try to do so too:

- **Head-to-head competitors** provide exactly the same service or exactly the same product as you do.

- **'Sometimes' competitors** provide a slightly different service or product, or are in a different location.

- **Left-field competitors** don't normally compete with you but, if circumstances were to change, could possibly do so.

Imagine you're a professional jazz musician (think smoky bars, Miles Davis and sleek horn solos). Your head-to-head competitors would be other jazz musicians in the same city; your 'sometimes' competitors would be musicians living in other cities or musicians playing other genres; your left-field competition could be those wretched poker machines that are taking over bars and seem to be sounding the death knell for live music.

In the same way, if you're an osteopath specialising in back pain, you might have three groups of competitors: Other osteopaths providing exactly the same service in the same area (head-to-head), allied health practitioners such as physiotherapists who specialise in back pain ('sometimes'), and pain-killing tablets sold by pharmacies (left-field).

Although figuring out who your competitors are may sound easy, your competitors may not always be so easy to spot. For example, a watchmaker repairing and selling watches 10 or 20 years ago would have probably thought that the main competition was other watchmakers. The idea that the mobile phone could almost completely annihilate this industry would seem a long shot.

When you're thinking about the competition for your proposed business, don't be too literal — think about where both your business and its industry are headed.

Homing in on head-to-head competitors

Mostly you want to spend your energy analysing the head-to-head competition. After all, these are the competitors that your customers are most often going to come across when they seek to purchase your goods or services.

One of the purposes of identifying competitors is so you can develop a competitive strategy to deal with each one (refer to the section 'Why Analysing Competitors is a Big Deal', earlier in this chapter, for more reasons). However, when you create a list of head-to-head competitors, this can sometimes be a long list. For example, if you're starting up a business as an electrician, you may find 50 other electricians are working in your local area. You don't want to have to come up with 50 different competitive strategies, so your best tactic is to try to group these competitors in some way.

Try this process:

1. **List your competitors in a small number of groups based on similarities.**

   For example, the electrician may split his list of 50 other electricians according to size of the business, focus of the business (maybe some focus more on repairs, others on hot water, others on new buildings), or by locality or suburb.

2. **Think about how you've organised these groups. Will a customer looking for your kind of business use these same criteria?**

   For example, if a customer is searching online for an electrician, are they going to search by suburb, by specialty, or by services provided (such as 24-hour call outs)?

3. **Have a think about where you belong in the scheme of things.**

   For example, the electrician may decide he wants to focus on solar systems but within a 50-kilometre radius only.

4. **Think to the future. Do you want to be in this same group in five years' time?**

   For example, maybe the electrician has a vision that ultimately he wants to offer not just solar installations, but home-energy consultations also.

By organising your competitors into groups, you can build a clearer idea about how to develop different competitive strategies, depending on what kind of competitor you're dealing with.

Thinking about future competitors

In Chapter 13, I talk about your vision for the future, and how important it is to keep your eyes open to trends in the economy, the environment and in your industry. This macro way of thinking is also useful at the early planning stages of your business, particularly if you spend a while thinking about not just who your competitors are right now, but also who your competitors could be in one, two or five years' time.

Why you can sometimes beat the big guys

When you're checking out competitors, you may come across lots of factors that make it tough for you to compete with the big guys in town, such as high capital costs, expensive IT systems or huge distribution networks. These factors are called *entry barriers*.

The flipside of entry barriers can be *exit barriers*. Sometimes competitors have invested so much in expensive rentals or specialised equipment, or sometimes competitors can be so management top-heavy, that they can't get easily out of the less profitable parts of their business, and also can't act quickly when opportunities arise.

For smaller businesses, these exit barriers sometimes point to opportunities. Maybe you can distribute product much more cheaply using the internet, while the competition is wedded to expensive retail rents. Similarly, maybe you can act quickly in response to new fads or fashions, creating and promoting products in a fraction of the time a big company takes to do the same thing.

Ask yourself questions relating to the following areas:

- **Automation potential:** Could any existing competitors automate their processes using advanced technology and, therefore, become more of a threat than they already are?

- **Big buys coming to town:** Could a franchise chain or large company move into your village, suburb or town and take lots of your customers? (In my village, the longstanding boutique wine store was decimated when two big liquor chains moved within 3 kilometres.)

- **Buyout of minor competitors by a larger competitor with more capital and muscle:** Could one of your existing competitors be bought out by someone with more capital and better distribution and, in the process, become a very formidable competitor? (Think about how some of the smaller gourmet food products have been purchased by supermarket chains and suddenly appear in every store.)

- **Changes in technology:** Could changes in technology mean your product or service becomes obsolete? (Think of the long-lost corner video store, the TV repairer or the 24-hour photo lab.)

- **Cheaper imports:** Could the goods you provide be substituted by imported goods if the exchange rate changes?

- **Customers doing it themselves:** Could your main customer or customers decide creating your product or providing your service in-house makes more sense? (Think of the big supermarket chains that now manufacture their own generic food lines.)

- **Life cycle of business idea:** Is the life cycle of your business reaching maturity or beyond, meaning numerous competitors and fewer profits to go around? (Think of the mobile coffee vans that were once a clever niche business but are now a dime a dozen.)

- **Offshoring of labour:** Could the services you provide be performed offshore instead? (Almost anything that's mostly labour and can be done on a computer is vulnerable to offshoring.)

- **Service offered online:** Could the service you provide be sold online and, therefore, open to international competition? (Even some things that I would never have imagined could go online have done so. I don't go to my local yoga class any more, but instead log onto a yoga website that offers hundreds of pre-recorded classes to fit any duration, level or style of yoga.)

Go to www.dummies.com/go/creatingbusinessplan to download a Future Competitor worksheet, which lists each of the questions shown in the preceding list. Make notes against each of these headings, and think about what the future may have in store for your business. You may also want to read through the first half of Chapter 13 at this point, and consider future competitors in light of overall industry trends.

Engaging in Cloak-and-Dagger Tactics

The time has come for you to don your dark sunglasses, felt hat and fake moustache. Adopt a foreign accent and pose as an undercover agent.

Doing a competitor profile

The earlier part of this chapter covers making a list of your key competitors (refer to the section 'Figuring Out Who Your Competitors Really Are' for more). Bad news is, just writing down the name of your competitor isn't enough. Your next step is to do a full-on assessment of each one. (This detailed assessment probably won't end up being part of your final business plan, but does form the basis for your marketing strategies.)

Predicting exactly what you need to include in your competitor dossier is a tad hard for me, because it depends so much on the type of industry you're in and also how practical it is to find out certain information. (Copying your competitors' bright ideas may be one thing, but hacking into their computer system is quite another.)

Your best source for all of this information is probably online (visiting your competitor's website or e-commerce store), but you may also be able to glean more information by checking out your competitors' stands if they go to trade shows, looking at competitor brochures, browsing through trade or business directories, chatting to suppliers or distributors, or talking to customers who have defected to your side of the fence. You may well have to go undercover and pose as a customer (or ask a family member to do so) — I know that such clandestine activity can feel a bit weird, but the results are usually worth it.

In Figure 3-1, I list a few questions you can use as your starting point with your competitors research.

The Competitor Analysis worksheet shown in Figure 3-1 is also available online at www.dummies.com/go/creatingbusinessplan.

Competitor Analysis

Competitor Name: _____ **Date:** _____

What customers does this competitor target in particular? ....

What are the hourly rates, or price per unit? ....

Do they offer any special pricing, discounts or pricing packages? ....

What image is this competitor trying to convey?...................................
....

Do they have an area of specialty or a particular niche? ....
....

Do they offer any services that I don't? ....
....

Does this competitor seem to be doing well? ....

How long has this competitor been around? ....

How many employees do they have? ....

How savvy is this competitor in regards to technology? ....

Is this competitor active in social media? ....

What distribution networks does this competitor have? ....
....
....

What are the likely competitive advantages that this competitor has? ....
....
....

Figure 3-1:
Building a
dossier for
each key
competitor.

Mirror, mirror on the wall . . .

Who's the fairest of them all?

One thing to remember when you compare yourself against others is that you don't need to be perfect, offer rock-bottom pricing or provide unbelievable service and availability. Instead, all you need to be is that little bit better than your competitor. For example, imagine an electrician starting up in a new town has decided he wants to be the cheapest (always a risky business strategy, but nonetheless this can sometimes be an okay way to get started). He discovers that the next cheapest competitor is working for $45 an hour. In order to be competitive on price, this electrician doesn't need to sell his services for $35 an hour — $42.50 will do just fine and will meet the needs for those customers hunting around for the cheapest hourly rate.

Of course, price isn't the only variable that you need to consider, and Table 3-1 shows a detailed competitive analysis where this electrician compares himself with four other electricians in his local area, rating his competitors according to what they do better (or worse) than him.

Table 3-1	Rating Head-to-Head Competitors			
Does this competitor . . .	*Sparkies*	*Ed Power*	*PlugItIn*	*Wire & Co*
Have cheaper pricing than me?	Yes	No	No	No
Offer longer opening hours or availability?	No	No	Yes	Yes
Offer specific services that I don't?	No	Yes	No	Yes
Have better distribution or service a wider region?	No	No	No	Yes
Offer a larger variety of pricing packages?	No	No	Yes	Yes
Have more expertise and a higher level of skill?	No	No	No	Yes
Service all the niches that I service?	No	No	No	No
Have respect and trust in the community?	Yes	No	No	Yes
Have an active social media presence?	No	No	Yes	Yes
Have a good online marketing strategy?	No	No	Yes	Yes
Have more capital and power to expand?	No	No	Yes	Yes

To do this competitive analysis for your own business, download the Current Competitor Analysis worksheet from www.dummies.com/go/creatingbusinessplan. You may want to insert additional criteria against which to compare yourself, or have more than four competitors in your analysis, but this template provides you with a starting point. The important thing is that you list your comparison criteria in the first column, and the names of the competitors that you're comparing yourself against in the first row. Below each competitor, write yes if they're better and no if you're better (or not applicable if this isn't relevant to you).

Choosing your competitive strategy

After you complete the rating process for each competitor (refer to the preceding section), grab a highlighter pen (or use the Fill function in Excel) and highlight any rows that have 'no' in every column. For example, in Table 3-1, the electrician has 'no' against the question of whether his competition services all the niches he services. The fact that he's servicing a specific niche that others aren't servicing (in this case, a consultation service to make homes energy-efficient) highlights a clear opportunity. Pricing is also potentially an opportunity for this business, given that he is cheaper than three out of four of his competitors.

So what next? To put it simply, the electrician has three possible competitive strategies. He can try to lead on price, he can attempt to differentiate his services in some way or other, or he can focus on a specific niche.

In fact, any business, including yours, is faced with these three possible competitive strategies: cost leadership, differentiation or niche. You may choose only one of the strategies, you could choose two, or you may choose a combination of all three:

✔ **You can choose to be the cheapest (cost leadership strategy).** With this strategy, you're not necessarily the cheapest across all products you offer, or the cheapest for every service but, in general, you're aiming to compete on price. Price leadership can be a tempting strategy — after all, customers are always looking for a bargain — but is risky over the long term. Unless you have a strategic advantage that enables you to deliver your product or service more cheaply than your competitors, competing on price can mean weak profitability. (On the other hand, if you're just getting started, choosing to be cheapest can be a good strategy for gaining clients and building up experience.)

✔ **You can set out to create a point of difference (differentiation strategy).** If you have a business that's very similar to your competitors both in price and the service you provide, you can set out to differentiate yourself in some way. For example, an electrician could seek to make response time and punctuality a point of difference ('We'll arrive within 30 minutes of the agreed time or the first hour is free'), or could make availability a point of difference ('24-hour call-out service, 7 days a week').

Ideally, if you choose differentiation as your competitive strategy, you want to find a synergy between this differentiation and your strategic advantage (for more about strategic advantage, refer to Chapter 2). For example, maybe a strategic advantage for this electrician is that his wife also has a trade license. Between them, they can offer a 24-hour service without worrying about leaving the kids unattended at home, and they don't have to pay the penalty rates that other businesses would normally have to pay if sending an employee out on a job in the middle of the night on a Sunday.

✔ **You can find a particular focus or niche (niche strategy).** With this strategy, your aim is to serve a specific market segment rather than dealing with the whole market. You can combine this niche strategy with a cost strategy, of course (by focusing on one specific niche, you may end up being the cheapest), and you can certainly combine a niche strategy with a differentiation strategy (because the differentiation itself becomes a niche). In *We Are All Weird*, written by Seth Godin and published by Brilliance Corporation, Godin argues that people are seeking choices more than ever, and that this competitive strategy is increasingly vital for any business.

You can choose cost leadership or differentiation as competitive strategies in their own right. However, if you choose a niche strategy, implicit in that is that you're also choosing a differentiation strategy. (In other words, you can choose differentiation as your competitive strategy without having a niche, but by its very nature choosing a niche as your competitive strategy means that you're also choosing to differentiate.)

If people can't find your product, how can they buy it?

If your business idea is based around a product that you've manufactured yourself, one key issue you'll need to address when comparing your product offering against that of competitors is distribution. After all, distribution is generally a business in its own right. Do you plan to do all the selling, packing and shipping as well as the manufacturing?

If your answer is yes, you may find that the problem is the number of products you offer. Distributors generally deal with a large number of products, and they gain efficiencies by doing so (in terms of sales representation, computer systems, freight costs, warehousing and so on). If you only manufacture one or two products, you won't have any of these efficiencies. Not only will you almost certainly find that distribution is very expensive, but you may also find that some retailers don't want to deal with you because they don't want to bother opening a new account for just one or two products.

Matching your competitive strategy to your strategic advantage

In Chapter 2, I talk about strategic advantage and explain that a true strategic advantage is something that your business has that offers real value to customers but that's hard for your competitors to copy.

If you managed to identify a strategic advantage, you may well find that this translates into a particular opportunity when you do your competitor comparison (as per Table 3-1, earlier in this chapter).

With these factors in mind, what you want to do is pick a competitive strategy (focusing on cost, differentiation or a particular niche) that complements both your strategic advantage and any opportunities you've identified in the competitive landscape.

Always try to pursue a clear strategy. If you choose to muddle along not doing anything that's clearly different to others, you will find it both difficult to compete and to establish a clear strategic advantage in the market.

Summarising Your Competitive Strategy

If you've been reading this book straight through, you may be feeling a little muddled by the way the concepts of strategic advantage, competitor analysis and competitive strategy all interrelate.

But interrelate they do, with each concept triggering off one another. In the following sections, you can see how these concepts relate and how you get to measure up the likely success of your business model.

Joining the dots

The thing about being in business is that your competitive environment is constantly changing. Maybe you have a particular advantage over competitors but then something changes that takes away that edge. Or maybe you've positioned yourself in a very specific way against a particular competitor but that competitor suddenly changes their business model entirely.

Figure 3-2 shows how the concepts of strategic advantage, competitor analysis and competitive advantage interrelate. You can see that the process of identifying your strategic advantage, comparing yourself against competitors and choosing a competitive strategy is a continuous cycle of using your analysis to assess your own business idea.

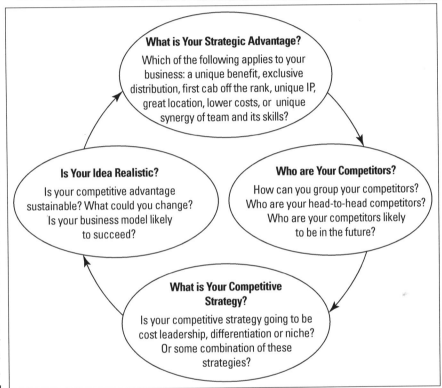

Figure 3-2:
Using your strategic advantage, competitor analysis and competitive strategy to continually improve your business idea.

The question of what your business can do better or differently than others goes to the heart of your business plan, and usually forms the essence of your likely business success. The first part of your business plan needs to include a summary of your strategic advantage (a topic I explain in Chapter 2), which then flows into an analysis of your competitors and a summary of your competitive strategy (which is what this chapter is all about). You may also choose to expand on your competitor analysis as part of the marketing section of your business plan (Chapter 12 explores marketing plans in detail).

Measuring up the risks

I mentor a start-up business group from time to time. One of the things we work on at each session is identifying what it is that a business is going to do better than others, and what the competitive strategy is going to be.

I sometimes find that when people do an honest appraisal of their business idea and the competition, the resulting business proposal is quite weak. Usually this is because the person starting up in business has limited skills or minimal capital, or because so many big guys are out there dominating the market that getting a foot in the door seems impossible.

I think a business plan that results in someone saying, 'This idea is a dud' or 'The idea is okay, but I'm not the right person to do it' is actually a very successful business plan. The plan, which has probably taken up many days or weeks of research but cost very little, has probably saved that person thousands of dollars, not to mention months or even years of his or her time.

More often, however, a plan that's built around a weak business idea (maybe it has no clear strategic advantage or strong competitive strategy, but nonetheless has some potential) provides no definitive answer as to whether that person should continue. In this situation, what becomes relevant is measuring up the risks. If starting (or continuing with) this business means little capital outlay and a few lost weekends and holidays, you could argue the person doesn't have much to lose. On the other hand, if this business involves someone's retirement savings and/or the threat of a failed relationship if things go wrong, the risk may be unjustifiable.

However much you want to believe in your business idea, if a high level of risk is involved (either personally or financially), do weigh this risk against the likely strength of your business model.

Preparing an Elevator Speech

Imagine you're in an elevator going up to the 25th floor and this guy who you've seen around a couple of times before gets in. You catch his eye and he says to you 'Hi, I'm Jim. I've see you here before. Remind me, what's your business all about again?'

You look at the orange numbers flickering on the elevator control panel. You're on the fifth floor, with 20 floors yet to go. You reckon you have about 30 seconds to convey what your business concept is, what you do, and what makes you so damned special. So, what do you reply?

Your answer, of course, depends on the context and the situation, but whatever wording you use, you should always start by thinking of your competitive strategy — what it is that makes you special in the eyes of your customers, and what makes you different from the competition (what this chapter focuses on).

Saying what you do in 30 seconds or less

Are you ready to take the challenge? Don't think about what you're going to say. Instead, click the Record button on your computer or smartphone, have a quick look at the clock, and answer this question in 30 seconds or less:

> 'What's your business all about?'

Tick, tick, tick ... stop. How did you go? Listen back and rate yourself out of 10.

Now have a go at doing your speech again but this time, make sure you include the following elements:

✔ Your name (and probably your business name too)

✔ The way that you help others

✔ What makes your business different from others

Sounds simple, but trust me, this 30-second snapshot is surprisingly demanding.

What to avoid with your elevator speech

When honing your elevator speech, steer clear of business-speak and gobbledegook and keep to simple, everyday terms. If you tell someone that your business aim is 'To achieve a user-centric portal framework' they're likely to die of boredom on the spot. They won't ever arrive at the 25th floor and you'll be stuck dealing with a string of paramedics.

Choose a clear, animated response for your elevator speech instead of business-speak, and give the following words the disdain they deserve: Client base, commitment, core, customer-orientated, empower, enhance, facilitate, implement, input, issue, integrated, maximise, outcome, outside the box, prioritise, scenario, synergy.

Avoiding the general slaughter of the English language isn't enough. Other no-noes include:

- ✔ **Don't start your speech with the words 'I am'.** Really. You can do better than this. Remember that this person wants to hear what *your business* can do for them, and this isn't the time to be talking about yourself.

- ✔ **Don't have a memorised speech that you stick to, word for word.** A good elevator speech changes with the context and the audience. What you say to a fellow parent in the queue at parent-teacher night is going to be different to what you say when sitting next to somebody at a conference dinner function.

- ✔ **Don't fail to mention what sets you apart.** This is your point of difference, the thing that makes you interesting and memorable. Even if you have a relatively everyday business — maybe you're an electrician or you tutor kids after school — you will be able to find something that sets you apart.

If an average 12-year-old kid can't understand what it is that you do after listening to your elevator speech, you need to start again.

Practice makes perfect

When I run business-mentoring courses, I talk about elevator speeches in the very first session. I explain how you don't necessarily have to be in an elevator; you get lots of situations such as dinner parties, conferences, business meetings and social groups where someone will ask you conversationally what it is that you do.

I go around the room and ask everybody to have a go at their elevator speech. Generally, only one or two people even come close to a decent speech in that first session. But then every single week thereafter I start the session by going around the room and getting everyone to do their 30-second spiel.

I find it fascinating how these speeches change as the weeks go by, and people get clearer and better at selling what it is they're doing. Doing an elevator speech puts you on the spot.

So in this first stage of getting your business off the ground, keep in mind that practice makes perfect. Say your speech aloud when you get in the shower, turn on the ignition of your car, or make yourself a cup of tea. Your family may think you're a little bit potty, but that's a small price to pay.

Visit www.dummies.com/go/creatingbusinessplan and follow the link to Preparing an Elevator Speech. I've provided three business cards here — click any of these cards to arrive at a link to that business owner's elevator speech.

Part II

Doing the Groundwork

Five Tips for Setting Prices for Your Service or Products

- ✔ **Don't be the cheapest:** Unless your business involves some technological breakthrough that allows you to produce things cheaper than anyone else, being the cheapest is a risky business strategy.

- ✔ **Value your product or service through the eyes of your customers:** Don't base pricing on costs but instead on what customers are prepared to pay.

- ✔ **Offer both premium and no-frill options:** If you can, think of a way to offer both premium and bare-bone pricing so you can exploit both ends of the market.

- ✔ **Look at ways to package your product or service:** Bundle products together, team up with another business or devise a bonus scheme.

- ✔ **Vary pricing for each situation:** Be prepared to charge different prices depending on customer location, order quantities, payment terms and customer loyalty.

Pricing and sales projections form an essential part of your business plan. Check out www.dummies.com/extras/creatingbusinessplan for a free online article about the psychology of sales projections.

In this part ...

- Follow a simple checklist to create a start-up budget for your new business, and figure out how much finance you need, who you can borrow from and what your loan repayments are likely to be.

- Set prices for your product and services, and look at ways to charge different prices for different things.

- Create a detailed sales forecast for the next 12 months using simple step-by-step techniques.

- Establish the true costs of your product or your service, and impress friends and family with bold chat about gross profit, profit margins and variable costs.

- Build a budget for expenses, and use business benchmarking to determine how realistic this budget really is.

- Keep that wolf from howling at your door — know how much you need to survive while your business gets established.

Chapter 4

Budgeting for Start-Up Expenses

. . . .

In This Chapter

▶ Making a list of everything you need, and how much it's likely to cost

▶ Differentiating between different types of expenses, and how to account for each one

▶ Thinking about how much finance your business requires to get off the ground

▶ Understanding interest, repayments and what you can afford

▶ Selling your soul to the devil, taking out loans and more

. . . .

*I*f you're planning to start a new business or expand your existing business in some way, chances are you're going to need a bit of cash behind you. The question is, of course, how much?

When starting a business, your budget must allow for not only new equipment, vehicles, stock and other big-ticket items, but also the variety of additional expenses you're bound to encounter in the first few months of trading. You may also need additional finance for living expenses until your business becomes profitable.

In this chapter, I talk about pulling together your start-up budget and working out different types of expenses, so that you can make a plan for how much cash you're going to need. I also talk about navigating the dark perils of finance, including the pros and cons of business loans, credit cards, equity partners, leases and last (but not least) borrowing funds from your benevolent and long-suffering family.

Creating a Start-Up Budget

Creating a budget for start-up expenses is a good idea, no matter how large or small your proposed business. Unless you know how much capital you're going to need to get started, you won't have any idea about how much finance is required, nor will you have a sense of the risk involved.

If you're still at the conception stage for your business — maybe you're testing your product at local markets or trialling the service that you offer — you're probably still working from home or manufacturing on a small scale. As part of the planning process and testing the long-term viability of your business idea, I suggest you create a start-up budget for how much money you would require if you were to manufacture your product on a large scale or if you were to set up a proper office servicing a wide range of clients.

Purchasing materials and inventory

If you're a manufacturer, retailer or wholesaler, your start-up budget must include the initial purchase of products for resale. In order to create this budget, you need the following information:

- **If you are a retailer:** Your start-up budget must include an estimate of the cost value of stock (including freight) you will need to have on your shelves on the first day that you open.

  Most retailers, other than those selling fresh produce, have at least two months' worth of stock at any one time. If you're importing goods from overseas, you will almost certainly require more than two months' worth of stock (either in your shop, or already in transit).

- **Manufacturers:** The initial stock that you require entirely depends on whether you're doing custom manufacturing (in which case you probably only need to invest in display goods) or whether you're doing bulk production (in which case you may need a minimum initial volume in order to keep your costs down).

- **Distributors/wholesalers:** The value of stock required depends on the lead time from your suppliers. If your suppliers can deliver to you overnight or within a couple of days, you'll need to hold much less stock than if you're importing goods from overseas.

From a bookkeeping perspective, when you buy goods that you plan to resell, or when you buy materials that you plan to manufacture into a finished product, these purchases aren't cost of goods sold, nor are they expenses. Instead, bookkeepers allocate stock purchases to asset accounts called Inventory, Stock on Hand or Raw Materials. This distinction between an asset and an expense is crucial to understand when you're assembling your financial projections. If you show all the stock or raw materials required for starting your business as an expense, your projected Profit & Loss could look very miserable indeed. (For more about the difference between cost of goods sold and expenses, see Chapter 6.)

Listing your start-up expenses

In Table 4-1, I show a possible format for listing start-up expenses. I suggest you create this list using spreadsheet software such as Excel. (This way, if your forecasted figures change, all the totals recalculate automatically.)

Go to www.dummies.com/go/creatingbusinessplan to access the budget shown in Table 4-1 as an Excel spreadsheet. Print out this document or open the spreadsheet on your computer and place a dollar estimate against each line.

Making your start-up expense estimates is pretty straightforward, but here are some pointers to help along the way:

✔ If an expense isn't relevant, just enter $0.00 as the value, or delete this row entirely.

✔ If something is missing from this list, just add another row. Remember, however, that you're budgeting for start-up expenses, not ongoing expenses. (If you're not sure what counts as a start-up expense, skip ahead to the section 'Separating Start-up Expenses from Operating Expenses', later in this chapter.)

✔ Have you already purchased some business assets using your own funds? See the section 'Including expenses paid for out of personal funds' later in this chapter for more details regarding whether to include these assets in your start-up expenses.

✔ If consumer tax applies in the country or state in which you're operating (for example, sales tax in the United States, VAT in Canada or the UK, or GST in Australia and New Zealand), and you know that you will be able to claim a refund for any tax you pay, show your start-up expenses excluding, rather than including, tax.

Table 4-1	Start-Up Expenses Budget	
New Equipment or Tools		$
Computer systems and peripherals		
Vehicles, including special fit-out, if required		
Office furnishings		
Retail equipment (cash register, point-of-sale software)		
Tools and equipment		
Other (describe here)		
Premises Fit-out		
Council fees, if necessary		
Fit-out of new premises		
Lease agreement fees		
Rental bond and rent in advance		
Other (describe here)		
Other Start-up Expenses		
Accounting fees (advice for new start-up)		
Consultant fees		
Incorporation of company		
Insurance (public liability/business indemnity/property insurance)		
Internet connection and networks		
Legal fees		
License fees		
Marketing materials and brochures		
Registration of business name		
Security bonds for electricity, gas and phone		
Signage		
Stock for resale		
Telephone connection		
Training of staff		
Website design and construction		
Other (describe here)		
TOTAL		$___.__

I often get asked how much is reasonable for a start-up budget. My answer is that I've seen business start-ups that require not one brass razoo, and others that require several million dollars. If you're not sure about the accuracy (or completeness) of your start-up budget, I suggest you bounce the figures off your accountant or business adviser.

One thing I have noticed is that people planning a new retail business often seem to underestimate start-up expenses. Items such as shop fit-out and opening stock for resale are invariably more expensive than expected. Make sure you're budgeting enough to cover all likely expenses.

Including expenses paid for out of personal funds

Have you already purchased an asset in your own name that you're intending to use for business purposes (likely examples are a computer or vehicle)? If so, should you show this item in your budget for start-up expenses? The answer depends, as follows:

- ✔ If you're setting up as a sole trader or a partnership, your start-up budget doesn't need to include assets that you've already purchased.

- ✔ If your business is going to have a company structure and you require the company to reimburse you straightaway for this asset, then yes, include this asset in your start-up budget.

- ✔ If your business is going to have a company structure but you're happy for the company to make use of an asset that you own while it's getting established, you don't need to include this asset in your start-up budget.

Adding enough to live on

Most businesses don't make any profit in the first six months and, in fact, many businesses make a loss during this time. For some businesses, the period before you see any profits may be even longer.

When budgeting for a new business, you not only need to budget for business expenses, but your own living expenses also. Quite how you do this depends on your circumstances, and whether you're continuing to work another job while your business gets established. Chapters 7 through to 9 explore business and personal budgets in detail, pulling together the different elements of your financial plan. When you complete this process, you should be able to ascertain whether you require any additional finance for living expenses.

Don't sink before you swim

A few years ago, a neighbour of mine decided to open a gift shop. She signed a lease in the main street and, while the shop stood empty for two months, spent up big on fitting out the premises, installing designer lights and top-of-the-range point-of-sale and security systems. The shop looked absolutely beautiful. The trouble was, by the time she was ready to open, she didn't have enough capital left to purchase adequate stock, nor enough capital to live on for the next 12 months while her business established itself. Within six months, she had to cut her losses and close down.

Business start-up expenses are often much higher than you imagine. If you're still at the initial planning stage, ensure you run your start-up budget past your accountant or business adviser.

While your budget for start-up expenses is an essential first step, this budget doesn't necessarily provide a clear indication of how much you need to borrow — you only know that for sure when you complete the rest of your business and personal budgets. See Chapters 7 to 10 for more on this.

Separating Start-Up Expenses from Operating Expenses

If you're new to business, you may find it hard to differentiate between start-up expenses and operating expenses. This difference is crucial in order for you to calculate how much start-up finance you require and in order for you to report accurately as regards business profitability.

A *start-up expense* is a one-off expense related to starting your business or purchasing an asset that your business requires. An *operating expense* is an ongoing expense that will feature as a regular part of running your business.

Dealing with initial start-up expenses

One of the tricky questions in the first stages of a business plan is how to treat initial start-up expenses. For example, if you spend $500 painting the inside of your new office, does this count as a business start-up expense, or is it just repairs and maintenance?

The answer — in terms of your business plan and financial reporting, but not necessarily your tax return — is that if something's a one-off expense that's related to getting your business started and you don't expect to have this expense again as part of day-to-day trading (or not for a little while at least), you should treat this as a start-up expense.

For example, if you rent a new office or shop and you spend money on fitting out the premises, building shelves, adding carpet or painting, these are good examples of start-up expenses. (However, if you repaint or re-carpet the office in a few years' time, this would count as repairs and maintenance.)

Other items such as logo design, business stationery, marketing materials or packaging design are also good examples of start-up expenses. Sure, you'll almost certainly spend money on more marketing materials in the future, but you're unlikely to have such a big expense all in one go.

What you're trying to do is distinguish between all those initial expenses that come in a rush when you first start up your business, and separate these from the ongoing expenses you're going to have with your business. This is the only way you can establish how profitable your business really is in those first financially delicate months of trading.

Putting theory into practice

I don't know about you, but despite the fact that *For Dummies* books are about as chirpy as can be when dealing with some pretty dry topics, I still tend to glaze over when reading about costs versus assets, profit and loss forecasts and budget estimates. So I'm going to take a real-life business and show how a budget for start-up expenses interacts with financial forecasts.

In this scenario, my friend Eva is starting up a small retail business. In Table 4-2, you can see what she reckons she's going to have to pay in the first four weeks of starting up her business (including the money she'll have to pay before she even opens her doors for trading).

Table 4-2	First Four Weeks Budget for Retail Business
Item	**$**
Eight weeks' rental bond	4,800.00
Four weeks' rent in advance	2,400.00
Signage and marketing brochures	1,500.00
Website design including first month's hosting (hosting is $100 per month)	1,100.00
Lease payment for air-conditioning unit	400.00
Cost value of stock purchased for resale	20,000.00
New shelving and computer equipment	15,000.00
Wages for the first month	3,000.00
Advertising for the first month	200.00
All other expenses for the first month (bank fees, electricity, internet, motor vehicle, telephone and so on)	800.00
Insurance for the first 12 months	2,400.00
Accounting fees for advice regarding starting a new business	1,600.00
TOTAL	**53,200.00**

Imagine that Eva sells $10,000 of goods in her first four weeks of trading. What do you think the projected Profit & Loss should be in her business plan for this period?

At a simplistic level, you could say that Eva is going to receive $10,000 as income, and she'll spend $53,200 in expenses, which would equate to a $43,200 loss. However, this basic approach doesn't give a true representation of what's going on, and no bank or investor is going to want a bar of a business that shows this kind of loss.

What Eva needs to do is separate her start-up expenses from her operating expenses. Table 4-3 shows how she does this.

Table 4-3	Start-up Expenses versus First Four Weeks Operating Expenses	
Item		**$**
Start-up Expenses		
Eight weeks' rental bond		4,800.00
Signage and marketing brochures		1,500.00
Website design excluding first month's hosting (hosting is $100 per month)		1,000.00
Cost value of stock purchased for resale		20,000.00
New shelving and computer equipment		15,000.00
Insurance for the first 12 months		2,200.00
Accounting fees for advice regarding starting a new business		1,600.00
TOTAL		**46,100.00**
Operating Expenses — First Four Weeks		
Four weeks' rent in advance		2,400.00
Website hosting		100.00
Lease payment for air-conditioning unit		400.00
Wages for the first month		3,000.00
Advertising for the first month		200.00
All other expenses for the first month		800.00
Insurance for the first month		200.00
TOTAL		**7,100.00**

Can you see how, if you view Eva's figures from this perspective, the projected Profit & Loss looks very different? If Eva makes 40 cents gross profit in the dollar, the business would have $10,000 in sales, $6,000 in cost of sales and $7,100 in operating expenses. The business would still show a loss of $3,100, but this is significantly less than a loss of $43,200.

Chapters 7, 8 and 9 look in more detail at piecing your financial projections together, but at the early stages of your business, the thing that's vital for you to understand is the distinction between start-up expenses and operating expenses. This distinction is important not just from the perspective of creating a business plan that paints a positive picture for a prospective business, but also from a business management point of view. After all, if you don't understand this distinction, you won't be able to calculate your true profitability with any accuracy in the early months of trading.

By the way, your accountant will almost certainly treat start-up expenses differently for tax purposes, choosing to write off items that you've shown as start-up expenses (and which you're essentially treating as assets), so that you minimise your tax bills. However, the treatment of expenses from a tax-management point of view is different to how you should treat expenses from a business-management point of view.

Assessing How Much You Really Need

If you've been reading through this chapter from the beginning, hopefully you have an idea of how much money you'll require to get your business started. You'll know how much you need for equipment, vehicles, office or shop fit-out, as well as how much you need (if anything) for opening stock. In addition, you've started thinking about whether you'll need additional funds to see you through the first few months of business while you get yourself established.

In other words, although you won't have a final figure for how much you may need in the way of finance, you should have a rough idea. At this point, you can start thinking about three things:

- ✔ If you don't have the necessary savings, will you be able to borrow the money?

- ✔ How much finance will you need, and what will the likely repayments be?

- ✔ Will repayments be affordable in the first year or two of your business — or will this level of borrowing bring an unacceptable level of risk and/or stress?

Depending on the answers to these questions, you may want to review your start-up budget. Although earlier in this chapter I stress the importance of giving your business every possible chance of success by budgeting enough (refer to the section 'Listing your start-up expenses'), you may find that you can pull back or delay on some spending without the business suffering unduly.

Here are some tips for pruning your start-up budget:

- ✔ **Consider leasing rather than buying assets outright.** Finance that's secured against an asset such as a vehicle is usually pretty easy to obtain, and preserves your cash so that it can be used as working capital instead.

✔ **Be realistic.** You may really want that brand new speed-machine, but unless your vehicle is an essential part of the brand and image of your business, you can almost certainly do without.

✔ **Consider buying stuff second-hand.** Again, second-hand stuff isn't as glamorous as new and shiny stuff, but may do the job just as well.

✔ **Look at renting equipment.** If your budget includes new equipment, consider whether you could rent this equipment on an occasional basis while your business builds up.

Always guard your *working capital* (that is, the difference between your current assets and current liabilities) as a tigress guards her cubs. Even if you think you have enough cash to purchase everything your business needs to get started, if your business is successful and grows at any kind of pace at all, the growth itself is likely to gobble up your ready cash. (This concept of growth gobbling cash is called the *limit of sustainable growth*, something I explore further in Chapter 10.)

Calculating Likely Loan Repayments

Unless you have the support of a sugar daddy (always a rather questionable strategy), securing finance for your business probably involves getting a loan. Nothing in life comes free, and whoever lends you money will usually charge you for this pleasure. So the next step when preparing your business plan is to figure out how much you're going to have to shell out in both repayments and interest expense.

You may be thinking you haven't gotten far enough yet with your plan to know how much finance you'll need. (After all, until you create budgets for your first year of trading, you won't know whether you'll require additional finance to pay for living expenses or cover for trading losses in those first few months.) The difficulty is, however, that you won't be able to create these budgets without having some idea of how much your loan repayments will be.

The answer to this chicken-and-egg dilemma is simple: Start by making an estimate of how much finance you require and what the likely loan repayments are going to be (I explain how to calculate loan repayments next in this chapter). Then assemble your financial projections, including your estimated loan repayments (which I explain in Chapters 5 to 10). If your projections predict that cash will be tight and these loan repayments unaffordable, return to your start-up budget and revise your plan.

This continual process of planning, budgeting, checking results and then returning to the plan to make adjustments is part of what being in business is all about. Nothing is ever cast in stone and you always have to be flexible about your plans and expectations, regardless of whether you're just starting out in business or you've been trading for 20 years.

Estimating loan repayment schedules

When estimating your business loan repayment schedule, keep in mind that the loan term for most business or personal loans is shorter than for home loans. (By *loan term*, I mean the number of years in which you agree to pay the loan back down to zero.) I mention personal loans here, not just business loans, because many small business start-ups find that banks are reluctant to lend money for a new business, but are happy to offer funds for a personal loan.

You can find oodles of loan repayment calculators online (simply type 'loan repayment calculator' into Google or your favourite search engine). However, for most situations I prefer the really simple loan calculator that Excel offers, because I can not only view my loan repayment schedule at a glance, but also save my workings for future reference.

Here's what to do:

1. **Open up Excel.**

2. **Go to the File menu and select New. Or, if you're using a Mac, select New From Template.**

3. **Type** loan calculator **within the Search Office.com for Templates box and press Enter.**

4. **Look for the template called Loan Calculator and Amortization Schedule and double click on it.**

   This popular template usually comes up first in the list.

5. **Enter the amount you want to borrow as the Loan Amount.**

6. **Enter the likely interest rate as the Annual Interest Rate.**

   To find out the likely interest rate, go to the website for your bank and look up current variable interest rates for business loans. Banks often slap a premium of up to 5 per cent additional interest on business loans, compared to home loans, to allow for the additional risk involved.

7. **Enter 5 as the Loan Period in Years.**

   You can enter a shorter period here if you prefer, but five years is a good estimate of the time in which you should aim to pay off a business loan. Note that banks are often reluctant to offer a longer loan term than this.

8. Enter the Start Date for this loan and press Enter.

In the blink of an eye, Excel calculates your monthly payments as well as the total interest and cost of the loan, similar to the workings shown in Figure 4-1.

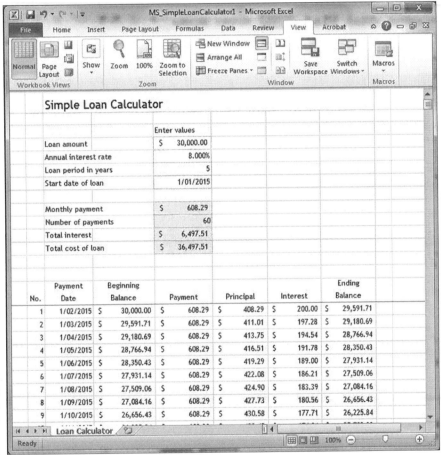

Figure 4-1:
Excel provides a simple loan repayment template you can use at any time.

You can find a copy of the Loan Calculator template at www.dummies.com/ go/creatingbusinessplan.

Calculating interest

When you do your financial projections (a spellbinding activity that I talk about in Chapters 8, 9 and 10), you have to split your loan repayments into *interest* and *principal*. Interest is the amount that the bank charges you each month for the pleasure of lending you money; principal (in this context) is how much you reduce the balance of your loan each month.

Looking at Figure 4-1, can you see how the monthly repayment is $608.29? Also, if you look at the first month's repayment, can you see how the interest is $200 and the principal is $408.29? This means that the first loan repayment reduces the balance of the loan by $408.29. As time goes on and the loan balance reduces, the monthly repayment stays the same but the amount of interest goes down and the amount of principal goes up.

In the context of your financial projections, the interest component is an expense in your Profit & Loss Projection. However, the whole value of the loan repayment shows as an outgoing in your Cashflow Projection.

If your business plan only includes a Profit & Loss Projection, you may be best to include the full value of the loan repayment in this report so that your projected net profit provides a better reflection of your likely cash position.

Thinking about whether you can really service this loan

After you calculate your predicted loan repayments, pause for a minute and ask yourself whether these repayments are realistic. The last thing you want to do while you're getting started is strangle your business with repayments that eat up your working capital and stifle growth.

If you're at all unsure about your calculated loan repayments, review your finance requirements carefully (refer to the section 'Assessing How Much You Really Need', earlier in this chapter). You may be better advised to plan on securing additional finance later down the track (when your business is hopefully growing and profitable) rather than saddling your new business with a high level of debt right from the start.

Understanding Different Finance Options

After deciding how much finance (if any) you require (refer to preceding sections), the next task is to find a willing victim to cough up the cash. A bank is usually the most obvious option, but other sources of funds include finance companies, equity partners, and family or friends.

At this point, spend some time confirming exactly how much you'll be able to borrow. If you have no steady income and no *collateral* (that is, assets such as your home against which the bank secures its loan), you may find that the bank refuses to lend you anything. This may mean you need to rethink your business plan or delay the start date while you save additional funds.

Getting into bed with the bank

Before you jump into a long-term relationship with any lender, be clear what you're getting into. Here's a quick summary of the kinds of finance available:

✔ A *business loan* usually works like an ordinary home loan — you borrow a fixed amount and commit to regular repayments over a certain number of years. A business loan is well suited for start-up finance, debt refinancing or financing business growth.

With business loans, the upside of structured repayments is that you're likely to pay off the loan relatively quickly. The downside is the bank usually offers a relatively short term on business loans (five years is quite standard) meaning that repayments are high even in the early years when the business can least afford it.

✔ A *business lease* can work in different ways depending on how you structure the lease. This kind of finance is almost always secured against a specific item of equipment or vehicle. Essentially, the finance company buys the asset on your behalf and then you make regular monthly payments for an agreed amount of time. Depending on the lease agreement, you will either own the asset outright at the end of the loan term, or you will be able to purchase it for a reduced price.

Leases are relatively easy to obtain for existing businesses (because they're secured against the asset itself) and help preserve your valuable working capital for things that are harder to obtain finance for (such as an increase in inventory or financing of accounts receivable).

✔ A *credit card* is the easiest type of finance to obtain, but is usually limited in how much you can borrow. Credit cards also involve the highest rate of interest. Generally, credit cards are best for short-term borrowing of relatively small amounts, and are a poor choice for start-up business finance.

✔ A *line of credit* works a little like a regular bank account, except the balance is in the red, not the black. You can use the loan for all your business banking, including both deposits and withdrawals. You have a credit limit on the account, and it's your choice whether you pay off the principal or pay interest only. Lines of credit are ideal for on-demand working capital and improved cashflow.

Although a line of credit offers great flexibility for your business, you do need to have a disciplined nature to force yourself to pay off the debt. (If you never reduce the principal outstanding on your line of credit, you end up paying more interest than on a regular business loan.)

Offering up collateral

Almost all banks require some security against borrowings and, unless you're still renting, the most obvious security is usually your own home. While you probably feel reluctant to offer your home as security, you may find that you don't have much choice in the matter, or that a business loan secured against your home attracts substantially less interest than a business loan that's unsecured.

Even if a business loan is in your name only, if you guarantee this loan against a property that's jointly owned, it's extremely likely that both parties (that is, both you and your best beloved) are jointly liable. This means that if the relationship breaks down, you get sick or even if you die, the other person may be legally obliged to repay the debt. For this reason, involving your better half in the decision about using the family home to secure a business loan is vital.

Crowd around

Crowdfunding (also sometimes called *crowdsourcing, crowd financing* or *crowd fundraising*) is an increasingly popular way to raise funds for your new business idea. The idea is that you set a goal for raising funds and ask for small contributions from many people, either offering a range of rewards or a small stake in your business in exchange for these contributions.

The rewards vary from project to project. For example, I recently contributed to a crowd-funding campaign for a friend who was raising funds to launch her CD. In exchange for my $25, I'll receive a copy of her CD when it comes out. I could also have chosen to contribute $500 in exchange for a house concert performance.

Are you wondering whether crowdfunding is a possible way that you could raise funds for your business? New crowdfunding platforms launch almost every day, but Indiegogo, Pozible, Kickstarter and Peerbackers are all platforms with solid reputations and high participation rates.

Seeking equity partners

In the preceding sections, I talk only about *debt finance*, meaning that to get cash for your business, you go into debt. However, the other major source of business finance is *equity finance*. With equity finance, you receive funding from an investor in exchange for a portion of ownership of your business.

The idea with most equity finance is that investors — sometimes referred to as *business angels* — buy into your company, offering funds and expertise in return for part-ownership. The investors don't receive interest on these funds, but instead are looking for a return through long-term capital gain. Because the investors are exposed to the risk of your company failing, they usually look for businesses with a strong history of growth and higher-than-average returns.

The advantages of equity finance include the ability to raise funds even if you don't have security or collateral to offer, meaning that your financial structure is more stable. In addition, your business can hopefully benefit from the investor's management expertise. On the downside, an outside investor means that you no longer have complete control of your business. You may find it hard not being able to make decisions without consulting others first, especially if you're used to running your own show, and conflict between you and the investor becomes a real possibility.

Borrowing from family

Borrowing from family can be both the easiest and the hardest way to secure finance, all at the same time.

When writing this chapter, I drafted these last couple of paragraphs about borrowing from family and friends and then decided 'Nah, I'll just delete this stuff — it's all so obvious.' And so I did. The very next day, I bumped into the sister of an old client of mine and we got chatting. The father of my client had lent my client a large sum of money many years ago, and my client had repaid his father assiduously in the intervening period until the debt was completely cleared. As far as I was concerned, this particular scenario was a happy one, where none of the stuff that so often goes awry with family loans had occurred. Little did I know, the sister of my client, many years after this loan had been offered and then repaid, was still upset. It turned out that she had approached her father for finance as well, but her father had said he couldn't, because he had no money left to lend. The sister had missed out on the purchase of the farm she wanted, and had nursed a resentment against her brother for years.

You will find many ways to make money in your lifetime but you will only have one family, and your family relationships are probably more valuable than anything else you have in your life. If you're considering borrowing from your family, pause first to think how other siblings may feel and what would happen if you fail to repay these funds. If your siblings could feel resentful or your family would suffer in any way if you fail to repay these funds (and failure in business, no matter how optimistic you currently feel, is always possible), then think again. You may be better to borrow from a different source.

Chapter 5

Figuring out Prices and Predicting Sales

In This Chapter

▶ Looking at different pricing strategies and thinking about what's best for you

▶ Mixing up price strategies so you can capture as wide a market as possible

▶ Applying price strategies to your business

▶ Keeping tabs on your pricing and not letting things slip

▶ Calculating how much you're likely to sell this week, this month and this year

▶ Building a sales forecast for the next 12 months

*I*f you're like most people starting out in business, you may be tempted to undercharge for your products or services. Maybe you're unsure about how much customers are willing to pay, or you're anxious that customers won't value your services. Maybe you're worried that you won't secure enough business to cover your expenses.

By undercharging, I'm talking about charging less than your customers are willing to pay. Precisely what this amount is can be tricky to judge, especially if you're pricing a service rather than a product. Calculating the value of your skills and expertise through the eyes of a customer is a very subjective process.

In this chapter, I talk about pricing strategies and how best to go about setting a price for your products or services. I also explain how to create your sales forecast for the next 12 months, one of the fundamental building blocks for any business plan.

Choosing a Pricing Strategy

Business educators use a heap of different terminology for price strategies, but essentially any price strategy boils down to one of three things: Cost-based pricing, competitor-based pricing or value-based pricing. In the following sections I explore each strategy in turn.

Setting prices based on costs

Cost-based pricing is where you start by figuring out what it costs you to make a product or provide a service, and then you add an additional amount to arrive at the profit that you're after.

For example, imagine I decide to start a business selling sunhats at the local markets. The hats cost $8 each to buy, the stall costs $100 rent for the day and I reckon I can sell 50 hats a day. I want to make $250 profit to cover my time, so this means I decide to charge $15 per hat. (Sales of $15 × $50 = $750; less the $400 for the cost of the hats, less the rent of $100, and I'm left with $250 in my hot, sticky hand.)

This pricing model may sound like perfectly logical, good business practice, but it's not, because this way of working doesn't pause to consider how much customers are actually prepared to pay for these hats. Maybe another stall opposite is selling the self-same hats for only $12. Maybe the hats are a real bargain and I should be charging $20.

From a strategic perspective, cost-based pricing is the weakest of all business models. On the one hand, if the resulting prices are too high in relation to the competition, the business will flounder; on the other hand, if resulting prices are less than people are prepared to pay, you'll miss out on the possibility of above-average profits.

Setting prices based on competitors

Competitor-based pricing is where you look at what your competitors are charging for similar products or services, and then set your prices accordingly. This pricing strategy is the most common strategy used by business.

As I mention in the introduction to this chapter, if you're just starting out in business, you may fall foul of the temptation to be cheaper than everyone else. However, unless everyone else in the industry is driving around in sports cars with money to burn, chances are your competitors' prices are the level they are for a very good reason. Unless you have a competitive advantage that enables you to produce products or provide your services cheaper than your competitors, setting your prices lower than everyone else is likely to lead to poor profitability for you, as well as a risky business model.

Instead of trying to undercut competitors, look at the prices that your competitors are charging and use this analysis as a reflection of what the market is prepared to pay. Then pitch your pricing accordingly.

Competing on price alone is always a dangerous strategy. Sure, you need to be aware of competitor pricing and factor this information into your pricing decisions. However, how you position and sell your products and services should almost always be based on a combination of many different factors, such as quality of product or quality of service, delivery times, location, availability and ambience, and never just price alone. (For more about identifying your competitive strategy, refer to Chapter 3.)

Setting prices based on perceived value

Value-based pricing is where you reflect on the products or services you provide, look at the customer demand, and then set your price according to how much you think customers will be prepared to pay.

Here are a few examples of value-based pricing:

- ✔ Apple use value-based pricing for many of their products (sought-after items such as iPads and iPods), where no direct head-to-head competition exists and customers are prepared to pay premium prices for a brand upon which they place a high value.

- ✔ The stallholders selling umbrellas outside the city train station close to where I live push up the price of umbrellas by $3 or $4 every time it rains. Why? Because customers place a much higher value on staying dry when the rain is bucketing down.

- ✔ I know of a very gifted and brilliant network engineer who has earned an almost god-like status among local businesses for being able to troubleshoot and solve network issues when everyone else has failed. He charges top dollar — significantly more than his competitors — but people will pay because they place such a high value on having reliable business systems, and getting those systems back up and running.

In many ways, value-based pricing represents the essence of good business sense and marketing. After all, how better to set your prices than by judging the maximum that customers are willing to pay? The only tricky thing about value-based pricing is that any judgement is subjective. For example, I love the design and funky look of Apple's gear and will happily pay premium dollars for a new iPad or shiny iPhone. My son Daniel, however, doesn't place much value on Apple's design and prefers generic products. Therefore, the value Daniel places on an iPad is significantly less than the value I place on the same item.

Building a Hybrid-Pricing Plan

So far in this chapter I've been talking about the theory of pricing and different pricing strategies. However, most successful businesses don't employ a single price strategy but instead employ a combination of strategies.

An example is a luxury inner-city hotel. Most of the time, they use *competitive-based pricing*, setting rates with the awareness of competitors' pricing very much in mind. However, with their premium rooms, they use *value-based pricing*, often improvising rates on the spot according to demand and what they think customers will be prepared to pay. Finally, for last-minute rates where they have a bunch of empty rooms and they know they won't be able to fill all of them, they use *cost-based pricing*, charging just enough above cost to make it worth their while to fill each room.

Using a combination of pricing strategies is called *hybrid pricing*, and is a key element in any successful business. The next part of this chapter explores ways to introduce hybrid pricing into your business, including premium products, no-frills products, package pricing and differential pricing.

Offering a premium product or service

With hybrid pricing, offering a premium product or service is only part of the picture. The idea is that as well as offering a premium product or service, you also offer a regular product or service. In other words, you target more than one type of customer.

Here are some examples:

- Amazon offers different pricing for freight, depending on how quickly you want your order delivered.
- My butcher sells two types of minced beef: Low-fat and not-so-low fat.
- The guy who mows our lawns offers two services: Regular just-with-a-lawnmower mowing and premium all-grass-edges-trimmed-within-an-inch-of-their-life mowing.

Pricing goods that you manufacture yourself

If you're manufacturing goods yourself, you must differentiate between what you charge at wholesale versus what you charge at retail. Even if you currently don't sell your goods at wholesale — maybe you're selling your wares at market stalls or direct to retail outlets — for your business model to be sustainable you almost certainly have to consider wholesale pricing at some point.

Why? Most manufacturers who work on a small scale (and I'm kind of assuming you do, because if you're the General Manager of Ford Motors you're probably not reading this book) don't have enough of a range or a broad enough sales team to service a wide range of retail stores. Range is always an issue for smaller businesses, as most large retailers don't want to bother with suppliers who only offer two or three products.

In addition, although you may be able to service retailers in your local area personally, chances are that you won't be able to visit retailers interstate or in regional areas. Servicing these retailers almost always involves selling the products you make to some kind of distributor or wholesaler.

The crunch in regards to your pricing will be that your wholesale price ends up being a relatively small percentage of the retail price. For example, a shopkeeper selling an item for $20 probably doesn't want to pay much more than $10 for that item. The wholesaler who receives $10 probably won't want to pay much more than $7. So out of a possible revenue of $20 you only receive $7, and out of that $7 you need to pay all the costs of production. This is fair, and reflects the reality of doing business and the costs of distribution, but can sometimes put a damper on what you may have been thinking is a great business idea.

Offering a premium product doesn't necessarily mean you compromise on the quality of your other products (a strategy that could risk your brand reputation). You can structure premiums in many different ways, such as faster service, guaranteed response time, additional services and complimentary extras.

Cutting back the frills

The flipside of premium pricing (refer to preceding section) is *no-frills pricing*. No-frills pricing doesn't necessarily mean inferior quality, but can include things such as off-peak pricing, lower service standards, longer response times or limited availability. Here are some examples:

- Frequent-flyer programs place restrictions on what flights are available for frequent-flyer points.

- Many gyms offer low-cost membership if you attend outside peak periods.

✔ Tourism operators employ no-frills pricing for off-peak periods.

✔ Supermarkets offer generic brands with basic product packaging.

My husband's recording studio business offers a no-frills product on Mondays and Tuesdays (traditionally the quietest days of the week for bookings). Musicians can visit the studio for a fixed duration of 8 hours to record and mix up to four tracks. John doesn't offer any flexibility with this model (you can only book on a Monday or Tuesday, you can't book less than 8 hours, and you don't get to choose your engineer), but nonetheless these days are almost always booked out, because there's always musicians looking for a good deal. With this no-frills deal, John manages to attract customers he would normally miss out on with his regular pricing.

Getting creative with packages

Package pricing, where one product or service is bundled together with something else, is another example of hybrid pricing. Package pricing can include things such as bundling two or more products or services together, offering bonus products, and extended warranties.

Examples of package pricing include

✔ A day spa offering a pedicure, waxing and massage as a package.

✔ A tourism operator offering flights, accommodation and meals as a package.

✔ A club offering a free giveaway of some kind for every membership renewal.

Fixed rate or by the hour?

For many types of services, you get a conflict between customers who want a fixed fee and business owners who want to charge by the hour. For example, a carpenter renovating a house would probably love to work on an agreed hourly rate, as he can be sure that he'll be paid properly for all his time and he doesn't risk being out of pocket if he underquotes. However, the home owners almost certainly want a fixed quote for this job, because they need to budget and can't afford for the costs to blow out.

For you as a businessperson, there's no right or wrong answer as to whether to charge a fixed fee or charge by the hour. However, be aware that you'll often find a natural tension between what customers prefer and what business owners prefer. If you're in an industry where you feel you're able to offer a specific service for a fixed fee, this can be an excellent marketing edge, especially if your competitors are charging by the hour.

If you're just starting up a new business, you may be pushed to think of how you could offer package pricing. Keep thinking creatively. Keep in mind that your business doesn't need to provide all elements of the package and that often the best approach is to team up with another business.

Charging different prices for the same thing

Yet another pricing strategy — and one that sounds kinda dodgy at first — is to charge different prices for the same thing (this is also known as *differential pricing*). Don't worry — I'm not proposing you breach trade practice guidelines. Instead, I'm talking about charging different prices depending on the quantity ordered, the total size of an order, the costs of shipping to customers, how promptly customers pay, how much the customer orders in the course of a year, and so on.

Differential pricing works really well for almost any business because it enables you to maintain your margins for regular sales, but generate extra income by selling to other customers at a discount.

You have so many ways to implement differential pricing that I'm going to spell out a fair few examples:

- **Pricing based on customer location:** Charging different rates (either for shipping or for on-site service) depending on where the customer is located makes good sense, although you still want to keep your pricing structure pretty simple.

- **Pricing based on loyalty:** Offering special pricing to customers who are members of your loyalty program or members of an affiliate organisation is a good marketing strategy and rewards customer loyalty.

- **Pricing based on order size or quantities ordered:** This kind of pricing makes intuitive sense straight off the bat. Almost any business will charge a different price for someone who buys 1,000 units rather than 10. (When you structure pricing according to quantity, this is called *quantity-break pricing*.)

- **Pricing based on payment terms:** Offering credit terms is expensive, not just in terms of using up working capital but also because of the risk of bad debt. Consider offering higher discounts for payment upfront or payment within 7 days.

- **Pricing based on total spending:** Providing reward incentives for total spending often features as part of loyalty programs and makes good business sense. For example, if customers spend more than $500 over the course of the year, they get something for free.

✔ **Pricing based on customer commitment:** Another clever strategy is to offer discount pricing but make the customer jump through hoops to get it. Money-back coupons where you have to post proof of purchase to the supplier, or price-match guarantees are examples of this kind of pricing.

Forming Your Final Plan of Attack

Previously in this chapter, I talk about a whole load of pricing strategies. Thinking about possible pricing strategies in this way may help spark off some new ideas and creative thinking in how you approach pricing your products or services. However, you may also be feeling a little overwhelmed and wondering where to start. So here's my specific recommendation for the process to follow:

1. **Do some research as to what you think customers will be prepared to pay.**

    This research will involve looking at what competitors are charging as well as thinking about how your product or service is different and what value customers are likely to place on this difference.

2. **Think about how you could vary your product or service to provide two or three 'levels' of pricing (no-frills, regular and premium).**

    Not every business can offer multi-level pricing (for example, I don't know that I'd seek out a surgeon offering a no-frills service), but you'd be surprised how many types of businesses can. (Refer to the section 'Building a Hybrid-Pricing Plan', earlier in this chapter, for more on pricing levels.)

3. **Investigate at least two ways to bundle or package your offering with other products or services.**

    'Getting creative with packages', earlier in this chapter, provides a few ideas on this topic.

4. **Find two or three ways to charge your customers different prices for the same things.**

    This pricing strategy (differential pricing) is probably the most crucial of all. Even if you can't figure out how to have more than one level of pricing, or you can't come up with a method to create a package, you should be able to incorporate some form of differential pricing in your strategy. 'Charging different prices for the same thing', earlier in this chapter, provides some pointers as to how you can do this.

Although the upside of a hybrid pricing strategy is that you maximise the number of customers you can reach, and hopefully make premium profits on at least some of your sales, you can risk confusing customers if you offer too many options. As your business grows and changes, experiment with different pricing combinations to see what works best and gets the best response from your customers.

Monitoring and Changing Your Price

If you've already been in business for a while, you may feel that your price strategies are pretty well settled and working just fine. That's good, but regardless of whether you're just starting out in business or you're running a 50-year-old family legacy, you still want to keep an eye on your pricing.

The biggest indication that your pricing may need to shift is if you have poor financial results. (Of course, poor results can be caused by many factors, not just pricing.) However, if you know that your competitors have just raised their price, your customers are commenting what good value you are, or you haven't raised your price in more than a year or two, it's probably time to do a price review.

Changing prices doesn't only mean raising prices. Always be open to new pricing plans, special offers, package pricing and so on. If you do decide to raise prices, try to do so incrementally and avoid big price hikes that may scare your customers. Alternatively, find ways to sneak price rises through the back door, such as only increasing prices on certain low-profile products or services, or getting rid of discounts.

Discount dramas

If you build discounts into your pricing strategies, be careful that when you offer discounts, your business receives something tangible in return. For example, if you offer a discount for cash payment rather than credit card, this makes sense because you normally pay merchant fees on credit card transactions. Similarly, if you offer a discount for prompt payment, this probably makes sense (depending on how much discount you offer) if you're currently in debt to the bank and paying interest.

Another example is if you discount over-stocked or end-of-season items. This makes sense because these slow-moving items are taking up valuable shop or warehouse space which could be better used for product that actually sells.

However, if you routinely offer discounts without receiving something that benefits your business in return, you risk eroding your profitability model. In addition, regular customers may get used to these discounts and come to expect them.

Building Your Sales Forecast

Once you have figured out your pricing strategy (what you intend to charge per hour, per unit or per service rendered), the next step in your business plan is to create a sales forecast for the next 12 months (or, if your business hasn't started yet, create a sales forecast for the first 12 months of operation).

Creating sales forecasts prompts all kinds of questions. If you're charging by the hour, what's a reasonable number of hours to bill for each week? If you're selling items, how do you know how many you'll sell? What if you sell lots of different items, at different prices? In the following sections, I talk about the details behind creating this kind of projection.

Calculating hours in a working week

If your business charges by the hour (maybe you're a bookkeeper, consultant, electrician, gardener, music tutor, maths tutor, plumber or some similar business), one of the first questions is how many hours can you reasonably charge for per week, per month or per year.

Imagine a recent music graduate (I'll call her Maddie) wants to set up a business as a maths tutor. Maddie reckons she can teach about 48 students a week (and if each lesson is 30 minutes, that's 24 hours of teaching), and that she's going to charge $60 per hour. With this in mind, she reckons that she'll earn $74,880 per year. (That's 24 multiplied by 52 weeks multiplied by $60.)

Is Maddie correct in her estimate of income for the next 12 months? I'm going to test her calculations using the following step-by-step method, which you can use as well:

1. **Estimate how many days you're going to work each week, and how many hours you can realistically charge for each day to arrive at your average number of billable hours per week.**

   When doing this calculation, remember to include billable hours only. Don't include travel time between locations, non-billable time due to administration/paperwork, or time spent running your business (bookkeeping, customer phone calls, marketing and so on).

2. **Estimate how much holiday you're going to take (or be forced to take) each year.**

Here, don't think in terms of lying on the beach watching the surf, but include both holidays where you go away and breaks where you may be available to work, but you can't. (For example, a school tutor probably won't get much work in school holidays, a gardener may find it hard to work in heavy rain or snow, or a business consultant may find that work grinds to a halt the month before and after Christmas.)

In Table 5-1, I've included 12 weeks against the holiday Maddie will take annually, because that's the number of weeks of school holidays each year.

3. **Make an allowance for public holidays.**

   Most people don't work public holidays. If you don't plan to (or maybe you can't because your customers will be unavailable), you have to allow for public holidays as well. Public holidays of ten days a year equates to an equivalent of two weeks per year. In Maddie's case, many public holidays also coincide with school holidays, so she only allows for five days (one week) of public holidays per year.

4. **Think of what will happen if you get sick.**

   My observation is that being a freelancer is one of the best possible ways of ensuring good health. Knowing that you won't get paid if you don't show up is a real incentive to getting out the door, however you're feeling. However, most people do get sick from time to time, and it's realistic to make an allowance for this.

5. **Calculate how many weeks per year you will be able to charge for.**

   In Maddie's case (see Table 5-1), after taking out holidays, public holidays and sick days she can likely work a full week (that's 24 billable hours) for only 38 weeks of the year. (Most businesses that aren't dependent on school terms can probably work more weeks per year than this, however.)

6. **Multiply the number of working weeks per year by the number of weekly billable hours, to arrive at your maximum billable hours per year.**

   As shown in Table 5-1, for Maddie this equals 38 weeks per year multiplied by 24 hours per week, making a total of 912 hours.

7. **Multiply your maximum billable hours per year by your hourly rate.**

   The result for Maddie is $54,720 per year, quite different from her initial estimate of $74,880.

Table 5-1	Calculating Maximum Billable Hours per Year
Number of days per week	4
Average number of billable hours per day	6
Total billable hours per week	*24*
Number of holiday weeks per year	12
Number of public holidays per year, expressed in weeks	1
Number of sick days per year, expressed in weeks	1
Total working weeks per year	38
Maximum possible billable hours per year	**912**
Hourly rate	$60
Maximum possible income per year	*$54,720*

Note: The method shown in Table 5-1 gives you the maximum billable hours per year for an example business. If you're still getting your business established, not only will your calculations be very different but it may be some time until you have enough customers to reach your maximum billable hours.

To apply the maximum billable hours per year method to your own business, go to www.dummies.com/go/creatingbusinessplan, where you can find the Calculating Billable Hours Excel worksheet.

Increasing sales with extra labour

If your business is primarily labour-based, don't forget to think beyond your own labour, how many hours you can pack into a week, and what you can charge for your time. Instead, expand your thinking to include delegating some of the work involved to employees or subcontractors.

Building a plan that involves employees servicing your customers (rather than just you servicing customers) is a vital part of any entrepreneurial conception. For example, don't just think of how many lawns you can mow, kids you can tutor or companies you can consult to. Instead, picture a team of people mowing lawns, a whole school of tutors or an entire posse of consultants.

If your business is labour-based, leveraging your expertise in this way is the only possible method by which you can hope to earn more than the industry average. For example, if you start up a business as a gardener, a music tutor or a physiotherapist, you can only work so many hours in the week. However, with a team of employees working for you, all delivering this service, you may be able to make a decent profit.

Predicting sales for a new business

If a business is still getting established, making an estimate of your first 12 months' sales can be really hard. Maybe people are going to flood through the door, maybe you're going to be a ten-week wonder, or maybe your business will grow steadily and organically over time. However, in order to build a business plan, you're going to have to make some kind of estimate.

To ensure your sales forecast is as realistic as possible, the more detail the better. Try to slice up sales targets by *market segment*, *product* or *region*:

- **Market segment targets:** *Market segment* is a fancy word that really means type of customer or type of work. For example, a building contractor may split his market into new houses and renovations, a musician may split her market into weddings, private functions and pub gigs. A handyman may split his market into private clients and real estate agents.

- **Product-based targets:** Product-based targets work best if you sell products rather than services. You can set sales targets according to units sold, or dollars sold, of each product. For example, a car yard could aim to sell at least 20 cars a month, a real estate agent could try to sell five houses every month, and a lawn-mowing business could set sales targets of 80 lawns per month.

- **Regional targets:** With regions, you set sales targets according to geographic regions. This works best for slightly larger businesses that typically have a dedicated salesperson or sales team in each region.

If you take on board any of the pricing strategy stuff I talk about earlier in this chapter (refer to the section 'Building a Hybrid-Pricing Plan' for more), chances are you're going to have a few different prices or packages on the go. This makes your sales forecast even more complicated. However, in Table 5-2, you can see how a few different businesses make a stab at constructing their initial estimates.

The idea behind any detailed sales forecast is that you start by itemising the different items that you sell or the different prices that you charge, and you try to make an estimate of weekly sales against each of these items.

Try to incorporate a decent level of detail into initial sales estimates, including all items you sell or services you provide.

Table 5-2	Initial Sales Estimates		
	Unit Price	Unit Sales per Week	Sales per Week
Cake Business			
Friands	$2.00	100	$200.00
Muffins — regular	$1.50	100	$150.00
Muffins — wholesale	$1.30	50	$ 65.00
Chocolate brownies	$2.20	130	$286.00
Teacakes	$7.00	60	$420.00
Total			**$1,121.00**
Hairdresser			
Women's cuts	$80.00	20	$1,600.00
Men's cuts	$50.00	10	$500.00
Colour — short hair	$85.00	10	$850.00
Colour — long hair	$110.00	5	$550.00
Cut and colour	$160.00	12	$1,920.00
Foils — half head	$120.00	8	$960.00
Foils — full head	$150.00	5	$750.00
Total			**$7,130.00**
Naturopath			
Short consultation	$65.00	20	$1,300.00
Long consultation	$130.00	5	$650.00
Consult + massage	$200.00	2	$400.00
Herbs	$45.00	15	$675.00
Phone consultation	$50.00	3	$150.00
Total			**$3,175.00**
Retail fashion*			
Clothing $11 to $20	$15.00	88	$1,320.00
Clothing $21 to $30	$25.00	32	$800.00
Clothing $31 to 40	$35.00	48	$1,680.00
Clothing $41 to 50	$45.00	30	$1,350.00
Clothing $51 to $60	$55.00	18	$990.00
Clothing $61 to $70	$65.00	6	$390.00
Total			**$6,530.00**

* Average unit cost shown for retail fashion business.

Go to www.dummies.com/go/creatingbusinessplan to download the spreadsheet shown in Table 5-2 — look for the Detailed Sales Forecasts worksheet. You can then adapt any of the business scenarios to fit yourself.

Predicting sales for an established business

If you've been running your business for a while, one of the most accurate ways of predicting sales is to analyse what sales have been for the last 12 months, and then build from there. Sure, you may have changed things — maybe you've switched to a new location, introduced new products or increased your pricing — but, nonetheless, your historical sales results are always going to provide you with the best indicator for future sales.

When basing sales forecasts on historical data, consider the following:

✔ When looking at sales figures for previous months, check whether these figures are shown including or excluding sales/consumer tax. (Most salespeople think in terms of the final value of each sale; accountants tend to look at sales figures net of any taxes collected on behalf of the government.)

✔ Does your business have significant seasonal variations? If so, have you factored this into your monthly forecasts?

✔ If you examine the trends, is the business growing or declining? Ideally, you should analyse trends over two or more years to truly get a sense of what's happening.

✔ Have any changes to pricing or product range occurred between last year and this year?

When looking at sales forecasts, also factor in personalities. Salespeople are often very buoyant with their predictions (this optimism tends to be part of the job), while accountants are typically gloom and doom. Hopefully, your business plan can arrive at a happy medium.

Creating Your Month-by-Month Forecast

At the simplest level, creating a forecast for the next 12 months can be as simple as listing the names of the months in one big row across a sheet of paper and writing an estimate underneath each one. However, this method is somewhat unsophisticated, to put it mildly.

Figures 5-1 and 5-2 show a couple of different possible formats. In Figure 5-1, I use the example of a kids' party business that offers three kinds of packages at different prices. This level of detail helps keep forecasts realistic — for example, the business owner in this example can see just how many parties they have to do during the month in order to meet expected sales. In Figure 5-2, I look at a business selling cakes to cafes. The sales projection provides a healthy dose of realism (this business has to sell a hell of a lot of friands and muffins to make even the most scant of income at these prices).

Now try doing the same for your own business. Here are some comments to help you along the way:

- ✔ If you're running a service business, go to www.dummies.com/go/ creatingbusinessplan and look for the 12-month Sales Forecast — Service worksheet. This template is very similar to Figure 5-1. If you're selling products rather than providing a service, go to www.dummies. com/go/creatingbusinessplan and look for the 12-month Sales Forecast — Retail or Products worksheet. This template is very similar to Figure 5-2. You can adapt either of these templates to suit your own needs, changing the months along the top, the item descriptions in the first column, and the prices and quantities in each row.

- ✔ If you've been thinking about your sales in terms of weeks, keep in mind that some months have four weeks and others have five.

- ✔ You need to factor in holidays and other seasonal aspects. For example, unless you run a Santa Claus for hire business, Christmas and early January are quiet months for most businesses.

- ✔ Show your sales before any consumer tax (sales tax, GST, VAT and so on) that you're obliged to charge to customers but have to then remit to the government.

Figure 5-1:
Building a 12-month sales forecast in Excel for a service business.

	A	B (Price)	C	D	E	F	G	H	I	J	K	L	M
1													
2	1 hour 30 Package	$170.00											
3	2 hour Package	$190.00											
4	2 hour Plus Package	$210.00											
5													
6			Jul-14	Aug-14	Sep-14	Oct-14	Nov-14	Dec-14	Jan-15	Feb-15	Mar-15	Apr-15	May-15	Jun-15
7	Parties with owner's labour												
8	1 hour 30 Package		12	12	12	12	12	12	12	12	12	12	12	12
9	2 hour Package		4	4	4	4	4	4	4	4	4	4	4	4
10	2 hour Plus Package		1	1	1	1	1	1	-	1	1	1	1	1
11													
12	Parties with subcontract labour												
13	1 hour 30 Package		8	12	13	8	12	80	4	5	12	13	18	22
14	2 hour Package		7	6	8	10	12	18	2	10	14	16	18	20
15	2 hour Plus Package		1	3	4	4	5	8	-	4	4	6	6	6
16													
17	Income Generated												
18	1 hour 30 Package		$ 3,400	$ 4,080	$ 4,250	$ 3,400	$ 4,080	$15,640	$ 2,720	$ 2,890	$ 4,080	$ 4,250	$ 5,100	$ 5,780
19	2 hour Package		$ 2,090	$ 1,900	$ 2,280	$ 2,660	$ 3,040	$ 4,180	$ 1,140	$ 2,660	$ 3,420	$ 3,800	$ 4,180	$ 4,560
20	2 hour Plus Package		$ 420	$ 840	$ 1,050	$ 1,050	$ 1,260	$ 1,890	$ -	$ 1,050	$ 1,050	$ 1,470	$ 1,470	$ 1,470
21	Total Sales		$ 5,910	$ 6,820	$ 7,580	$ 7,110	$ 8,380	$21,710	$ 3,860	$ 6,600	$ 8,550	$ 9,520	$10,750	$11,810

Figure 5-2:
Building a 12-month sales forecast in Excel for a business selling products.

		Jul-14	Aug-14	Sep-14	Oct-14	Nov-14	Dec-14	Jan-15	Feb-15	Mar-15	Apr-15	May-15	Jun-15	Annual Totals
Friands	$ 2.00													
Regular Muffins	$ 1.50													
Wholesale Muffins	$ 1.30													
Chocolate Brownies	$ 2.20													
Teacakes	$ 7.00													
							Sales Forecast for July to June for Cakes to Cafes							
Friands		400	400	420	440	460	480	500	500	500	500	500	500	5600
TOTAL		$ 800	$ 800	$ 840	$ 880	$ 920	$ 960	$ 1,000	$ 1,000	$ 1,000	$ 1,000	$ 1,000	$ 1,000	11,200
Regular Muffins		400	400	400	400	400	400	400	400	400	400	400	400	4800
TOTAL		$ 600	$ 600	$ 600	$ 600	$ 600	$ 600	$ 600	$ 600	$ 600	$ 600	$ 600	$ 600	7,200
Wholesale Muffins		200	200	200	300	300	300	400	400	400	400	400	400	3900
TOTAL		$ 260	$ 260	$ 260	$ 390	$ 390	$ 390	$ 520	$ 520	$ 520	$ 520	$ 520	$ 520	5,070
Chocolate Brownies		520	520	520	520	520	520	520	520	520	520	520	520	6240
TOTAL		$ 1,144	$ 1,144	$ 1,144	$ 1,144	$ 1,144	$ 1,144	$ 1,144	$ 1,144	$ 1,144	$ 1,144	$ 1,144	$ 1,144	13,728
Teacakes		250	250	250	250	250	250	250	250	250	250	250	250	3000
TOTAL		$ 1,750	$ 1,750	$ 1,750	$ 1,750	$ 1,750	$ 1,750	$ 1,750	$ 1,750	$ 1,750	$ 1,750	$ 1,750	$ 1,750	21,000
GRAND TOTAL		$ 4,554	$ 4,554	$ 4,594	$ 4,764	$ 4,804	$ 4,844	$ 5,014	$ 5,014	$ 5,014	$ 5,014	$ 5,014	$ 5,014	$ 58,198

Are you dreaming?

I have a friend who trained as a naturopath, spending years of study with the expectation that this is how she would make her living in the years to come. However, after she graduated and started out on her own, she found it very difficult to make much money out of her practice. After a year or two, she started attending monthly network meetings with fellow naturopaths. Through these meetings she learnt that it wasn't just her who was having a hard time building up her practice, and that the pickings naturopaths typically survive upon are scant indeed.

If you're starting off on a brand new business, how can you assess how realistic your sales forecasts are? If your business is something that has been done before, I suggest you do some research first. Research industry

benchmarks, talk to your accountant, chat to people already working in the industry, or go to industry conferences and network meetings. So long as the quality of your product or service is up to scratch and you have decent marketing materials, you can probably expect to achieve similar results to those already working in the industry.

Things are trickier if you've invented a new product or you're launching a specialist service of some kind. In this situation, it's very hard to measure customer acceptance or interest in your product without first testing the market in some way. Ways of testing the market may include selling at markets, launching your service or product on a small scale locally or possibly (depending on the product) launching your product online.

Can you see how in the template for Figure 5-1, I separate services that the owners plan to provide themselves, and services that they plan to use employee or subcontract labour for? I do this because the costs of labour are so different. For example, the owner of the party business does the entertainment at many of the kids' parties herself, and for each of these parties she earns at least $170. However, if she pays for someone else to go to the party, she earns only $50. Separating out services in this way, analysing what services you'll provide and what services you plan to use subcontractors for, make good sense when you get to predicting costs in the next stage of your business plan (a topic I cover in Chapter 6).

Chapter 6

Calculating Costs and Gross Profit

In This Chapter

▶ Working out the costs for every sale you make

▶ Getting a feel for gross profit and how to crunch the numbers

▶ Focusing on the profit margins for your own business

▶ Creating a gross profit projection for the next 12 months

*T*he summer just past stretched into weeks of long, sunny days. The next-door kids, Callum and Rhys, hatched a plot to make homemade lemonade and sell it to thirsty passers-by. Most days I'd stop and buy a glass and the kids would happily announce how much profit they'd made so far. The school holidays were almost at a close the afternoon I bumped into their mother in the supermarket. She had a trolley piled high with lemons. 'This profit the boys are making is costing me a fortune,' she laughed.

Chances are that such halcyon days belong only to childhood and that, in your business, you're going to have to be seriously realistic about what everything costs. No more lemons for free.

In this chapter, I talk about calculating the costs for each sale that you make, and how to relate these calculations to your gross profit margins. And I show you how to build upon your sales projections to include these costs so that you can create a forecast of your gross profit for the year ahead.

Calculating the Cost of Each Sale

The focus of this chapter is the costs that go up and down in direct relation to your sales. For example, if you manufacture wooden tables, your costs include timber. If you sell books, your costs include the purchase of books from publishers.

If you run a small service-based business and you have no employees, you may find that you have no costs of this nature (and, hence, most of this chapter is irrelevant to you). However, before abandoning this chapter willy-nilly, do read through the first couple of sections ('Identifying your variable costs' and 'Costing your service'), just to make sure.

Identifying your variable costs

In order to complete the expenses part of your Profit & Loss Projection for the next 12 months, you first need to grasp the difference between variable costs and fixed expenses. *Variable costs* (also sometimes called *direct costs* or *cost of goods sold*) are the costs that go up and down in direct relation to your sales.

This theory may seem all very well, but you need to understand how it applies in the context of your own business. Here are some examples that may help:

- ✔ If you're a manufacturer, variable costs are the materials you use in order to make things, such as raw materials and production labour. (For the boys next door making lemonade, their variable costs were lemons and sugar.)

- ✔ If you're a retailer, your main variable cost is the costs of the goods you buy to resell to customers. Other variable costs, particularly for online retailers, may include packaging and postage.

- ✔ If you're a service business, you may not have any variable costs, but possible variable costs include sales commissions, booking fees, equipment rental, guest consumables or employee/subcontract labour.

Fixed expenses (also sometimes called *indirect costs* or *overheads*) are expenses that stay constant, regardless of whether your sales go up and down. Typical fixed expenses for your business may include accounting fees, bank fees, computer expenses, electricity, insurance, motor vehicles, rental, stationery and wages.

Not sure which variable costs apply to your business? Figure 6-1 provides a question-based checklist to prompt you to think about your business and what variable costs it may have.

The checklist shown in Figure 6-1 is also available to download from www.dummies.com/go/creatingbusinessplan — look for the Identifying Variable Costs checklist.

IDENTIFYING VARIABLE COSTS FOR YOUR BUSINESS

Do you use raw materials to create new products?
Examples: Ingredients, foods, timber, metals, plastics, paper

Do you purchase finished products or materials for resale?
Examples: A clothes shop buys clothes, a cafe buys coffee beans, and a landscaper buys soil and plants

Do you purchase any materials for packaging?
Examples: Cardboard, bubble wrap, bottles, caps, envelopes

Do you use any energy as part of manufacturing items?
Examples: Electricity or gas in the factory

Do you employ any labour when manufacturing items?
Examples: Factory wages, subcontractor wages, production wages

Do you employ any labour for which you charge clients or customers directly?
Examples: An electrical company employs electrical contractors and charges customers by the hour for the contractors' time

Do you pay any commissions on sales?
Examples: Sales commission, sales bonuses, sales rebates, sales discounts

Do you have any expenses relating to importing goods from overseas?
Examples: Inwards shipping costs, customs fees, external storage costs

Do you have costs relating to distributing or shipping items?
Examples: Outwards freight, couriers, warehouse rent, warehouse staff

Figure 6-1:
Identifying
variable
costs
for your
business.

Costing your service

I mention near the beginning of this chapter that if you're providing a service, you may not have any variable costs associated with your business. However, you may well have some minor costs associated with providing your service and, as soon as your business grows, you will have the cost of hiring employees or contractors to provide the service on behalf of your business.

Table 6-1 shows some examples where variable costs apply.

Table 6-1	Variable Costs Examples for Service Businesses
Type of Business	*Likely Variable Costs*
Contract cleaning	Cleaning staff wages, cleaning materials
Holiday house	Guest consumables, booking commissions
Massage therapist	Daily room hire
Home maintenance business	Building materials, cost of subcontractors
Medical practitioner	Medical supplies, pathology

If you're unsure whether something is a variable cost or a fixed expense, ask yourself this: Do you spend more on this item as sales increase? If your answer is yes, chances are this item is a variable cost.

Costing items that you buy and sell

When calculating costs for items that you buy and then sell you have two types of costs to consider:

- **Incoming costs:** These are the costs involved in getting the goods to your door. Incoming costs often include freight and, for importers, may also include customs charges, duties and tax. Incoming costs may also vary significantly depending on the quantity you order.

- **Outgoing costs:** These are the costs involved in making the sale and getting the goods to your customer. Outgoing costs include sales commissions, discounts, outwards freight, packaging and storage.

In Table 6-2, I show a costings worksheet for a wholesaler. You can see that, at first glance, the wholesaler's buy price is $9.00 and the sell price is $18.00, making for a handsome margin of 50 per cent. Browse through the figures in more detail, however, allowing for freight, storage, commissions and so on, and you can see that the final margin is something much closer to a paltry 24 per cent. (For more on gross profit and gross profit margin, see the section 'Understanding Gross Profit', later in this chapter.)

Table 6-2	Calculating True Costs and Margins	
	Percentage of Sell Price	*$*
Sell Price (Before Taxes)		*$18.00*
Less **Variable Costs**		
Buy price for this item	50%	$9.00
Inwards freight to warehouse	5%	$0.90
Storage costs warehouse	2%	$0.36
Early payment discount	2%	$0.36
Agent commission	10%	$1.80
Outwards freight to customer	6%	$1.08
Packaging	1%	$0.18
Total costs of selling		**$13.68**
Gross Profit		**$4.32**
Gross Profit Margin	*24%*	

Adding import costs

If you decide to import goods from overseas, doing your product costings carefully is particularly important. Even if current exchange rates make your prices look cheap as chips, this rosy picture may soon fade when you add the costs of freight, customs, distribution and taxes. Work through your final product costings *before* you consider exporting or importing anything anywhere.

A whole scad of jargon goes hand-in-hand with export and import. Terms such as FOW (Free on Wharf), FOB (Free on Board) and CIF (Costs, Insurance and Freight) are all there ready to trap the unsuspecting novice. For importers, understanding what price your suppliers quote is vital because the extras of freight, insurance, agent commissions and duty can easily add a further 40 or 50 per cent to the cost of product.

If you're restricted to buying and selling in different currencies — maybe you buy in US dollars but sell in Euros — take the time to generate multiple pricing models and make sure you can still be profitable even if the exchange rate changes substantially.

Creating product costings for manufacturers

If you manufacture products, one of the most crucial steps in your business plan is to create an accurate costing worksheet for each product that you sell. This process can be pretty tedious, but without knowing exactly what everything costs, you can't move forward and plan.

Tables 6-3 and 6-4 show two possible product costings and the kind of information to include. I've taken both of these examples from businesses that I've mentored — the first example is a family member who started a business making homemade gourmet sauces, the second example is a friend who made kid's clothing and sold it at the markets.

Table 6-3	Cost of Producing One Bottle of Pickle	
Item	*$*	*Notes*
100g fresh tomato	$0.80	Based on seasonal average
30g onion	$0.05	
20g sugar	$0.03	Based on buying in bulk 50-kg bags
5g salt	$0.01	Based on buying in bulk 10-kg bags
Cost of labour	$0.88	Average 400 bottles per day, with labour $350 per day
Kitchen rental	$0.38	Average 400 bottles per day, with rental $150 per day
Bottle plus lid	$0.45	
Label	$0.35	
Packaging	$0.40	$3.20 per custom box, 8 bottles per box
Total	**$3.35**	

Table 6-4	Cost of Producing Children's Dungarees*	
Item	*$*	*Notes*
Corduroy fabric	$2.50	Based on 0.8 square metre of fabric
Labour	$12.06	Average 40 minutes labour per dungaree set
Thread	$0.05	
Label	$0.03	
Packaging	$0.10	
Total	**$14.74**	

*Sizes 6 to 8

Can you see how both examples in Tables 6-3 and 6-4 put a value on labour? You may think this doesn't apply to you, because chances are if you're just starting out in business, you're contributing your own labour for free. However, when creating a product costing, you're best to include a realistic allowance for how much the labour would cost if you were to pay for someone else to create the product. This way, you can see the 'true' profitability of each product, and you get a better sense of the long-term potential of your enterprise.

The other interesting thing to consider is volume discounts. For example, in the product shown in Table 6-3, the cost of sugar is based on buying 50 kilograms at a time. However, how much would this business save if the owner was able to buy 100 kilograms at a time? (Even if your business can't afford to buy in large quantities yet, just knowing that your costs may reduce dramatically as your business grows is an important part of the business planning process.)

If you use accounting software, you can usually set up 'kits' or 'assemblies' for each product you manufacture. In other words, you can create an inventory item that's made up of several other items. The benefit of working in this way is that the software calculates product costs automatically; the downside, especially for a small business, is that this method of accounting for every gram of salt or squirt of glue used can be hideously time-consuming.

The dangers of custom manufacture

Over the years, I've observed that almost any business doing custom manufacture struggles to make a profit. Why? The very nature of creating one-off pieces — whether these be original sculptures, handmade furniture, custom spiral staircases or hand-built guitars — means that you are engaging with the unknown.

The unknown factor may be materials that cost more than you expect, a customer who isn't happy with the first prototype, underestimating the cost of labour, or many other factors. The time taken up discussing a job with a customer, drawing up designs, communicating changes and working out how to do something is almost always more than you expect.

When you create one-off items, you don't have the same ability to control your costs in the way that you do when you make the same item over and over again.

Am I warning you never to engage in this kind of business? No, not quite. After all, without custom manufacturers our society would be without potters and artists, sculptors and artisans, furniture makers and craftspeople. However, if you're planning this kind of business and you want to make a profit, you will need to be particularly brutal about quotations and costings, and you need to be prepared to reject jobs where the margins are too slight.

Understanding Gross Profit

You've almost certainly heard of the terms *gross profit* or *gross profit margins* but are you entirely clear what these terms mean and why an understanding of these terms is so crucial to your business plan? If you have even a moment's hesitation in answering 'yes' to this question, then read on . . .

Calculating gross profit

Put simply, gross profit is equal to sales less variable costs. A few examples may help bring this concept to life:

- ✓ A fashion retailer buys a skirt from the wholesaler for $20 and sells it for $50. Her gross profit is $30.

- ✓ A massage therapist charges $80 per massage but the therapy centre takes $25 as a booking and room fee. His gross profit is $55.

- ✓ A carpenter charges $800 for fixing a veranda. Materials cost $200 and labour for her apprentice costs $100. Her gross profit is $500.

Sounds okay so far? Just bear in mind:

- ✔ Gross profit equals sales less variable costs
- ✔ Gross profit is always more than net profit
- ✔ The more you sell, the more gross profit you make

Figuring gross profit margins

Following on from the examples in the preceding section, if a fashion retailer buys a skirt for $20 and sells it for $50, her gross profit is $30. Sounds easy, but how do I figure out her *gross profit margin*? As follows:

> *Gross profit margin* = gross profit divided by sales multiplied by 100

In this example, the retailer's gross profit margin equals $30 divided by $50 (that's gross profit divided by sales) multiplied by 100, which is 60 per cent.

As I mention earlier, the more you sell, the more gross profit you make. However, if your costs stay constant, your gross profit margin stays the same, regardless of how much you sell. For example, if this retailer sells four skirts, her sales would be $200, her costs would be $80, her gross profit would be $120, but her gross profit margin would still be the same, at 60 per cent.

Table 6-5 shows the gross profit and gross profit margins for the three examples from the preceding section.

Table 6-5	Calculating Gross Profit and Gross Profit Margin		
	Fashion Retailer	*Massage Therapist*	*Carpenter*
Sell price	$50.00	$85.00	$800.00
Costs	$20.00	$25.00	$300.00
Gross Profit	$30.00	$60.00	$500.00
Gross Profit Margin	**60%**	**71%**	**63%**

Unless you know that something cost more to buy or to make than what you sold it for, both your gross profit and your gross profit margin should always be a positive figure.

Looking at margins over time

So far in this chapter, the examples I use talk about gross profit per unit sold or hour worked. However, in real life gross profit margins often vary from one transaction to the next (shopkeepers make a higher margin on gourmet jams than they do on milk, for example).

For this reason, it's good to be able to calculate your average gross profit margins over a period of time. Here's how some different kinds of businesses go about calculating their gross profit:

- ✔ A builder constructs a house that then sells for $250,000. He spends $180,000 on materials and labour to build this house. His gross profit on the job is $70,000, and his gross profit margin is 28 per cent.

- ✔ A couple making homemade chilli sauce that they sell in all different shapes and sizes, and at different prices, can see that they made $80,000 in sales over the last 12 months and spent $20,000 on ingredients, bottles, labelling and freight. Their gross profit for the year is $60,000, and their average gross profit margin is 75 per cent.

- ✔ A woman who buys second-hand clothes and resells them on eBay can see that she sold $2,500 on eBay during the month and spent $1,300 on buying clothes and postage. Her gross profit for the month is $1,200, and her average gross profit margin is 48 per cent.

Analysing Margins for Your Own Business

Have you been reading this chapter and thinking to yourself that this theory is all very well, but you're not a retailer, a carpenter or a massage therapist? If so, never fear. In the following sections I explain how to apply the principles of gross and net profit to your own business.

Calculating margins when you charge by the hour

If you have a service business and you charge by the hour, calculating your gross profit can be blindingly easy. Why? Because sometimes, a service business has no variable costs, and gross profit equals 100 per cent of income. Read on to find out more.

Here's how you work out your gross profit and gross profit margin if you have a service business:

1. **Write down your hourly charge-out rate, not including any taxes that you charge to customers (such as GST, VAT or sales tax).**

2. **Ask yourself whether any variable costs are associated with your service and, if so, calculate how much these costs are per hour.**

    The most likely cost for a service business is employees or subcontract labour. For example, when I ran a contract bookkeeping service, I paid my contractors an hourly rate for doing bookkeeping. This was a variable cost associated with my service.

    If you're a sole owner-operator with no employees, you may find that no variable costs are associated with your service.

3. **Subtract the cost you calculated in Step 2 from the hourly rate from Step 1.**

    This is your gross profit for this service. If you have no variable costs associated with your service, your hourly gross profit is the same as your hourly charge-out rate.

4. **Divide the gross profit you calculated in Step 3 by the hourly rate from Step 1, and divide your result by 100.**

    If you have no variable costs associated with your service, your gross profit margin will be 100 per cent.

5. **Consider the profitability of your service model.**

    Most service businesses need a decent gross profit margin in order to survive. If you're subcontracting out your services, don't underestimate the margin you'll need in order to cover all your business expenses. For example, if you're charging customers $50 per hour but paying employees $35 per hour, leaving yourself with a measly gross profit margin of 30 per cent, you're almost certainly going to be doing things tough.

Calculating margins when you sell products

If you buy or manufacture items that you sell to others, each item has a separate gross profit margin. If you have accounting software and you use this software to track your inventory, you'll be able to generate reports that calculate gross profit margins for you. However, if you don't have this resource, grab a calculator and work through the following for each item you sell:

1. **Write down the sell price of this item, not including any taxes that you charge to customers (such as GST, VAT or sales tax).**

   If the sell price varies depending on the customer, do the analysis for each price you sell this item for.

2. **Write down the cost of this item.**

   If you buy this item from someone else, write down the total cost of purchasing this item, including freight but not including any taxes that you can claim back from the government (such as GST or VAT). If you manufacture this item, write down the total cost of all materials and production labour.

3. **Subtract the cost you calculated in Step 2 from the sell price you calculated in Step 1.**

   This is your gross profit for this item.

4. **Divide the gross profit you calculated in Step 3 by the sell price you calculated in Step 1, and divide your result by 100.**

5. **Consider the results and your fate in life.**

   Number crunching is not an end in itself. Does this margin seem reasonable? If you're not sure, ask around other people who work in the same industry as yourself, and try to get a sense of what margins you should expect.

Always bear in mind that, so long as your pricing policies remain consistent, your gross profit margin should stay relatively constant, no matter how much you sell.

Calculating margins if you do big projects

If you do lots of big projects over the course of a year — maybe you're a builder, you do custom manufacturing or you do big contract consultancy jobs — you're going to find it tricky to calculate your hourly gross profit, or your gross profit per unit sold. A different tack is required:

1. **Look at your total sales for 12 months, not including GST.**

   I'm talking about total sales for all the different products that you sell, combined. If you're looking at a Profit & Loss report to get this figure, don't include things such as interest income, or sundry income from services.

2. **Add up your total variable costs for 12 months, not including GST.**

   If you're an owner-operator with no employees running a service business, you may find that no variable costs are associated with your service. Otherwise, if you're unsure how to figure out what your variable costs are, refer to 'Identifying your variable costs', earlier in this chapter.

3. **Subtract the total costs you calculated in Step 2 from the total sales you calculated in Step 1.**

   This is your gross profit for the past 12 months.

4. **Divide the gross profit you calculated in Step 3 by the total sales you calculated in Step 1, and divide your result by 100.**

5. **Review your overall profitability.**

   What makes an acceptable gross profit margin varies from business to business. However, what's important for you is to be aware of your gross profit margin and ensure that it stays consistent over time.

Building Your Gross Profit Projection

In the earlier chapters in this book, I talk about clarifying your business idea and competitive strategies (Chapters 2 and 3), creating a budget for start-up expenses (Chapter 4), and setting prices and creating your first sales projection (Chapter 5). Next on the road map is expanding your sales projection to add an estimate of direct costs so that you can arrive at a projection of your gross profit for the next 12 months.

Note: I'm assuming here that you've already made a stab at predicting sales for the next 12 months. If you haven't, scoot back to Chapter 5 to complete this process. What you're aiming for is a monthly estimate of total sales for the next 12 months. This could be a single total for each month, or you may choose to split sales into several categories (similar to the first few rows of Figure 6-2).

What you do next depends on what kind of business you're working on.

If you have a service business with no employees and no variable costs

This type of business has the simplest of financial forecasts. Simply enter the heading 'Variable Costs' and leave the figures in this row blank. However, note that if you forecast substantial growth for your business, you may not be able to do all the work yourself, and you may need to hire subcontractors or use employee labour. In which case, you'll need to show the variable costs of this labour (read on to find out more . . .).

If you have a service business and you use employee or subcontract labour

In this section, I'm talking about a service business that uses employee or subcontract labour to provide at least some of the services. In this context, the employee or subcontract labour becomes a variable cost because the cost of this labour goes up or down in direct relation to sales. (I'm not talking about a service business where the owner provides all the services but maybe has an admin employee working in the office. This scenario is different, because the business isn't actually hiring out the admin worker to clients.)

Examples of this kind of business could be a plumber who subcontracts out some work, a party business that pays employees a casual rate to go to parties, a builder who uses labourers, or a consultant bookkeeping service that hires lots of bookkeepers.

Here's how to create a gross profit projection for this kind of business:

1. **Complete your sales projections for the next 12 months.**

   You should have a spreadsheet file with the months along the top, details regarding sales below, and a grand total sales forecast for each month along the bottom. In Figure 6-2, the first 21 rows show this information. (Refer to Chapter 5 for more information on sales projections.)

2. **If you haven't done so already, separate out sales where you're going to do the work, and sales that you'll get employees or subcontractors to do the work.**

   Figure 6-2 shows how this is done. The reason you separate the two is because you're going to have variable costs associated with the services that employees or subcontractors provide.

If you have a company structure, rather than a sole trader or partnership structure, you will receive some kind of salary. Usually in financial projections, director salaries are shown in the expenses part of the projection, not as a variable cost, but if you feel strongly that you want to show the cost of your labour here, you can do so. The format of a business plan has no absolute rights or wrongs; the only condition is that the structure needs to be logical and make sense not just to yourself, but also to others.

3. **Insert costs next to each of your prices.**

   Can you see how I've inserted the costs for each service in the first few rows of column C in Figure 6-2?

4. **List your variable costs below the sales.**

   I've inserted a separate row for each service provided here, because the cost is different for each one.

5. **Calculate the value of variable costs by multiplying the number of times the service is sold by the cost of each service.**

   For example, the formula in cell B24 is =**B13*C2**.

I often add names to cells, rather than specifying cell references. For example, in the spreadsheet for Figure 6-2, I give cell C2 the name 'Cost1hr30'. This way, my formula for cell B24 becomes =**B13*Cost1hr30**. I talk more about naming cells in Chapter 8.

6. **Add a row that calculates gross profit.**

   Gross profit is equal to sales less variable costs. For example, in Figure 6-2, the gross profit for July equals $5,910 less $1,975, equalling $3,935. The formula for this gross profit in July is =**B21-B27**.

7. **Save this spreadsheet with the name 'Gross Profit Projection'.**

   Of course, you can save this spreadsheet with any name you like. However, I do refer to this file in Chapter 8 and so if you save the file by this name, you'll find my instructions in that chapter make more sense.

	Price	Cost										
1 hour 30 Package	$ 170.00	$ 115.00										
2 hour Package	$ 190.00	$ 130.00										
2 hour Plus Package	$ 210.00	$ 145.00										
	Jul-14	Aug-14	Sep-14	Oct-14	Nov-14	Dec-14	Jan-15	Feb-15	Mar-15	Apr-15	May-15	Jun-15
Parties with owner's labour												
1 hour 30 Package	12	12	12	12	12	12	12	12	12	12	12	12
2 hour Package	4	4	4	4	4	4	4	4	4	4	4	4
2 hour Plus Package	1	1	1	1	1	1	-	1	1	1	1	1
Parties with subcontract labour												
1 hour 30 Package	8	12	13	8	12	80	4	5	12	13	18	22
2 hour Package	7	6	8	10	12	18	2	10	14	16	18	20
2 hour Plus Package	1	3	4	4	5	8	-	4	4	6	6	6
Income Generated												
1 hour 30 Package	$ 3,400	$ 4,080	$ 4,250	$ 3,400	$ 4,080	$15,640	$ 2,720	$ 2,890	$ 4,080	$ 4,250	$ 5,100	$ 5,780
2 hour Package	$ 2,090	$ 1,900	$ 2,280	$ 2,660	$ 3,040	$ 4,180	$ 1,140	$ 2,660	$ 3,420	$ 3,800	$ 4,180	$ 4,560
2 hour Plus Package	$ 420	$ 840	$ 1,050	$ 1,050	$ 1,260	$ 1,890	$ -	$ 1,050	$ 1,050	$ 1,470	$ 1,470	$ 1,470
Total Sales	$ 5,910	$ 6,820	$ 7,580	$ 7,110	$ 8,380	$21,710	$ 3,860	$ 6,600	$ 8,550	$ 9,520	$10,750	$11,810
Costs												
1 hour 30 Package	920	1,380	1,495	920	1,380	9,200	460	575	1,380	1,495	2,070	2,530
2 hour Package	910	780	1,040	1,300	1,560	2,340	260	1,300	1,820	2,080	2,340	2,600
2 hour Plus Package	145	435	580	580	725	1,160	-	580	580	870	870	870
	1,975	2,595	3,115	2,800	3,665	12,700	720	2,455	3,780	4,445	5,280	6,000
Gross Profit	$ 3,935	$ 4,225	$ 4,465	$ 4,310	$ 4,715	$ 9,010	$ 3,140	$ 4,145	$ 4,770	$ 5,075	$ 5,470	$ 5,810

Figure 6-2: Building a gross profit projection for a service with employees or sub-contactors.

If you're not too sure about how to proceed with this stage of your Profit & Loss Projection, you can download a Service Business With Employees template from www.dummies.com/go/creatingbusinessplan. The template shows how to set up your projections if you run a service business where employees or subcontractors are part of providing the service.

If you buy and sell a small number of products

For this kind of business, I'm talking about someone who buys or manufactures a few specific products and then resells them. Examples could include someone making homemade jams, a baker selling pastries, a cafe selling a limited range of items or a cabinet-maker producing a limited range of furniture.

In the next example, I show how to create a gross profit projection for this kind of business. (The final profit here is rather pitiful considering the amount of goods sold, but this example is probably quite realistic. The first time you do a gross profit projection for your business, you often find your business model isn't strong enough.)

Here's how to create a gross profit projection for a business buying and selling a small number of goods:

1. **Complete your sales projections for the next 12 months.**

   You should have a spreadsheet file with the months along the top, details regarding sales below, and a grand total sales forecast for each month along the bottom. In Figure 6-3, the first 28 rows show this information. (Refer to Chapter 5 for more information on sales projections.)

2. **Insert costs next to each of your products.**

   I've inserted the costs for each of my products in the first few rows of column C in Figure 6-3.

   Earlier in this chapter, I talk about creating detailed product costing worksheets for each product (refer to 'Creating product costings for manufacturers'.) If you're feeling clever, you may want to link each of the costs at the top of this worksheet to your product costing worksheets. This would mean that the moment you update a product costing, your gross profit projection is automatically updated as well. Chapter 8 talks more about linking one worksheet to another.

3. **List your variable costs below the sales.**

   I've inserted a separate row for each product provided in Figure 6-3, because the cost is different for each one.

4. **Calculate the value of variable costs by multiplying the number of units sold by the cost of each service.**

   For example, the formula in cell C31 is =**C13*D2**.

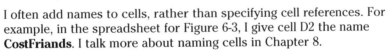

   I often add names to cells, rather than specifying cell references. For example, in the spreadsheet for Figure 6-3, I give cell D2 the name **CostFriands**. I talk more about naming cells in Chapter 8.

5. **Add a row that calculates gross profit.**

   Gross profit is equal to sales less variable costs. For example, in Figure 6-3, the gross profit for January equals $5,014 less $1,594, equalling $3,420. The formula for this gross profit in January is =**I28-I36**.

6. **Save this spreadsheet with the name 'Gross Profit Projection'.**

   Of course, you can save this spreadsheet with any name you like. However, I do refer to this file in Chapter 8 and so if you save the file by this name, you'll find my instructions in this chapter make more sense.

Figure 6-3: Building a gross profit projection for a business selling a small number of different products.

		Sell Price	Costs											
	Friands	$ 2.00	$ 0.66											
	Regular Muffins	$ 1.50	$ 0.80											
	Wholesale Muffins	$ 1.30	$ 0.80											
	Chocolate Brownies	$ 2.20	$ 1.20											
	Teacakes	$ 7.00	$ 3.00											

		Sales Forecast for July to June for Cakes to Cafes											
		Jul-14	Aug-14	Sep-14	Oct-14	Nov-14	Dec-14	Jan-15	Feb-15	Mar-15	Apr-15	May-15	Jun-15	Annual Totals
Friands		400	400	420	440	460	480	500	500	500	500	500	500	5600
TOTAL		$ 800	$ 800	$ 840	$ 880	$ 920	$ 960	$ 1,000	$ 1,000	$ 1,000	$ 1,000	$ 1,000	$ 1,000	11,200
Regular Muffins		400	400	400	400	400	400	400	400	400	400	400	400	4800
TOTAL		$ 600	$ 600	$ 600	$ 600	$ 600	$ 600	$ 600	$ 600	$ 600	$ 600	$ 600	$ 600	7,200
Wholesale Muffins		200	200	200	300	300	300	400	400	400	400	400	400	3900
TOTAL		$ 260	$ 260	$ 260	$ 390	$ 390	$ 390	$ 520	$ 520	$ 520	$ 520	$ 520	$ 520	5,070
Chocolate Brownies		520	520	520	520	520	520	520	520	520	520	520	520	6240
TOTAL		$ 1,144	$ 1,144	$ 1,144	$ 1,144	$ 1,144	$ 1,144	$ 1,144	$ 1,144	$ 1,144	$ 1,144	$ 1,144	$ 1,144	13,728
Teacakes		250	250	250	250	250	250	250	250	250	250	250	250	3000
TOTAL		$ 1,750	$ 1,750	$ 1,750	$ 1,750	$ 1,750	$ 1,750	$ 1,750	$ 1,750	$ 1,750	$ 1,750	$ 1,750	$ 1,750	21,000
GRAND TOTAL		$ 4,554	$ 4,554	$ 4,594	$ 4,764	$ 4,804	$ 4,844	$ 5,014	$ 5,014	$ 5,014	$ 5,014	$ 5,014	$ 5,014	$ 58,198
LESS: VARIABLE COSTS														
Friands		$ 264	$ 264	$ 277	$ 290	$ 304	$ 317	$ 330	$ 330	$ 330	$ 330	$ 330	$ 330	3,696
Regular Muffins		$ 320	$ 320	$ 320	$ 320	$ 320	$ 320	$ 320	$ 320	$ 320	$ 320	$ 320	$ 320	3,840
Wholesale Muffins		$ 160	$ 160	$ 160	$ 240	$ 240	$ 240	$ 320	$ 320	$ 320	$ 320	$ 320	$ 320	3,120
Chocolate Brownies		$ 624	$ 624	$ 624	$ 624	$ 624	$ 624	$ 624	$ 624	$ 624	$ 624	$ 624	$ 624	7,488
Teacakes		$ 750	$ -	$ -	$ -	$ -	$ -	$ -	$ -	$ -	$ -	$ -	$ -	750
TOTAL VARIABLE COSTS		$ 2,118	$ 1,368	$ 1,361	$ 1,474	$ 1,488	$ 1,501	$ 1,594	$ 1,594	$ 1,594	$ 1,594	$ 1,594	$ 1,594	18,894
GROSS PROFIT		$ 2,436	$ 3,186	$ 3,213	$ 3,290	$ 3,316	$ 3,343	$ 3,420	$ 3,420	$ 3,420	$ 3,420	$ 3,420	$ 3,420	39,304

If you're not too sure about how to proceed with this stage of your Profit & Loss Projection, you can download a Sales Business With Different Products template from www.dummies.com/go/creatingbusinessplan. The template shows how to set up your projections if you run a business selling a small number of different products.

If you sell many different products or your variable costs are a percentage of sales

Sometimes, the idea with variable costs is that they are a stable percentage of income. For example, if you pay commissions on sales, these commissions are normally a certain percentage. Or if you're a retailer, the cost of the goods you buy is probably a similar percentage of sales each time you make a sale.

If your variable costs are always a pretty stable percentage of sales, the trick is to set up your gross profit projection so that your variable costs calculate automatically. In other words, set up your worksheet so that if you increase sales, variable costs automatically increase as well.

For example, in Figure 6-4, the online bookseller knows that for every $100 of full-price books he sells, it costs him $60 to buy the books. In other words, his variable costs represent 60 per cent of sales. Similarly, he knows that postage costs him, on average, 25 per cent of the sale value.

Here's how to build your gross profit projection if you sell lots of products, meaning the easiest way to calculate variable costs is as a percentage of sales:

1. **Complete your sales projections for the next 12 months.**

    You should have a spreadsheet file with the months along the top, details regarding sales below, and a grand total sales forecast for each month along the bottom. In Figure 6-4, the first 18 rows show this information. Notice that in contrast to a business that only sells a handful of different products, in this example the bookseller calculates sales projections according to the type of goods he's selling, and the average profit on each. (Refer to Chapter 5 for more information on sales projections.)

2. **Think of how much it costs you to buy each kind of item that you sell, and express this is a percentages of the sale value next to each price.**

    For example, a fashion retailer always doubles the cost when pricing shoes. So her variable costs for shoes would be 50 per cent.

3. **List your variable costs below the sales.**

    Insert a separate row for each kind of product that you sell.

4. **Calculate the value of variable costs by multiplying the average value of each sale by the percentage that this item normally costs.**

    For example, the formula in cell C21 is =C10*D2.

I often add names to cells, rather than specifying cell references. For example, in the template for Figure 6-4, I give cell D2 the name **CostFPBooks**. I talk more about naming cells in Chapter 8.

5. Add a row that calculates gross profit.

Gross profit is equal to sales less variable costs. For example, in Figure 6-4, the gross profit for July equals $21,590 less $15,153, equalling $6,437. The formula for this gross profit in July is =**C18-C25**.

6. Save this spreadsheet with the name 'Gross Profit Projection'.

Of course, you can save this spreadsheet with any name you like. However, I do refer to this file in Chapter 8 and so if you save the file by this name, you'll find my instructions in this chapter make more sense.

Go to www.dummies.com/go/creatingbusinessplan to download the Gross Profit Projection Many Products worksheet shown in Figure 6-4.

Figure 6-4:
Building a gross profit projection for a business selling lots of different kinds of products, or calculating costs on a percentage basis.

		Average Sell Price	Cost as a % of sales												
Full-price books		$ 24.99	60%												
Remainder books		$ 19.99	20%												
DVDs		$ 17.99	60%												
Postage & Packaging			25%												
					Sales Forecast for July to June for Online Books										
		Jul-14	Aug-14	Sep-14	Oct-14	Nov-14	Dec-14	Jan-15	Feb-15	Mar-15	Apr-15	May-15	Jun-15		Annual Totals
Full-price books		400	400	420	440	460	480	500	520	490	540	600	500		5750
TOTAL	$	9,996	$ 9,996	$ 10,496	$ 10,996	$ 11,495	$ 11,995	$ 12,495	$ 12,995	$ 12,245	$ 13,495	$ 14,994	$ 12,495		143,693
Remainder books		400	410	420	430	440	450	460	470	480	500	520	540		5520
TOTAL	$	7,996	$ 8,196	$ 8,396	$ 8,596	$ 8,796	$ 8,996	$ 9,195	$ 9,395	$ 9,595	$ 9,995	$ 10,395	$ 10,795		110,345
DVDs		200	200	200	300	300	300	400	400	400	400	400	400		3900
TOTAL	$	3,598	$ 3,598	$ 3,598	$ 5,397	$ 5,397	$ 5,397	$ 7,196	$ 7,196	$ 7,196	$ 7,196	$ 7,196	$ 7,196		70,161
GRAND TOTAL	$	21,590	$ 21,790	$ 22,490	$ 24,988	$ 25,688	$ 26,388	$ 28,886	$ 29,586	$ 29,036	$ 30,686	$ 32,585	$ 30,486		324,199
LESS: VARIABLE COSTS															
Full-price books	$	5,998	$ 5,998	$ 6,297	$ 6,597	$ 6,897	$ 7,197	$ 7,497	$ 7,797	$ 7,347	$ 8,097	$ 8,996	$ 7,497		86,216
Remainder books	$	1,599	$ 1,639	$ 1,679	$ 1,719	$ 1,759	$ 1,799	$ 1,839	$ 1,879	$ 1,919	$ 1,999	$ 2,079	$ 2,159		22,069
DVDs	$	2,159	$ 2,159	$ 2,159	$ 3,238	$ 3,238	$ 3,238	$ 4,318	$ 4,318	$ 4,318	$ 4,318	$ 4,318	$ 4,318		42,097
Postage & Packaging	$	5,398	$ 5,447	$ 5,622	$ 6,247	$ 6,422	$ 6,597	$ 7,222	$ 7,397	$ 7,259	$ 7,671	$ 8,146	$ 7,621		81,050
TOTAL VARIABLE COSTS	$	15,153	$ 15,243	$ 15,758	$ 17,802	$ 18,317	$ 18,831	$ 20,875	$ 21,390	$ 20,843	$ 22,085	$ 23,539	$ 21,595		231,431
GROSS PROFIT	$	6,437	$ 6,547	$ 6,732	$ 7,187	$ 7,371	$ 7,556	$ 8,011	$ 8,196	$ 8,194	$ 8,601	$ 9,046	$ 8,891		92,768

Gross profit, parrots, fraud and more

Understanding and monitoring your gross profit margin is an essential part of managing almost any business.

At the early stages of a business plan, understanding your gross profit margin is crucial for creating accurate budgets and experimenting with different business models. For example, look at your sales figures and ask yourself, what difference would a 5 per cent increase in gross profit make in the bottom line of your Profit & Loss? Often an increase of just 5 per cent can make the difference between business survival and death.

As your business becomes more established, your gross profit margin becomes an indicator of the health of your business. Similar

to a parrot down the mine, an unusual result in profit margins on your Profit & Loss report is often the first indicator that something is astray.

I remember getting a call a few years ago from a private investigator who'd been asked to investigate an alleged fraud in a computer retail company. The owner of the company suspected his bookkeeper of siphoning off funds, but couldn't identify how it was happening. The reason for these suspicions? The gross profit margin of his company had always been stable at 35 per cent, but in recent months it had fallen to 32 per cent. (I did assist with the investigation and, sadly, we were able to confirm the owner's worst fears.)

The neat thing about showing variable costs as a percentage in the top-left corner of your worksheet is that if you change one of these percentages, your variable costs change automatically too.

The beauty of developing financial projections in the method shown in the preceding steps is that you can experiment with different scenarios. For example, imagine that this is your business and you're thinking of switching suppliers. The service is much better, but the cost of books from this supplier will be 65 per cent of sales, rather than 60 per cent. By changing one figure in the top of your worksheet, you can see instantly the impact this change would make to your profitability.

Don't feel ill at the thought of all this technical stuff — if you can count to ten, then you can master creating a formula in a spreadsheet. Go to www.dummies.com/go/creatingbusinessplan and follow the Relating Costs to Income link to view a nifty video on this very topic.

Chapter 7

Planning for Expenses

In This Chapter

▶ Creating a 12-month forecast for business expenses

▶ Tweaking your forecast so it's as accurate as can be

▶ Comparing your business with others similar to you

▶ Understanding where taxes and loan repayments fit into the picture

▶ Figuring out how much money you need to keep that hungry wolf at bay

Although a business plan takes many shapes and sizes, pretty much every business plan includes a projection of both income and expenses for the next 12 months ahead. (Some business plans extend further than this, for three or even five years; however, for most purposes, 12 months usually does just fine.)

In this chapter, I focus on the expenses element of this 12-month forecast. Estimating future expenses isn't some idle form of crystal-ball gazing where you pluck some figures out of the air until you arrive at a final prediction of profit that makes you sleep easy. Instead, planning each expense in detail provides you with an opportunity for a reality check, even if this reality can prove rather chilling at times.

In this chapter, I also suggest that if you're creating your first business plan, you look at not only your likely business expenses for the next 12 months, but also your personal expenses. After all, in the absence of benevolent fairy godmothers or inheritances from wealthy great-aunties, starting a business that requires your full-time input but doesn't generate enough profits for you to survive is never going to fly.

Concentrating on Expenses

I accept that this book provides no gripping plot, murders or sex scenes, and that few people picking up this book are going to start at Chapter 1 and read through to the end. Instead, you'll probably flick through the pages, picking and choosing the bits you're interested in, which is generally okay. However, when you're working on financial projections, simply jumping in at whatever chapter catches your eye can be a time-wasting exercise.

As I explain in Chapter 1, the typical financial planning cycle involves creating a start-up budget, followed by estimating prices, costs and expenses. You then use this information to create Profit & Loss Projections, break-even analysis reports and Cashflow Projections.

If you've been working through this cycle chapter by chapter, you'll be about halfway through this process. (Chapter 4 focuses on budgeting for start-up expenses, Chapter 5 on prices and rates, Chapter 6 on product costs and gross profit and Chapter 7 — that's this chapter — on expense budgets. Chapters 8, 9 and 10 then complete the financial planning process.)

So, if you've just picked up this book and plunged in at this chapter, pause for a moment and check that you've already covered the initial stages of your financial plan (that is, creating a start-up budget, setting prices and calculating product costs). If you haven't, take the time to get these foundations in place first.

Separating start-up expenses and variable costs from ongoing expenses

When planning for business expenses, always separate *start-up expenses* from *ongoing expenses*:

- *Start-up expenses* are one-off expenses that you encounter when you first start a business, such as new equipment, company formation expenses, legal expenses and signage. I talk lots about start-up expenses in Chapter 4.

- *Ongoing expenses* are the kind of expenses that occur year in and year out, and which form a regular part of everyday trading. Ongoing expenses are the focus of the next part of this chapter.

When you're working with Profit & Loss Projections in your business plan, you only include ongoing expenses. Start-up expenses — if relevant to you — are shown separately.

Similarly, remember the difference between *variable costs* and *fixed expenses*.

- *Variable costs* (also sometimes called *direct costs* or *cost of goods sold*) are the costs that go up and down in direct relation to your sales.

- *Fixed expenses* (also sometimes called *indirect costs* or *overheads*) are expenses that stay constant, regardless of whether your sales go up and down.

This chapter focuses on fixed expenses only. For more about creating a worksheet that forecasts variable costs, refer to Chapter 6.

Thinking of what expenses to include

If you've been running your business for a while, you already have a good idea of what your expenses are going to be. However, if you're just getting started with your business plan, thinking of the types of expenses you may encounter can be tricky. Are you going to take out insurance? What about accounting fees? Will you need to pay any professional memberships? What expenses could you face that you haven't even thought of yet?

Figure 7-1 shows a Business Expenses worksheet that lists expenses in the first column, how often they occur in the second column, and an estimate of the amount in the third. The monthly total shown in the fourth column calculates automatically. You can download this worksheet from www.dummies.com/go/creatingbusinessplan.

To use the Business Expenses worksheet, here's what to do:

1. **Go to** www.dummies.com/go/creatingbusinessplan **and download the Business Expenses worksheet template. Save this onto your computer, and then open it up in Excel.**

   You can also open up this template in most other spreadsheet software, if you prefer.

2. **For each expense account, make a stab at how much you think this expense will be for your business, and whether this expense occurs weekly, fortnightly, quarterly, monthly or annually.**

If you haven't started trading yet and you're still creating a business plan, estimating expenses can be very tricky. See 'Staying Real with Benchmarks' later in this chapter for ways to improve the accuracy of your estimates.

If your business is already trading, the best way to make estimates is to look at what you've spent in the past. Old supplier invoices, accounting software transaction journals and monthly Profit & Loss Statements are all good sources for this information.

Round all amounts to the nearest $20 or so — forecasts aren't meant to be a science.

3. **Delete any expenses that aren't relevant to your business.**

    The list of expenses in this worksheet is pretty comprehensive, so you'll almost certainly find that some of these expenses aren't relevant to you. If that's the case, simply delete that row in the worksheet. (Highlight the row, right-click with your mouse, and then select Delete.)

4. **Add any expenses that are relevant to your business but aren't included on this list.**

    To insert a row, right-click where you want the row to be, select Insert, and then Entire Row.

    Don't insert any variable costs (costs of purchasing goods for resale, or costs of production). What you're focusing on in this chapter is fixed expenses only. (For more about variable costs, refer to Chapter 6.)

5. **Check the monthly estimates for each expense make sense.**

    Excel automatically calculates how much each expense will cost every month, depending on the frequency you select. At this point, look at these calculations and see if they make sense to you.

6. **Review the totals at the bottom of the Monthly Total column.**

    The Total Expenses row automatically adds up all the rows above it. This means that if you change a figure, the total recalculates automatically.

    To get a spreadsheet to do this calculation, you have to insert a formula. In Excel, the easiest way to do this is to press your AutoSum button (the one with a Greek symbol that looks a bit like an 'E'). However, if you're using the template downloaded from www.dummies.com/go/creatingbusinessplan, this formula is already there.

7. **Ignore the figures in the individual month columns.**

    I talk more about these in the following section.

	A	B	C	D
7	**Type of Expense**	**Freqency**	**Estimate**	**Monthly total**
8	Accounting Fees	Annually	$1,500	$125
9	Advertising	Monthly	$1,200	$1,200
10	Bank Charges	Monthly	$100	$100
11	Cleaning Expenses	Weekly	$50	$217
12	Computer Consumables	Monthly	$150	$150
13	Consultant Expenses	Monthly	$300	$300
14	Couriers	Monthly	$80	$80
15	Customer Consumables	Monthly	$60	$60
16	Electricity	Quarterly	$500	$167
17	Equipment Rental	Monthly	$200	$200
18	Freight Fees	Monthly	$300	$300
19	Gas	Quarterly	$300	$100
20	Hire Purchase Payments	Monthly	$650	$650
21	Insurance	Annually	$3,000	$250
22	Interest Expense	Monthly	$520	$520
23	Internet Fees	Monthly	$150	$150
24	Lease Expenses	Monthly	$800	$800
25	License Fees	Annually	$1,200	$100
26	Merchant Fees	Monthly	$320	$320
27	Motor Vehicle rego & insurance	Annually	$1,500	$125
28	Motor Vehicle Fuel	Weekly	$80	$347
29	Motor Vehicle Repairs & Maint	Annually	$2,000	$167
30	Motor Vehicle Tolls	Weekly	$70	$303
31	Office Supplies	Monthly	$150	$150
32	Parking	Weekly	$35	$152
33	Professional Memberships	Annually	$1,800	$150
34	Rates	Quarterly	$400	$133
35	Rental Expense	Fortnightly	$1,500	$3,250
36	Repairs and Maintenance	Annually	$6,000	$500
37	Replacements	Annually	$3,000	$250
38	Security Expenses	Monthly	$120	$120
39	Staff Amenities	Monthly	$300	$300
40	Storage Expenses	Monthly	$150	$150
41	Subcontractor Expenses	Monthly	$520	$520
42	Subscription and Dues	Annually	$2,200	$183
43	Telephone (inc mobile)	Monthly	$550	$550
44	Travel Domestic	Monthly	$350	$350
45	Travel Overseas	Annually	$3,500	$292
46	Wages and Salaries	Weekly	$3,500	$15,167
47	Wages oncosts	Weekly	$350	$1,517
48	Website expenses	Monthly	$850	$850
49	**Total Expenses**			**$29,672**

Figure 7-1:
In this
Business
Expense
worksheet,
start by
estimating
an amount
for each
expense,
along with
how often
it occurs.

Why is a month not four weeks?

I sometimes come across business plans where an expense such as rent is, say, $300 a week, and the business has shown $1,200 a month in its monthly business expense worksheet. At risk of sounding like a finicky fusspot, the budget for a month is not four times the budget for a week.

To calculate a monthly budget for something you pay weekly, you need to first multiply the weekly amount by 52, and then divide it by 12. In this example, $300 a week rent multiplied by 52 equals $15,600. Divide this by 12 and you get $1,300 a month (not $1,200).

Building a 12-month projection

Figure 7-2 shows an example of possible expenses for a relatively small business. You can see the months running along the top, the names of the expenses down the first column, and an estimate of how much each expense will be along each row.

Looks good? Then it's time for you to give it a go:

1. **Open up your Business Expenses worksheet.**

   Refer to the preceding section for more on this worksheet. Hopefully you've already completed the first three columns of this worksheet, and added or deleted expense accounts so that this worksheet is relevant for your business.

2. **Change the names on the months along the top row.**

   My example has January as the first month, but obviously you're going to start with the month that corresponds to the period of your business plan. For example, if you plan to open in August, August is going to be the first month in this worksheet.

3. **Complete dollar estimates for expenses, month by month.**

   If the template is working as it should, the monthly estimates will appear automatically (and correctly) for all weekly, fortnightly or monthly expenses. However, with expenses that you pay out only quarterly or annually, you'll need to change the amounts so that they fall in the right months. For example, in the Accounting Fees row at the top, I have a single amount in October, when these fees normally fall due. (To make this change, I simply scroll across this row, deleting the monthly amounts, and type the whole year's allocation into the October column.)

If you use accounting software, you may be able to export a month-by-month summary of all expenses out of your accounting software and into Excel. If you think that your expenses are likely to be similar in the next 12 months to what they were in the previous 12 months, this method provides a quick and efficient way to populate the amounts in your Business Expenses worksheet.

4. **Have a further think about the nature of annual expenses.**

    You'll find some expenses occur only once a year (such as accounting fees or membership dues). For these expenses you can simply enter the whole budget for the year in the month when payment is going to fall due.

    For other expenses, however, you may have an idea of how much the annual total will be, but you don't know when payment will be due. Vehicle repairs are a good example. I know that my car usually clocks in at approximately $2,000 of repairs per year, but I never know when these bills are going to fall due. With these kinds of expenses, I just enter an annual estimate (as you can see I do in row 29 of Figure 7-2), and leave a monthly amount in place.

5. **Check the formula for Total Expenses.**

    The idea of the Total Expenses row is that it automatically adds up all the rows above it. To get your spreadsheet to do this calculation, you have to insert a formula. In Excel, the easiest way to do this is to press your AutoSum button (the one with a Greek symbol that looks a bit like an 'E').

    This formula is already in the Business Expenses template, but if you've inserted or deleted rows, you may have knocked it out of whack. Click on the formula and check it still makes sense. (For example, =**SUM(G12:G48)** means that Excel is going to add up every figure from cell G12 down to cell G48.)

6. **Save your work and ponder.**

    With your final worksheet complete, spend a generous amount of time checking it over, ensuring it makes sense and is realistic.

Type of Expense	Frequency	Estimate	Monthly total	Jan	Feb	Mar	Apr	May	Jun	Jul	Aug	Sep	Oct	Nov	Dec
Accounting Fees	Annually	$1,500	$125										$1,500		
Advertising	Monthly	$1,200	$1,200	$1,200	$1,200	$1,200	$1,200	$1,200	$1,200	$1,200	$1,200	$1,200	$1,200	$1,200	$1,200
Bank Charges	Monthly	$100	$100	$100	$100	$100	$100	$100	$100	$100	$100	$100	$100	$100	$100
Cleaning Expenses	Weekly	$50	$217	$217	$217	$217	$217	$217	$217	$217	$217	$217	$217	$217	$217
Computer Consumables	Monthly	$150	$150	$150	$150	$150	$150	$150	$150	$150	$150	$150	$150	$150	$150
Consultant Expenses	Monthly	$300	$300	$300	$300	$300	$300	$300	$300	$300	$300	$300	$300	$300	$300
Couriers	Monthly	$80	$80	$80	$80	$80	$80	$80	$80	$80	$80	$80	$80	$80	$80
Customer Consumables	Monthly	$60	$60	$60	$60	$60	$60	$60	$60	$60	$60	$60	$60	$60	$60
Electricity	Quarterly	$500	$167	$500			$500			$500			$500		
Equipment Rental	Monthly	$200	$200	$200	$200	$200	$200	$200	$200	$200	$200	$200	$200	$200	$200
Freight Fees	Monthly	$300	$300	$300	$300	$300	$300	$300	$300	$300	$300	$300	$300	$300	$300
Gas	Quarterly	$300	$100	$300			$300			$300			$300		
Hire Purchase Payments	Monthly	$650	$650	$650	$650	$650	$650	$650	$650	$650	$650	$650	$650	$650	$650
Insurance	Annually	$3,000	$250										$3,000		
Interest Expense	Monthly	$500	$520	$520	$520	$520	$520	$520	$520	$520	$520	$520	$520	$520	$520
Internet Fees	Monthly	$150	$150	$150			$150			$150			$150		
Lease Expenses	Monthly	$800	$800	$800	$800	$800	$800	$800	$800	$800	$800	$800	$800	$800	$800
License Fees	Annually	$1,200	$100	$700									$500		
Merchant Fees	Monthly	$320	$320	$320	$320	$320	$320	$320	$320	$320	$320	$320	$320	$320	$320
Motor Vehicle rego & insurance	Annually	$1,500	$125									$1,500			
Motor Vehicle Fuel	Weekly	$80	$347	$347	$347	$347	$347	$347	$347	$347	$347	$347	$347	$347	$347
Motor Vehicle Repairs & Maint	Annually	$2,000	$167	$167	$167	$167	$167	$167	$167	$167	$167	$167	$167	$167	$167
Motor Vehicle Tolls	Weekly	$70	$303	$303	$303	$303	$303	$303	$303	$303	$303	$303	$303	$303	$303
Office Supplies	Monthly	$150	$150	$150	$150	$150	$150	$150	$150	$150	$150	$150	$150	$150	$150
Parking	Weekly	$35	$152	$152	$152	$152	$152	$152	$152	$152	$152	$152	$152	$152	$152
Professional Memberships	Annually	$1,800	$150		$1,800										
Rates	Quarterly	$400	$133	$400			$400			$400			$400		
Rental Expense	Fortnightly	$1,500	$3,250	$3,250	$3,250	$3,250	$3,250	$3,250	$3,250	$3,250	$3,250	$3,250	$3,250	$3,250	$3,250
Repairs and Maintenance	Annually	$6,000	$500	$500	$500	$500	$500	$500	$500	$500	$500	$500	$500	$500	$500
Replacements	Annually	$3,000	$250	$250	$250	$250	$250	$250	$250	$250	$250	$250	$250	$250	$250
Security Expenses	Monthly	$120	$120	$120	$120	$120	$120	$120	$120	$120	$120	$120	$120	$120	$120
Staff Amenities	Monthly	$300	$300	$300	$300	$300	$300	$300	$300	$300	$300	$300	$300	$300	$300
Storage Expenses	Monthly	$150	$150	$150	$150	$150	$150	$150	$150	$150	$150	$150	$150	$150	$150
Subcontractor Expenses	Monthly	$520	$520	$520	$520	$520	$520	$520	$520	$520	$520	$520	$520	$520	$520
Subscription and Dues	Annually	$2,200	$183	$200		$500						$300	$1,200		
Telephone (inc mobile)	Monthly	$550	$550	$550	$550	$550	$550	$550	$550	$550	$550	$550	$550	$550	$550
Travel Domestic	Monthly	$350	$350	$350	$350	$350	$350	$350	$350	$350	$350	$350	$350	$350	$350
Travel Overseas	Annually	$3,500	$292											$3,500	
Wages and Salaries	Weekly	$3,500	$15,167	$15,167	$15,167	$15,167	$15,167	$15,167	$15,167	$15,167	$15,167	$15,167	$15,167	$15,167	$15,167
Wages oncosts	Weekly	$350	$1,517	$1,517	$1,517	$1,517	$1,517	$1,517	$1,517	$1,517	$1,517	$1,517	$1,517	$1,517	$1,517
Website expenses	Monthly	$850	$850	$850	$850	$850	$850	$850	$850	$850	$850	$850	$850	$850	$850
Total Expenses			$29,672	$29,972	$30,122	$28,522	$29,072	$28,322	$28,022	$29,072	$28,302	$33,022	$33,772	$28,322	$28,022

Figure 7-2: Forecasting expenses for the months ahead.

A budget, projection or cashflow?

People tend to use the words 'budget', 'projection' and 'cashflow' synonymously, but there are subtle differences. A *budget* is about setting sales targets and expense limits. In larger businesses, for example, part of the responsibility for each manager is to meet agreed sales budgets, and ensure spending doesn't exceed allocated expense budgets.

On the other hand, a *projection* often looks further into the future than a budget. Rather than being a document that sets out expectations and responsibilities, a projection is more a statement of what might be possible. I often use projections to experiment with 'what-if' scenarios, looking at what would happen to my profits if sales were to slump by

10 per cent, or expenses increase by a similar amount. (In this chapter, when I talk about building an expenses worksheet, I'm still really at the projection stage. Later on, if the plan shows that the business model is viable, I can take these projections and use them to create budgets.)

A *cashflow* is a different report again, and looks at the actual cash flowing in and out of a business. For example, if you receive a $20,000 loan from the bank, this appears on your Cashflow Projection but doesn't show on your budget or your Profit & Loss Projection. (Why not? Because a loan doesn't count as income.) Chapter 10 talks lots more about cashflow reports and how they work.

Finetuning Your Worksheet

With the first draft of your expenses worksheet complete, you're ready to finetune it so you can be sure that your projections are as accurate as possible. Look at relationships between expenses, think about irregular payments, and focus on large expenses in a bit more detail.

Recognising relationships

One important thing to muse over is whether any expense categories are directly related to one another. For example, staff oncosts such as insurance or superannuation usually go up or down in direct proportion to wages.

The trick is to tell your spreadsheet about relationships so that it calculates them for you automatically. In Figure 7-2, for example, you can see a figure for wages in Row 46. I know that wages oncosts average 10 per cent of wages, so my formula for wages oncosts is =**C46*10%**. The neat thing about specifying relationships in this way is that when you change one figure in the spreadsheet, other figures change automatically, too.

Allowing for irregular payments

When creating expense projections, take a while to consider expenses that vary from month to month or change with the seasons. Here are a few specifics to consider:

- ✔ As I mention earlier, fuel bills, such as electricity and gas, often fall due every two or three months, rather than every month.

- ✔ If you pay wages every week, bear in mind that every third month you'll get a month with five paydays, not four.

- ✔ Think about seasonal variations. Depending on your business, expenses can increase or decrease dramatically at different times of year.

- ✔ If you're a small owner-operated business, think about when you may take holidays, and whether you need to increase your wages expense during this time.

Playing with the 10 per cent rule

I have a technique that I've developed over the years as a way of ensuring that my expense estimates are more likely to be accurate. What I do is go through the worksheet and identify any expenses that make up more than 10 per cent of the total expenses. For example, if you look at Figure 7-2, you can see that wages make up almost 50 per cent of total expenses. For such a small business, this wages bill makes up a huge proportion of outgoings.

If your expenses worksheet includes any one expense that's more than 10 per cent of total expenses, see if you can split this expense up in more detail. In the example shown in Figure 7-2, I would suggest to the business that they add more detail about wages in the worksheet — for example, listing each staff member separately, or listing each category of wages separately.

Staying Real with Benchmarks

You can find out how other businesses in your industry are faring by using something called *business benchmarking*. Business benchmarking results are compiled using survey results from other business owners. Individual results are always kept confidential, and it's only the averages (or highs and lows) that are reported, as well as percentages. For example, if I'm planning to open a boutique bar and I'm working on my business plan, I could look at the benchmarks for bars and clubs and see what percentage of sales I could expect to spend on alcohol, food, rental, wages and so on, or how much profit an average bar in a city suburb makes each year.

Business benchmarks provide an excellent way for you to check whether your financial projections are realistic, especially if you haven't started your business yet.

Locating benchmarks for your business

Depending on the nature of your business, you can hunt for benchmarks at a few places:

- ✔ **Banks:** Banks often have industry-specific information useful for benchmarking.

- ✔ **Benchmarking services:** Search online using the word 'benchmarks' or 'benchmarking' to find organisations specialising in the collation and resale of benchmarking data.

- ✔ **The 'big 5' accounting practices:** The major accounting and consulting firms such as KPMG, PWC or EY (formerly Ernst & Young) usually publish reports on key industries that are available for a fee. Call to find out what reports are available for your industry.

- ✔ **Boutique accounting practices:** Some accountants specialise in particular industries. For example, I know of someone who has a boutique accountancy practice specialising in medical practitioners and dentists. Specialist accountants will be very conversant with their industry and can quickly advise you whether your financial projections fall within industry standards. If you can't find a specialist accountant for your industry, ask your own accountant. Most accountants service a wide range of businesses and will have a good instinct as to whether a set of figures is reasonable, or not.

- ✔ **Government departments.** Government departments can be surprisingly forthcoming regarding what expenses are reasonable to expect for specific industries. (Tax office staff in particular are interested in this data, because they use specialist software to compare business tax returns with others in the same industry to assess whether the figures seem reasonable, or whether it's likely that the business owner is not declaring cash-in-hand income.)

- ✔ **Industry associations:** Industry associations almost always have some reference materials regarding benchmarks and are usually willing to advise members.

✔ **Networking meetings:** If you have colleagues working in the same industry but not in direct competition (maybe you're all in professional practice of some kind but specialising in different areas), you may find these colleagues are willing to share information regarding rent, wages or other expenses as a percentage of sales. (However, most business owners will be reticent regarding the actual amount paid for these items.)

Other country-specific benchmarking resources include:

✔ In Australasia, visit www.benchmarking.com.au, the ANZ's small business hub, the Dunn & Bradstreet calculator at www.bankofmelbourne.com.au or the Management Research web page of Waikato University at wms-soros.mngt.waikato.ac.nz.

✔ The American Express Open Forum website in the US is a great starting point for free and low-cost industry financial data. Go to www.openforum.com and search for 'benchmarking'.

✔ The Canadian government's Industry Canada webpage offers its online SME benchmarking tool, which will generate a report by industry type and province for you on the spot. Search on SME Benchmarking Tool at www.ic.gc.ca.

Using benchmarks as part of your plan

With a topic such as benchmarking, I like to use a detailed example to bring the whole concept to life.

In this fictional example, imagine a doctor (I'll call her Kate) has recently opened a new medical practice. As part of her business plan, she has purchased a set of benchmarks from a benchmarking organisation (see Table 7-1).

In Table 7-1, you can see that the average medical practice has a turnover of $822,000. The lowest practice in the survey has a turnover of $274,600 and the highest has a turnover of $1,691,500. Sounds interesting enough, but the real practical stuff for you — in planning your business — are the percentages. For example, can you see that the average medical practice spends 5.5 per cent of turnover on rent, and 25.3 per cent on wages?

Table 7-1	Using Business Benchmarks		
Indicator	*Average*	*Low*	*High*
Total income (thousands)	$822.2	$274.6	$1,691.5
Drugs, supplies, consumables	2.16%	0.76%	3.59%
Wages and salaries (staff only, not owners)	25.30%	15.10%	39.34%
Rent of premises	5.52%	1.92%	9.09%
Staff on-costs	2.23%	1.11%	3.87%
Non-vehicle depreciation/lease/hire purchase	2.70%	0.56%	5.18%
Net profit (bps)	49.22%	30.21%	67.31%
Support staff per practitioner	1.52	1.00	2.35
Average consult length (minutes)	15	10	19
Average no. of consults per doctor per week	156	105	200
Opening hours per day	9.51	8.00	11.00
Opening days per week	5.50	5.00	6.10

Now look at Figure 7-3, which shows Kate's first year's Profit & Loss report. Can you see how in the final column, Kate has calculated how much each expense is as a percentage of sales? For example, her rent at $34,200 per year is 12 per cent of sales (that's $34,200 divided by $285,000 multiplied by 100). Compare this rent against other medical practices, and you can see that Kate is paying way above the average rent of 5.5 per cent. Similarly, Kate is spending 30 per cent on wages, well above the average of 25.3 per cent.

You may be wondering how to apply the preceding example to your own business — after all, chances are that you're not a medical practitioner. Here's what to do:

1. **Complete your sales, cost of sales and expenses projection for the next 12 months.**

For more detail on how to do these projections, refer to the first part of this chapter, along with Chapters 5 and 6. Alternatively, if your business has already been trading for a while, you could generate a Profit & Loss report for the most recent 12 months of trading, and send this report to Excel.

2. **Right-click in the cell where Total Income appears, click Define Name, type** Total Income **and then click OK**

   In Figure 7-3, Total Income appears in cell D3. Naming cells makes Excel formulae easier to understand.

3. **Add a column for % of sales, and create a formula for % of sales against each row.**

   Can you see the column of percentages in Figure 7-3? You can create this column by inserting a formula against the first cost of sales row and then copying this formula to all the other rows. For example, the formula that I type in cell E6 (next to Medical Supplies) is '=**D6/Income'**. I then click the % button on my menu bar to show this figure as a percentage.

4. **Get hold of benchmarks for your industry.**

   I talk about how to find benchmarks earlier in this chapter (refer to 'Locating benchmarks for your business').

5. **Compare your business plan against the industry averages.**

   For example, if you're running a cafe and benchmarks show that the average cafe spends 30 per cent on wages, compare this percentage with your projections and see whether you're spending, relatively speaking, more or less.

You may find it tricky to find benchmarks that are relevant to you. Maybe you've invented a totally new product or maybe your business is an unusual combination of many different activities. In this scenario, try to locate a set of benchmarks for a business type that's at least similar to yours in some way or other.

If you've already been trading for a couple of years or more, you can also benchmark your financial projections against Profit & Loss reports from your own business for previous years. For example, if results from previous years show that your wages usually average 30 per cent of sales, but your Profit & Loss Projection shows that wages only equal 25 per cent of sales, you have probably made an error in your calculations.

	A	B	C	D	E	F
1						
2					% of sales	
3		Total Income		$ 285,000		
4						
5		Cost of Sales				
6			Medical Supplies	$ 5,700	2.0%	
7			Medications	$ 2,850	1.0%	
8			Pathology Services	$ -	0.0%	
9		Total Cost of Sales		$ 8,550	3.0%	
10						
11		Gross Profit		$ 276,450	97.0%	
12						
13		Expenses				
14			Accounting Fees	$ 1,995	0.7%	
15			Bank Fees	$ 2,565	0.9%	
16			Computer Consumables	$ 1,425	0.5%	
17			Depreciation Expense	$ 5,700	2.0%	
18			Electricity	$ 7,200	2.5%	
19			Insurance - Business	$ 8,550	3.0%	
20			Maintenance	$ 3,800	1.3%	
21			Office Supplies	$ 2,567	0.9%	
22			Professional Development	$ 12,922	4.5%	
23			Postage	$ 540	0.2%	
24			Rent	$ 34,200	12.0%	
25			Subscriptions	$ 2,332	0.8%	
26			Salaries			
27			Staff Amenities	$ 6,213	2.2%	
28			Superannuation	$ 7,695	2.7%	
29			Wages & Salaries	$ 85,500	30.0%	
30			Telephone	$ 6,722	2.4%	
31			Travel & Entertainment	$ 3,500		
32		Total Expenses		$ 193,426	67.9%	
33						
34		Operating Profit		$ 83,024	29.1%	
35						

Figure 7-3:
Looking at expense percentages is part of the bench-marking process.

Thinking about Taxes and Loan Repayments

Spend a while browsing any reading matter about business planning and you soon stumble across righteous statistics about how the 30 per cent or so businesses with formal business plans do a squillion times better than the 70 per cent that don't. Sounds wonderful, but these statistics fail to mention the suffering that the 70 per cent went through before they abandoned business plans in disgust, feeling the experience akin to some medieval torture.

In the following sections, I touch on some of the pain points that you're likely to encounter at this stage of your plan, hopefully supplying straightforward answers to some of the more complicated of questions.

Allowing for personal and company tax

One of the questions people often ask is whether to include personal or company tax in the worksheet. The answer depends on whether your business is structured as a sole trader, partnership or company.

If you're a sole trader or partnership, you're responsible for paying tax on any profit that the business makes. The amount of tax you pay depends on many factors, including whether you have any sources of income other than the business. Generally, I don't include personal income tax as an expense on any business plan.

If your business has a company structure, you do need to include company tax expense on your expenses worksheet. In Chapter 8, I explain how to pull all the different elements of your business plan together, starting with your income worksheet, deducting your cost of sales and business expenses, calculating net profit, and finally adding two rows called Company Tax Expense, and Net Profit After Company Tax.

Understanding where other taxes fit in

What about taxes such as sales tax, VAT or GST? The answer depends on where you live.

If your business is subject to any kind of value-added tax (known, for example, as VAT in Canada and the United Kingdom, or GST in Australia and New Zealand), you don't include this tax in any of your expenses. Instead, you show the value of each expense before tax is applied. (Why? Because this kind of tax applies only to the final sale to the consumer — as a business, you're entitled to claim back any tax of this nature that you pay.) On the other hand, if your business pays a sales tax (something that applies in almost every state within the United States), you should include sales tax in your expenses, showing the value of each expense inclusive of the tax that you pay. (Why? Because this tax forms part of the cost of this expense — you can't claim this tax back from the government.)

Dealing with loan repayments and interest

If your business has borrowed money and you're paying off a business loan, deciding how to show loan repayments in your expenses worksheet can be quite tricky.

Imagine that you have a bank loan and your repayments are $1,000 per week. You've almost paid off this loan, and you currently have only $15,000 left to repay. The interest on this loan equals only about $15 per week.

Any accountant will gladly explain that in terms of the profit of your business, the only expense that you can claim is the interest. However, when you're doing a business plan, this kind of analysis is too simplistic. The interest may be inconsequential, but budgeting $1,000 a week in repayments is not.

The best way to show loan repayments in your business plan depends on the circumstances:

✔ If you decide to include both a Profit & Loss Projection and a Cashflow Projection in your business plan (and if you're not sure yet, skip ahead to Chapter 10), you should show the value of the interest expense in your Profit & Loss Projection, and the value of the whole loan repayment in your Cashflow Projection.

✔ If your business plan only requires a Profit & Loss Projection, stay on the side of caution and show the full value of the loan repayment in your expenses worksheet. This way, the final net profit that you arrive at in your projections will be as close as possible to your likely surplus in cash.

Factoring Personal Expenses into the Equation

If you're starting a new business and you have very little savings or start-up capital, you may find you have very little to live on while building up your business. In this scenario, I can't stress enough how important it is to create a budget not only for business expenses, but also for personal expenses.

Dave, one of the students in a business start-up course I was running, had recently been retrenched from a high-stress high-income job in construction management. Disillusioned and disheartened, he had decided to leave the corporate world and instead start up a handyman business. His business concept seemed solid enough and, when working on his income projections, he was realistic that it could take some time to build up clients and a good income base. However, when we worked on his personal budget, my hair stood on end. Dave's commitments were huge. He had two car leases, three kids at private school and whopping mortgage repayments. With his savings, he only had about six weeks to go before everything would come crashing down around his ears. When Dave weighed everything up, he realised that he (and his wife) couldn't bear to downsize, shift his kids to public school and sell his cars. Besides, he didn't have time to make all these changes in the six weeks he had left until his savings ran out. Instead, he went back to the corporate world, with a plan to maybe return to his idea of a handyman business at a point when his commitments weren't quite so scary.

Even if your business is already up and running, creating a budget for personal expenses is usually still a good idea. You must ensure that your business is going to generate enough income to cover your personal expenses. If not, you may need to make changes to your business plan (such as adjusting expenses or increasing income) or, alternatively, make some changes to your personal spending patterns.

Identifying income

When building a personal budget, the first step is to make a list of all your non-business sources of income. (Of course, if you're already running your own business rather than in the start-up phase, you may have no income that doesn't come from your business.) To prompt you, here's a list of other possible sources of income:

- ✔ **Income from employment:** When doing a personal budget, remember to factor in income after tax, not before tax. In other words, if your pay is $800 a week but your employer deducts $200 a week, only include $600 as your income.

- ✔ **Rental property income:** If you have a rental property, you can either show income from your rental property in the income section of your personal budget and expenses from the property in the expense section, or you can simply show the net income (that's income less expenses) on the income side of your budget.

✔ **Interest from savings accounts:** Include any income you receive from invested cash. (While I'm on the topic, if you have any funds stashed away that aren't earning interest, now's the time to shift these funds to an online saving account that earns its keep.)

If you receive wages weekly and you're doing an expenses budget on a monthly basis, you need to multiply your wages by 52 then divide them by 12 to arrive at how much income you receive each month.

Figuring how much you need to live

Your budget for personal expenses works in much the same way as your budget for business expenses, except for the fact that the kinds of expenses you'll have in your private life are very different from those in your business life. Table 7-2 prompts you with a list of the many kinds of expenses you may have.

Cut that credit down

In my opinion, the best kind of credit card is one that you cut in half and chuck in the bin. With banks being seemingly indiscriminate in offering large credit limits, credit card debt is easy to build up. Before you know it, you can accumulate a large amount of debt with interest rates so high that you're unable to keep up with your payments. At this point, your debt will grow faster than your ability to pay it off.

The other danger of credit card debt is that if you fail to make a repayment on time, you can damage your credit rating very quickly. This in turn may make it tricky for you to take out business loans.

If you have a credit card, try to avoid using it for business purposes, and instead keep it for personal spending only. Ask the bank to reduce your limit to a low amount of $1,000 or so. If you have debt above this amount, see if you can convert this credit card to a lower interest personal loan. (And if you do so, ensure you close those credit card accounts so you can't ever use them again!)

Table 7-2		Listing Personal Expenses		
Expense	*$*	*Expense*	*$*	
Loans and repayments		**Getting around**		
Rent or mortgage		Car registration and insurance		
Car loan repayment		Car petrol		
Other loan repayments		Car maintenance		
Credit card interest		Road tolls		
Child support payments		Bus/train/ferry fares		
Home expenses		Other		
Council rates		**Shopping**		
Water rates		Supermarket groceries		
Repairs & maintenance		Fruit/veg/meat		
Strata-title fees		Clothing/shoes		
Home and contents insurance		Toiletries		
Home bills		Gifts		
Electricity		eBay		
Gas		Hairdressers/grooming		
Internet		**Fun/discretionary**		
Telephone		Coffee		
Mobile telephone		Lunch/takeaways		
Cable TV		Eating out/bars/clubs		
Other		Alcohol		
Education		Cigarettes		
School fees		Movies/gigs/theatre		
Textbooks		Holidays and travel		
University/college fees		Books and publications		
Other study		Charity/donations		

Expense	$	Expense	$
School uniforms			
Excursions			
Private music/dance/sport lessons			
Other			
Health			
Health insurance			
Doctor's fees			
Dentist fees			
Optometrist/physio			
All other practitioners			
Gym membership			
Medications			
Life insurance			
Other			

Many software applications are available to help you to track your personal expenses (including lots of new smartphone apps). However, I find that Excel is ideal for setting out all my expenses month by month so I can plan for the whole year ahead.

I've created a template in Excel that you can use as a starting point for your own budget too. To access the Personal Expenses worksheet, go to www.dummies.com/go/creatingbusinessplan.

Here's how to use the Personal Expenses worksheet:

1. **Go to** www.dummies.com/go/creatingbusinessplan **and download the Personal Expenses worksheet template. Save this onto your computer, and then open it up in Excel.**

   You can also open up this template in most other spreadsheet software, if you prefer.

   This template will look similar to Figure 7-4.

2. **For each expense, make a stab at how much you think this expense will be, and whether this expense occurs weekly, fortnightly, quarterly, monthly or annually.**

If you're at all unsure how much an expense is, document every single cent you spend for at least the next four weeks using a smartphone or notebook. Although Excel probably works best for mapping out expenses for the next 12 months on a single page, smartphone apps are great for helping you document your expenses as they occur. Recording every itsy-bitsy bit of spending can be tedious, but if you spend a few weeks doing this, you'll end up with a very incisive insight into your financial affairs. Alternatively, use a small notebook and carry this everywhere you go, writing down every time you spend money.

3. **Add any expenses that are missing or remove any expenses that aren't relevant to you.**

   To insert a row, right-click where you want the row to be, select Insert, and then Entire Row. To delete a row, right-click where you want to delete a row, select Delete, and then Entire Row.

4. **Change the names on the months along the top row.**

   My example has January as the first month, but obviously you're going to start with the month that corresponds to the period that you're doing the budget for.

5. **Review the monthly totals.**

   If the template is working as it should, the monthly estimates will appear automatically (and correctly) for all weekly, fortnightly or monthly expenses. However, with expenses that you pay out only quarterly or annually, you'll need to change the amounts so that they fall in the right months.

6. **Write down your non-business monthly income after tax (if you have any, that is).**

   I talk about what income to include earlier in this chapter (refer to the section 'Identifying income').

7. **Add up your total monthly expenses.**

   If you're using the Excel template, this total calculates automatically.

8. **Look at the difference between your monthly income and monthly expenses.**

   Unless you plan to change your spending habits, the shortfall between monthly income generated from non-business sources and monthly expenses is the *minimum* amount of after-tax profit that your business must generate in order for you to be able to survive. Write this figure down and ponder!

When you look at each month for the next 12 months, can you see any months where expenses are particularly high or income particularly low? (For people working casual jobs, Christmas is often one of these times.) If you can plan ahead for these times, maybe slotting some money away into a savings account, this can make life less stressful and help you feel that your personal budget is under control.

Figure 7-4: For new businesses, budgeting for personal expenses is as important as planning for business expenses.

		Total	Monthly total	Jan	Feb	Mar	Apr	May	Jun	Jul	Aug	Sep	Oct	Nov	Dec
Loans and repayments															
Rent or mortgage	Weekly	200	$867	$867	$867	$867	$867	$867	$867	$867	$867	$867	$867	$867	$867
Car loan repayment	Monthly	350	$350	$350	$350	$350	$350	$350	$350	$350	$350	$350	$350	$350	$350
Other loan repayments	Fortnightly	100	$217	$217	$217	$217	$217	$217	$217	$217	$217	$217	$217	$217	$217
Credit card interest	Monthly	80	$80	$80	$80	$80	$80	$80	$80	$80	$80	$80	$80	$80	$80
Child support payments	Monthly	220	$220	$220	$220	$220	$220	$220	$220	$220	$220	$220	$220	$220	$220
Home expenses															
Council rates	Quarterly	400	$133	$400			$400			$400			$400		
Water rates	Quarterly	300	$100		$300			$300			$300			$300	
Repairs & Maintenance	Annually	2000	$167	$167	$167	$167	$167	$167	$167	$167	$167	$167	$167	$167	$167
Strata-title fees	Monthly	150	$150	$150	$150	$150	$150	$150	$150	$150	$150	$150	$150	$150	$150
Home and contents insurance	Annually	1500	$125									$1,500			
Home bills															
Electricity	Quarterly	700	$233		$700			$700			$700			$700	
Gas	Quarterly	500	$167	$500			$500			$500			$500		
Internet	Monthly	80	$80	$80	$80	$80	$80	$80	$80	$80	$80	$80	$80	$80	$80
Telephone	Monthly	120	$120	$120	$120	$120	$120	$120	$120	$120	$120	$120	$120	$120	$120
Mobile telephone	Monthly	80	$80	$80	$80	$80	$80	$80	$80	$80	$80	$80	$80	$80	$80
Cable TV	Monthly	120	$120	$120	$120	$120	$120	$120	$120	$120	$120	$120	$120	$120	$120
Other	Monthly	30	$30	$30	$30	$30	$30	$30	$30	$30	$30	$30	$30	$30	$30
Education															
School fees	Monthly	1200	$1,200	$1,200	$1,200	$1,200	$1,200	$1,200	$1,200	$1,200	$1,200	$1,200	$1,200	$1,200	$1,200
Textbooks	Annually	500	$42	$42	$42	$42	$42	$42	$42	$42	$42	$42	$42	$42	$42
University/college fees	Quarterly	0	$0	$0	$0	$0	$0	$0	$0	$0	$0	$0	$0	$0	$0
Other study	Monthly		$0												
School uniforms	Annually	350	$29	$350											
Excursions	Annually	700	$58	$58	$58	$58	$58	$58	$58	$58	$58	$58	$58	$58	$58
Private music/dance/sport lessor	Weekly	80	$347	$347	$347	$347	$347	$347	$347	$347	$347	$347	$347	$347	$347
Other	Monthly		$0												
Health															
Health insurance	Monthly	250	$250	$250	$250	$250	$250	$250	$250	$250	$250	$250	$250	$250	$250
Doctors fees	Annually	1200	$100	$100	$100	$100	$100	$100	$100	$100	$100	$100	$100	$100	$100
Dentist fees	Annually	500	$42	$42	$42	$42	$42	$42	$42	$42	$42	$42	$42	$42	$42
Optometrist/physio	Annually	400	$33	$33	$33	$33	$33	$33	$33	$33	$33	$33	$33	$33	$33
All other practitioners	Annually	800	$67	$67	$67	$67	$67	$67	$67	$67	$67	$67	$67	$67	$67
Gym membership	Weekly	35	$152	$152	$152	$152	$152	$152	$152	$152	$152	$152	$152	$152	$152
Medications	Monthly	80	$80	$80	$80	$80	$80	$80	$80	$80	$80	$80	$80	$80	$80
Life insurance	Monthly	110	$110	$110	$110	$110	$110	$110	$110	$110	$110	$110	$110	$110	$110
Vet bills	Annually	400	$33	$33	$33	$33	$33	$33	$33	$33	$33	$33	$33	$33	$33
Other	Monthly	0	$0	$0	$0	$0	$0	$0	$0	$0	$0	$0	$0	$0	$0

Sheet1 / Sheet2 / Sheet3

What if I can't bear to do a personal budget?

Scrutinising one's personal spending has to be one of the more depressing ways to spend a rainy afternoon. Alternatively, a rough-and-ready way to figure out how much you need to live is to write down how much you've earned the last 12 months, look up how much you've saved or how much savings you've used, and calculate the difference. Unless your personal circumstances have changed, this difference is going to be approximately the same as how much you need to live.

However, if you're starting or growing a business and you're willing to live a little leaner while things get off the ground, this method isn't good enough. The only way to really get a handle on your finances is to make a budget and try to live by it. This is the only way to see if you're spending more or less than you can afford.

Setting goals and budgets

In the preceding section, I suggest you write down everything you currently spend each week or each month, and analyse how much your expenses are going to be each month. However, this is a very different process from creating a budget for each type of expense.

For example, maybe you've been monitoring your spending for the last eight weeks and you can see you spend an average of $100 per week eating out. The question you need to ask yourself is this: Given your overall financial goals, is this amount reasonable?

One way to identify where you can save money is to categorise each expense as to whether it's essential or optional, and whether it's a fixed amount or variable. Table 7-3 provides examples for each of these categories. Generally, you won't have much influence — certainly in the short term — over essential expenses that are a fixed amount each month. However, you will almost certainly have room to save money on all other kinds of expenses.

What you're trying to develop here are good habits regarding personal spending. These habits are more important at some stages of life than others (a family with young children and a mortgage probably need to be much more careful about money than a young person with no commitments in a big share house). However, the skills you develop in regards to your personal spending tend to spill over into skills you can use in your business, and vice versa.

As part of this planning process, I recommend you set a clear goal for what you want to achieve financially. Do you want to save $10,000 within the next

12 months? Get rid of all your debt within three years? Or be a millionaire by the time you're 40?

Goals can be short term or long term. Short-term goals are things you can achieve in the next couple of weeks or months. Long-term goals are what you want to achieve in the next one to five years. And, of course, even longer term goals are what you want to achieve in the next 10 to 20 years.

Table 7-3	Categorising Different Kinds of Personal Expenses
Type of Expense	*Examples*
Essential expense, no flexibility to decrease	Rent, mortgage payments, loan payments, insurance premiums
Essential expense, flexibility to decrease	Food, electricity, telephone
Optional expense, no flexibility to decrease	Gym membership, cable TV, music lessons, subscriptions
Optional expense, flexibility to decrease	Eating out, takeaways, alcohol, cigarettes, clothing, holidays

Recognising why personal and business budgets connect

You may be wondering why I devote so much space in this chapter to talking about personal budgets when this is meant to be a book about business. I do so because I've seen many new businesses flounder because of a failure by the owners to understand their personal spending. Here are the kinds of traps you want to avoid:

✔ I knew a couple who started a business at the beginning of the holiday season and had a few bumper months of trading. They drew all the available cash out of the business in order to survive, but then when the business needed cash to get it through lean times, there was none.

✔ Former clients of mine started up a business that did very well right from the start. However, they hadn't created a realistic budget for personal spending, and despite the business thriving, it didn't generate enough profit in that first year to cover mortgage repayments and school fees. Although they did muddle through in the end, that first year of trading was very stressful and left a legacy of huge credit card debt.

✔ A friend of mine started up a business that soon built to generate a steady but modest income. Being a happy-go-lucky personality, she spent money from her business pretty much as soon as it came in. However, 18 months after she opened doors for trading, she lodged her first tax return. She hadn't set any money aside for tax, and had to take out a personal loan to cover the debt.

Seeing where you can scrimp and save

As I mention in the introduction to this section, if your personal expenses look as if they're likely to exceed the profit your business generates, and you don't have any other source of income or savings, one of your options is to see if you can cut back on your personal expenses.

You may be surprised to find how cheaply you can live if you really have to. Your flexibility depends on your stage of life — announcing that you're about to start a business as a street performer two weeks before your wife is due to give birth to twins is never going to go down well — but, mostly, you'll be surprised how you can simplify even the most complicated of lives. Here are some ideas, in order of desperation:

✔ Cut out all takeaways

✔ Quit going out with your friends

✔ Replace alcohol with tap water

✔ Announce to your family and friends that birthdays/Christmas gifts are temporarily suspended

✔ Cancel all holidays

✔ Avoid all shopping malls and retail precincts

✔ Sell your car and buy a cheaper one

✔ Pull your kids out of private school

✔ Move out of your rental property into a cheaper one

✔ Move back in with your parents (desperate times call for desperate measures)

✔ Move back in with your ex (just kiddin')

Sometimes a business can survive, but leave a broken relationship in its wake. One reason business plans are so important is that they can help you to understand the risks involved not just on a financial level, but on a personal level also.

And on that cheery note, this chapter comes to a close.

Part III
Checking Your Idea Makes Financial Sense

Five Reasons Profit on Paper is Different from Cash in the Bank

- **Customers owe you more money now than they did before:** If customers owe you $25,000 more now than they did six months ago, your cash situation is going to be $25,000 worse than your Profit & Loss report for the same period.

- **You've been having too much fun:** If your business has a sole trader or partnership structure, any money you take out of the business for personal use doesn't show up as an expense. This means that if you've been living the high life, your Profit & Loss can show heaps of profit, but your cash position can paint a very different picture.

- **You've accumulated stock holdings:** If you have $10,000 more in stock than you did six months ago, your cash situation will be $10,000 worse than whatever appears on your Profit & Loss report.

- **You've repaid a loan:** Loan repayments don't appear on your Profit & Loss report but they sure chew up cash.

- **You've purchased new equipment:** If you purchase expensive new equipment, this equipment doesn't appear on your Profit & Loss report but, again, does reduce your cash.

Read more about how to manage expenses if cash gets tight. Visit www.dummies.com/extras/creatingbusinessplan.

In this part ...

✔ Take control of your future and discover how to create a Profit & Loss Projection for the next 12 months.

✔ Think carefully about how much profit you're likely to make. Is this venture looking too risky? If so, find out what you can do to improve the bottom line.

✔ Calculate your break-even point — in other words, the level of sales you need to generate every week or every month in order to cover your expenses.

✔ Decide whether you need your break-even point to cover business expenses only, or whether you want to factor personal expenses into the equation as well.

✔ Understand why your business can be awash with profit yet you have no cash in the bank, and learn vital skills to create your own Cashflow Projection reports so that you can predict cash shortages ahead of time.

Chapter 8

Assembling Your Profit & Loss Projection

In This Chapter

▶ Getting acquainted with some spreadsheet theory

▶ Arriving at the moment of truth: Your 12-month Profit & Loss Projection

▶ Looking at your net profit and rate of return

▶ Creating different scenarios and assessing your level of risk

*I*n this chapter, I pull together all the information that goes into a Profit & Loss Projection, including pricing and sales projections, costs and gross profit projections and expense projections. This helps you arrive at an estimate of just how much profit your business is likely to generate over the next 12 months.

Looking at your likely profits can be an emotional turning point, especially if this is the first Profit & Loss Projection you've ever made. Few of us go into business without wanting to make a profit and, if the Profit & Loss Projection shows limited profits for what's likely to be a heap of work, you'll probably feel rather discouraged.

Feeling discouraged is okay. If your business model is a dud, you're better to quit now while you're still ahead than spend another year or two on an idea that will never fly. On the other hand, if you suspect that your essential idea is still strong, this part of the planning process gives you another chance to look at all your figures and experiment with pricing, costs and expenses.

Of course, you may find that your financial projections predict a business with a rosy future. That's great. Nothing is better than a promising business plan. However, in the last part of this chapter, I spend a bit of time exploring scenario analysis. What if sales were 10 per cent less, or expenses 10 per cent more? Take some time to follow this process so you can assess how robust your plan is, the likely risk involved, and whether those rose-colour glasses are likely to fade.

Understanding More About Spreadsheets

Last year, we had a young visitor from overseas stay with us. One evening, she talked about the sports education at her very traditional school. It turned out that after six years of high school education she knew the dimensions of a soccer, basketball or cricket field by heart, as well as the number of players and the many rules involved in each sport. Yet she had never once kicked a ball, scored a goal or wielded a cricket bat.

This kind of education seems daft to me, in the same way that explaining the theory of financial projections without talking about spreadsheets also seems daft. A spreadsheet is the only viable tool for creating financial projections, and to pretend otherwise is simply to make the job harder than it needs to be.

If you're already comfortable with using spreadsheets, and getting spreadsheets to share data, feel free to skim read (or skip) the first few pages of this chapter. Otherwise, stick around for a quick theory lesson. The concepts may be a little tricky at first, but I promise you that 30 minutes spent now understanding spreadsheets will save you countless hours in the months ahead.

Naming worksheets within a single workbook

When you're in business, you often end up with different bits of information in different places or files. For example, maybe you have your product costings in one spreadsheet file, your expense budget in another, and your sales projections in another.

With Excel, you can link data between different worksheets, so that updating one bit of information automatically updates the same bit of information in another worksheet. For example, imagine you have detailed product costings in one worksheet, and the bottom line of each worksheet calculates the final product cost. Then imagine you have a separate worksheet that calculates gross profit, and simply refers to the final product cost when calculating profit. By linking these two worksheets, you can automatically update gross profit projections every time you update your product costings. Working in this way saves time and reduces the chance for error.

The easiest way to get your head around this concept is to give it a go, starting with naming worksheets in a single workbook:

1. **Open up Excel (or any other spreadsheet software for that matter).**

   Any new spreadsheet file consists of single worksheets within a workbook. A *workbook* is the file that you create using spreadsheet software and, by default, every new workbook in Excel contains three *worksheets*, each one of which is a single page.

2. **Look at the tabs running along the bottom which say Sheet1, Sheet2 and Sheet3.**

   You're currently in Sheet1, so this tab appears in white, not grey.

3. **Rest your mouse on the tab that says Sheet1 and right-click.**

   Or, if you're using a Macintosh, hold down the control button and then click with your mouse.

4. **Click Rename and then type** SalesDetail **as the name.**

   You have now renamed this tab, similar to the tab shown in Figure 8-1.

5. **Now rest your mouse on the tab that says Sheet2 and right-click to rename this tab to become** SalesSummary.

   Or, if you're using a Macintosh, hold down the control button and then click with your mouse.

   All done? Great. You have now created and named two separate worksheets within a single workbook. The first worksheet is called SalesDetail and the second worksheet is called SalesSummary.

6. **Go to the File menu and save this workbook.**

   For this example, give the workbook an easy-to-remember file name such as 'testing'.

Figure 8-1:
Renaming the first two worksheets in Excel.

Linking one worksheet to another

Once you've created two worksheets within a single workbook (refer to the preceding section if you're wondering what I'm talking about), you're ready to link one worksheet to another. Here goes:

1. **Open up your file with the SalesDetail and SalesSummary worksheets.**

   Refer to the preceding section for how to create this file. You may still have this file open, of course, in which case you don't need to do anything.

2. **Type the information you can see in Figure 8-2. When you get to the total, click the AutoSum symbol so that the total calculates automatically.**

   If you can't see the AutoSum symbol, type this formula instead: =SUM(B1:B3).

Figure 8-2:
Entering data into the SalesDetail worksheet.

	A	B	C	D	E	F	
1	Sales Product A	$ 3,000					
2	Sales Product B	$ 1,000					
3	Sales Product C	$ 20,000					
4	Total Sales	$ 24,000					
5							
6							
7							
8							

Book4

SalesDetail / SalesSummary / Sheet3

3. **Highlight the data in row 4 (cells A4 and B4) and click Copy.**

   You can find the Copy and Paste commands by right-clicking with your mouse on a PC, pressing the command button and clicking the mouse on a Mac, or by clicking the Copy and Paste buttons on the top menu bar.

4. **Click the SalesSummary tab to move to that worksheet.**

   The worksheet will be completely blank at this stage.

5. **Click Paste Special.**

   You can find the Paste Special commands by right-clicking with your mouse on a PC, pressing the command button and clicking the mouse on a Mac, or by selecting Paste Special from the Paste button on the top menu bar.

   You'll see a dialogue box similar to Figure 8-3.

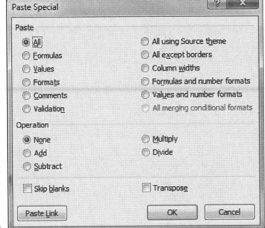

Figure 8-3:
The Paste
Link
command
appears
in the
bottom-left
of the Paste
Special
window.

6. **Click the Paste Link button that appears in the bottom-left of the Paste Special window.**

   Check Figure 8-3 if you can't spot the Paste Link button. In a heartbeat, your total sales now appear in row 1.

7. **Check out the formula that shows in the formula bar for cell B1 (=SalesDetail!B4).**

   This formula tells Excel to go to the worksheet called SalesDetail, find whatever value is in cell B4 and then dump it in this cell in the SalesSummary worksheet. (If you can't see the formula bar, go to the View menu and ensure that the Formula Bar option is clicked.)

Feeling underwhelmed? Don't be. Flick back to the SalesDetail tab, and change one of the sales figures. Then return to the SalesSummary tab and you'll see that the total has updated automatically. Seems simple, but this concept will help to connect your Gross Profit and Expenses Projections into a single dynamic document.

Using names to identify important cells

I want to share one more spreadsheet concept before leaping into the practicalities of your business plan, and that is how to name important cells.

The idea of naming cells is that when you open up a workbook a few weeks or months later and you're trying to remember what on earth you were trying to do, the formulae that use names make much more sense than formulae that use cell references. Cell names also provide an efficient way to copy formula from one worksheet to another.

Here's an example of how cell naming works:

1. **Open up the file where you've linked two worksheets.**

   Refer to the preceding section for more on this file. You may still have this file open, of course, in which case you don't need to do anything.

2. **Go to the SalesDetail tab. Right-click on cell B4 and click Define Name.**

   The New Name window appears, similar to that shown in Figure 8-4.

Figure 8-4: Naming cells makes your worksheets easier to understand.

3. **As the Name, type** Total_Sales, **then click OK.**

   Note that you can't have a space in the name (so I can't call this cell 'Total Sales').

4. **Click in cell A6 and type** Cost of Sales.

5. **Click in cell B6 and type** =Total_Sales*50%. **Then press the Enter key.**

   In the blink of an eye, B6 should show as $12,000.

You may be wondering what the big deal is. After all, I could have typed **=B4*50%** rather than **=Total_Sales*50%**. However, cell names work well for two reasons: The first reason is that cell names are easier to understand if someone else tries to use this worksheet (for example, the term 'Total Sales' is way more meaningful than 'B4'). The second reason is that if you want to refer to this cell more than once (maybe many costs will end up being a percentage of total sales), copying formula from one cell to another is much more efficient if you use cell names.

For more details about naming cells, and how cell names can help you create worksheets with a minimum of fuss, see the Naming Cells video at www.dummies.com/go/creatingbusinessplan.

Building Your Profit & Loss Projection

So you're ready to create your first Profit & Loss Projection for the next 12 months? Then make yourself a hot cup of something and get ready to see how all the bits of your plan fit together.

Step one: Insert your projected sales forecasts

The top of any Profit & Loss Projection always starts by showing income, then cost of sales, then gross profit. I talk about calculating gross profit in detail in Chapter 6, so if you haven't already worked through your gross profit projections, scoot over to Chapter 6 first. With these workings in place, you're ready to go:

1. **Using Excel (or any other spreadsheet software), open up your Gross Profit Projection worksheet.**

   Refer to Chapter 6 for more about this worksheet. The idea is that you've already created a worksheet estimating both your sales and your cost of sales for the next 12 months.

2. **Rest your mouse on the tab at the bottom of this worksheet that says Sheet1 and right-click.**

   Or, if you're using a Macintosh, hold down the control button and then click with your mouse.

3. **Click Rename and then type** GrossProfit **as the name.**

4. **Rest your mouse on the tab that says Sheet2 and right-click.**

5. **Rename this tab to become** ProfitLoss.

   You have now created and named two separate worksheets within a workbook. The first worksheet is called GrossProfit and the second worksheet is called ProfitLoss.

6. **On the second worksheet, label the months along the top (in row 1).**

7. **Go to your GrossProfit tab, and highlight the row where you recorded the grand total for sales each month. Right-click with your mouse (or control then click if you're on a Mac) and select Copy.**

8. **Return to the ProfitLoss tab and click on cell B2.**

   Cell B2 is where the first month of total sales is going to show.

9. **Right-click (or control then click for Mac users) and select Paste Special.**

10. Click the Paste Link button that appears in the bottom-left of this dialogue box.

Before your eyes, the sales for each month should appear right across row 2, similar to Figure 8-5. (I just show the first few months here, but you get the general idea.)

Are you wondering why I've gone to all the trouble of creating multiple worksheets and linking one sheet to another, rather than just copying and pasting the estimated total sales? The reason I suggest you work in this way is so your total sales will update automatically whenever you tweak your detailed sales. For example, maybe I want to see what would happen if I lift my pricing by 10 per cent. All I have to do is tweak the pricing in my Sales Projection worksheet and this flows automatically through to my Profit & Loss Projection.

	A	B	C	D	E	F	G	
1		July	Aug	Sep	Oct	Nov	Dec	
2	Total Sales	31,070	35,440	41,150	36,450	47,260	174,890	1
3								
4								

GrossProfit / ProfitLoss / Sheet3

Figure 8-5: Total sales form the first line of your Profit & Loss Projection.

Of course, if you're a very small business and you don't want to go to the trouble of splitting up your income in any kind of detail — you just want to type in an estimated dollar total for each month — then you don't need to bother creating a separate worksheet for sales projections.

Step two: Bring across variable costs

The next stage is to bring across your variable costs. Again, you need to have your gross profit projections complete before you do this step. If you haven't, you may need to have a quick look through the last few pages of Chapter 6 before you continue.

1. **Go to the GrossProfit tab, and highlight the rows where you recorded the total for cost of sales and gross profit for each month. Right-click with your mouse (or control then click if you're on a Mac) and select Copy.**

2. **Return to the ProfitLoss tab and click on cell A4.**

3. **Right-click (or control then click for Mac users) and select Paste Special.**

4. Click the Paste Link button that appears in the bottom-left of this dialogue box.

Your total cost of sales for each month, as well as Gross Profit, should now appear below your sales. (If a bunch of zeros appear in row 5, which may happen because row 5 is blank in the Gross Profit worksheet, simply delete these zeros.)

5. Format the cells if necessary.

Sometimes the formatting doesn't come across when you link one worksheet to another. So feel free to add bold to your headings and format the amounts to include dollar signs.

6. Check your results.

By the time you're done, your worksheet should look similar to Figure 8-6, showing total sales, cost of sales and gross profit for the next 12 months. This worksheet has exactly the same figures as your gross profit projection, but with the difference that it displays much less detail. This less detailed format is what many investors or bank managers would expect to see as an overall financial projection.

	A	B	C	D	E	F	G
1		July	Aug	Sep	Oct	Nov	Dec
2	Total Sales	31,070	35,440	41,150	36,450	47,260	174,890
3							
4	Total Cost of Sales	19,095	22,035	25,930	22,780	30,125	116,560
5							
6	Gross Profit	11,975	13,405	15,220	13,670	17,135	58,330
7							

GrossProfit / ProfitLoss / Sheet3

Figure 8-6: Cost of sales and gross profit show below total sales on your Profit & Loss Projection.

Step three: Add your expenses budget

Step three in building your Profit & Loss Projection is to add detail regarding your expenses. Chapter 7 explains how to create a worksheet that accurately forecasts business expenses on a monthly basis, and I'm going to assume here that you've already completed this worksheet.

Here's how to add expenses to your Profit & Loss Projection:

1. With your Profit & Loss Projection workbook open, right-click the tab called Sheet3, select Rename and call this tab Expenses.

With the instructions in the next page or two, I often tell you to right-click with your mouse. But if you're one of those sensible people who use a Mac, you need to press the command button and then click instead.

2. **Open up your expenses worksheet.**

   Refer to Chapter 7 for details on how to create this spreadsheet.

3. **Highlight every single cell that has anything in it.**

   In other words, click in the top-left cell and drag your mouse down to the bottom-right cell.

4. **Right-click and select Copy.**

5. **Go to your Profit & Loss Projection workbook and click the Expenses tab.**

6. **Go to the top-left cell in this worksheet, then right-click and select Paste.**

   Cool. You've just copied everything from your expenses worksheet into your Profit & Loss worksheet. All good so far.

7. **Now highlight the names of the expenses in Column A, right-click and select Copy.**

   I'm just talking the labels of your expenses here, such as Accounting Fees and Advertising Expenses.

8. **Go to the ProfitLoss tab, click cell A8 and select Paste Special, followed by Paste Link.**

   What you're doing here is linking the list of expenses in your Expenses Worksheet to the list of expenses in your Profit & Loss Projection.

9. **Back on the Expenses tab, highlight the total value for each month, right-click and select Copy.**

10. **Go to the ProfitLoss tab of your worksheet, click cell B8 and select Paste Special, followed by Paste Link.**

    There you have it. You now have a Profit & Loss worksheet that starts with sales, then shows cost of sales and gross profit, and finally lists all your expenses. Figure 8-7 shows how these expenses come across (although for the sake of fitting everything onto the page, I've hidden some of the expense rows).

Are you wondering why I suggest you copy across all the expense totals from your worksheet, rather than just a single total for expenses in the same way as you did for sales and cost of sales? The reason is partly historical. Accountants, bank managers and investors are accustomed to a standard format for Profit & Loss projections, and this format typically provides a summary of sales and cost of sales, and more detail for expenses.

	July	Aug	Sep	Oct	Nov	Dec	Jan	Feb	Mar	Apr	May	Jun	Total
Total Sales	31,070	35,440	41,150	36,450	47,260	174,890	13,400	31,350	50,850	56,770	69,070	79,670	667,370
Total Cost of Sales	19,095	22,035	25,930	22,780	30,125	116,560	7,200	19,330	32,580	36,620	44,970	52,170	429,395
Gross Profit	11,975	13,405	15,220	13,670	17,135	58,330	6,200	12,020	18,270	20,150	24,100	27,500	237,975
Accounting Fees	-	-	-	-	-	-	-	-	-	1,500	-	-	
Advertising	1,200	1,200	1,200	1,200	1,200	1,200	1,200	1,200	1,200	1,200	1,200	1,200	14,400
Bank Charges	100	100	100	100	100	100	100	100	100	100	100	100	1,200
Cleaning Expenses	217	217	217	217	217	217	217	217	217	217	217	217	2,600
Computer Consumables	150	150	150	150	150	150	150	150	150	150	150	150	1,800
Consultant Expenses	300	300	300	300	300	300	300	300	300	300	300	300	3,600
Couriers	80	80	80	80	80	80	80	80	80	80	80	80	960
Telephone (inc mobile)	550	550	550	550	550	550	550	550	550	550	550	550	6,600
Travel Domestic	350	350	350	350	350	350	350	350	350	350	350	350	4,200
Travel Overseas	-	-	-	-	-	-	-	-	3,500	-	-	-	3,500
Wages and Salaries	3,683	3,683	3,683	3,683	3,683	3,683	3,683	3,683	3,683	3,683	3,683	3,683	44,200
Wages oncosts	368	368	368	368	368	368	368	368	368	368	368	368	4,420
Website expenses	850	850	850	850	850	850	850	850	850	850	850	850	10,200
Total Expenses	17,340	17,490	15,890	16,440	15,690	15,390	16,440	15,990	20,390	21,140	15,690	15,390	203,280
Net Profit	5,365 -	4,085 -	670 -	2,770 -	1,445	42,940	10,240 -	3,970 -	2,120 -	990 -	8,410	12,110	34,695

Figure 8-7: Your completed Profit & Loss Projection.

Step four: Look at the bottom line

The next step of building your 12-month Profit & Loss Projection is the easiest of all, and that's calculating net profit.

Net profit is simply your gross profit less your expenses. So all you have to do is add a line that says Net Profit at the bottom of your worksheet, and insert a formula that subtracts Total Expenses from Gross Profit. In Figure 8-7, the formula for July's net profit would be =**B6-B49**. Your formula will be different because you're bound to have a different number of rows for your expenses, but I'm sure you get the general idea.

Notice that in Figure 8-7, I also added a final column showing the total for each row, so that I can see the total sales, gross profit, expenses and net profit for the whole 12 months combined.

Step five: Think about tax

If you're a sole trader or partnership, the amount of personal tax you pay depends on many factors, including whether you have any other sources of income other than the business. For this reason, I suggest that you don't include personal income tax as an expense on your Profit & Loss Projection, but that you make an allowance for tax when calculating how much you require in personal drawings. (See 'Assessing whether your net profit is reasonable, or not' later in this chapter for more info.)

However, if your business has a company structure, you need to include company tax as an expense on your Profit & Loss Projection based on the profits you make. To do this, simply add a final line to your Profit & Loss report called Company Tax Expense. Calculate this expense at the correct percentage of company tax and then add a final line to your worksheet called Net Profit After Tax. Figure 8-8 shows an example, with the company tax rate calculated at 30 per cent.

54 **Net Profit**	$ 8,467	$ 11,374	$ 16,652	$ 12,909	$ 20,989	$ 109,372
55						
56 Company Tax Expense	$ 2,540	$ 3,412	$ 4,995	$ 3,873	$ 6,297	$ 32,811
57						
58 **Net Profit After Tax**	$ 5,927	$ 7,962	$ 11,656	$ 9,036	$ 14,692	$ 76,560

Figure 8-8: Adding an extra line to show company tax.

What about that dream of yours?

At some point in your business-planning process, it's good to think about your goals. (In fact, in Chapter 7, I suggest you try to establish some financial goals for yourself, both short and long term.)

In this respect, I'm not really talking about the kind of goal you dream up down at the pub one night (to be a millionaire within 12 months, or to buy your own private jet plane within

three years), but instead more practical goals in terms of your annual income and general savings.

Now is a good time to look at the projected net profit of your business and think about whether the plan seems on track to achieve the goals you want for yourself. (If not, either the plan or your goals will need to change.)

Checking you've got it right

You're not quite done yet. The last step is to check that you got everything right. (Spreadsheets are great in the way they calculate everything for you, but get one formula wrong, and the error can spread like a naked celebrity shot on Twitter.)

So here's your checklist:

- ✔ Save your workings and then re-open your Gross Profit Projection worksheet. Temporarily change your prices to $10 for every product, change your unit costs to $1, and change the unit sales to 100 units per month. Check that your gross profit comes out at $900 every month. Then quit without saving.

- ✔ Grab a calculator and manually check the sums for the first and the last month in your forecast. Check total sales, gross profit, total expenses and net profit.

- ✔ If your business is already up and running, print out your Profit & Loss report for the most recent month. Plug in the figures from this report into the first month of your Profit & Loss Projection and check that the net profit in your projection matches with the report.

All good? Then you're ready to move onto the next part of your business plan, which is where you get to ponder whether the forecasted profit is what you need it to be . . .

Analysing Net Profit

As I mention in the preceding section, one of the primary purposes of your Profit & Loss Projection is to figure out how much profit you'll be left with at the end of the day. This result enables you to decide whether you want to continue with this business, whether you need to change your business model in some way, and whether you're making a reasonable rate of return on your investment.

Calculating net profit margins

So, to do a quick recap:

- ✔ Gross profit equals sales less variable costs.
- ✔ Net profit equals gross profit less fixed expenses.
- ✔ Gross profit is always more than net profit.
- ✔ The more you sell, the more gross profit you make.
- ✔ The more you sell, the more net profit you make.

To calculate your net profit margin, you first calculate your net profit, and then you divide this amount by the value of total sales and multiply the result by 100. For example, if my sales are $200,000 a year and my net profit is $6,000, my net profit margin is 3 per cent (that's $6,000 divided by $200,000 multiplied by 100).

Assessing whether your net profit is reasonable, or not

There is no such thing as a specific percentage rate at which you can say that a net profit margin is reasonable, because too many variables affect this judgement. However, you should be able to establish for yourself a rate that you think is reasonable, and run with that.

The biggest factor to take into account is whether the net profit on your Profit & Loss Projection includes payment for your time. If your business has a sole trader or partnership structure, the final net profit on your Profit & Loss Projection represents the profit that your business generates before you see a single cent in payment for your time. Therefore, the net profit (and hence the net profit margins) need to be much higher than for an equivalent business with a company structure. (In contrast, if your business has a company structure, you need to include your monthly wages as part of your expenses, and so payment for your time is already accounted for.)

Another approach is to think about how much you need to live comfortably. If the net profit of your business is more than what you require to live (or, if you're a company, the net profit plus your wages), this figure is probably reasonable. However, if the net profit doesn't cover your personal expenses, your business has a problem. (For more about budgeting for personal expenses, refer to Chapter 7.)

When looking at your projected net profit, I recommend that you look at the margin for error. If your Profit & Loss Projection shows a high level of sales and a similarly high level of expenses, with only a narrow net profit margin left at the end of the day, you must ask yourself whether you have enough room for error. (I talk about this topic later in this chapter, in 'Measuring Risk and Your Comfort Factor'.) If a reduction of only 10 per cent in sales could mean you can't make your mortgage repayments, this net profit is probably not quite enough.

Thinking ahead further than 12 months

In this chapter (and most other chapters in this book) I suggest you work on financial projections for the next 12-month period only. I make this suggestion for two reasons: First, if you're just getting started in business, trying to make financial projections for two, three or even five years into the future can quickly feel like a make-believe exercise, because so much about what lies ahead is unknown. Second, what I'm trying to do in this book is to get you to create financial projections yourself, and I don't want to discourage you by making things any trickier than they need to be.

However, if you only do financial projections for 12 months into the future, you may not get a true picture of what lies ahead, particularly if you have strong growth patterns or your business is just getting started. Sometimes, you need to extend your forecasts for 24 or even 36 months ahead in order to predict at what point your business will really start to flourish and generate decent profits.

Extending your Profit & Loss Projection is easy — simply copy and paste the results from the 12th month across to additional columns, and then change the figures as need be. All the same principles apply — you're simply extending the forecast for another year or two.

Looking at your rate of return

One final factor that I think is worth considering when you look at your net profit is your *return on investment ratio*. This ratio calculates the return that you make on any money that you're investing (or have already invested) in the business, and answers the all-important question of whether this rate of return is reasonable.

What if the figures aren't good enough?

I've been called many things in my time, but one of the nicknames that I'm fond of, in a perverse kind of way, is 'the smiling assassin'. I earned this title for my ability to deliver bad news in a warm and fuzzy way that leaves people wondering what the hell just happened.

As someone who spends a lot of time looking at the financial performance of businesses, and interpreting results for business owners, this smiling assassin role is very familiar. Too often businesspeople slog away at their business, earning just enough to survive, too busy to face the reality that their trading model is flawed, the future is gloomy, or that they're sinking ever quicker into debt. They ask me for advice, because they know that something has to change, but in their heart of hearts they often don't want to hear what it is I have to say.

I can't sit with you, dear reader, and look at your financials with a beady eye. However, I can encourage you to take a long, hard look at your financial projections and ask yourself whether the projected final profit is likely to be enough to justify the work you're going to put in.

When I work on the business mentoring course, probably one quarter of the class decide not to proceed with their business idea at the end of the course, and another quarter

of the class end up making major changes to their plan. To me, even for the people who ditch their business idea completely and return to their day job, the business plan has been successful. Why? Because that person hasn't wasted a whole load of time and money on a dud idea.

Of course, maybe all your business idea needs is some tweaking at the edges. What if you could increase sales or prices by just 10 per cent, decrease costs by a similar amount, and cut expenses to the bone? Would your idea work then? Or do you need additional products, a different distribution model, a revised manufacturing process or a new location?

In Chapter 1, I show an image of the financial planning cycle, commencing with your start-up budget, moving on to prices, then calculating costs and expenses, and finally calculating net profit, break-even and cashflow. At the end of this cycle, I return to reviewing your business model and competitive strategy.

Keep this cycle in mind when working on the financials of your plan. Don't think of your financial projections as being the culmination of the planning process, but rather look at these projections as an opportunity to return to your business model and make improvements.

For example, imagine that to get your business going you're going to put in $200,000 of your personal savings and you plan to work full-time on the business. You calculate that a reasonable wage in return for your time is $75,000 per year. In this scenario, you would ideally want your business to generate profits of at least this amount plus a return of, say, 5 per cent on the funds you've invested.

The formula for calculating your return on investment (ROI) is this:

ROI = Net profit (after wages) divided by investment in the business

To continue with the example, imagine that in the last three years, after paying yourself a decent wage for the hours you spend working in the business, you've averaged a net profit of $5,000 per year. Your return on investment is $5,000 divided by $200,000 multiplied by 100, which equals 2.5 per cent.

In theory, if the interest rates for term deposits are more than 2.5 per cent — and they almost always are — you could spare yourself the hassle and risk of running a business and instead make more by investing your assets elsewhere.

Although number crunchers love this kind of pillow talk, I don't always agree. Looking at percentage rates of return doesn't take into account some of the more intangible benefits of being in business for yourself, such as the work/lifestyle balance, being your own boss, doing something you're passionate about, or being able to live in a regional area where jobs are scarce.

Measuring Risk and Your Comfort Factor

If you're doing a plan for a new business or a business that's currently undergoing significant change, one of the major challenges is how unknown everything is. For example, maybe you're planning to open up a new fashion outlet, a dentistry practice or a health spa. When it comes to forecasting your sales, you may feel that you're just plucking figures out of the air.

Figure-plucking (a highly technical term that I'm particularly fond of) is a dangerous thing. In an attempt to discourage this process, in Chapter 5 I focus on planning for sales in detail, analysing the number of items or services you have to sell in order to reach projected monthly sales totals. In Chapter 7, I also talk about benchmarking, and explain how important it is to research industry averages. (I suggest talking to your accountant, looking up benchmarking services, going to networking meetings, or contacting industry associations.) However, even with all this solid groundwork in place, you may still be wondering about the accuracy of your financial projections.

In this situation, I recommend you do a bit of scenario analysis, varying your income, cost of sales and expenses upwards or downwards by 10 or 20 per cent to see what happens. Although this process is slightly technical, it's probably the only way to assess how robust your plans are, and how much wriggle room you have to play with.

If you're new to Excel, I'll readily admit that scenario analysis can get a tad technical. For that reason, I provide an explanation in this chapter, as well as a template that you can download and a short video that shows how to create a template of your own. To download the Building Scenarios worksheet or view the Building Scenarios video, visit www.dummies.com/go/creatingbusinessplan.

Feeling confident? Then fire up Excel and have a stab at following these instructions:

1. **Complete your Profit & Loss Projection as per Figure 8-7.**

   You should have two worksheets: One that says GrossProfit and one that says ProfitLoss.

2. **Click the tab that says Sheet3 and rename this worksheet** Scenarios.

   For more about naming worksheets, refer to 'Naming worksheets within a single workbook' earlier in this chapter.

3. **Return to your ProfitLoss worksheet, highlight the whole page and click Copy.**

   If you're in any doubt as to how to do this, watch the video.

4. **Go to the Scenarios tab, click in the top-left cell (cell A1), select Paste Special, followed by Paste Link.**

   For more about pasting links, refer to 'Linking one worksheet to another', earlier in this chapter.

5. **Tidy up the rows full of zeros and reapply formatting.**

   When you copy links in this way, the formatting drops off. So you'll need to highlight all the figures and format these as dollar amounts. Also, any blank rows on the source worksheet come across as rows of zeros. Simply delete these zeros to get this worksheet looking good.

6. **Insert three rows at the top of this worksheet and type** Variations **followed by** Sales, Cost of Sales **and** Expenses, **with** 100% **next to each one, exactly as you see in Figure 8-9.**

   You need to format the percentage cells as percentages (click the % button on the toolbar to do this).

	A	B	C	D	E	F	G	H
1				VARIATIONS				
2		Sales	100%	Cost of Sales	100%	Expenses	100%	
3								
4		July	Aug	Sep	Oct	Nov	Dec	Jan
5	Total Sales	$ 31,070	$ 35,440	$ 41,150	$ 36,450	$ 47,260	$ 174,890	$ 13,400

Figure 8-9: Setting up a worksheet for scenario analysis.

7. **Right-click on cell C2, select Define Name and name this cell** VariationSales. **Similarly, name cell E2** VariationCostofSales **and name cell G2** VariationExpenses.

   For more about naming cells, refer to 'Using names to identify important cells' earlier in this chapter.

8. **In cell B5, change the formula from** =ProfitLoss!B2 **to become** =ProfitLoss!B2*VariationSales.

   This means that whatever appears in cell B2 on your Profit & Loss Projection copies automatically to this scenario, and cell B5 on this worksheet is multiplied by whatever percentage is in cell B2.

9. **Now copy and paste the formula from cell B5 across the whole row.**

10. **Repeat this concept for cost of sales and expenses, multiplying each one by the variation.**

    I'm being very brief here, because this whole concept is pretty tricky to express in words, and the video does a much better job of explaining what you have to do. So please, if you're at all unsure, head to www. dummies.com/go/creatingbusinessplan and watch the video.

11. **Redo your formulas for gross profit and net profit.**

    You want these to calculate automatically based on the revised figures for this scenario; you don't want to link these calculations to the Profit & Loss Projection worksheet. By this time, your worksheet hopefully looks similar to Figure 8-10.

Figure 8-10: Scenario analysis enables you to see very quickly what would happen if sales or expenses change.

VARIATIONS — Sales: (blank); Cost of Sales: 90%; Expenses: 110%, 110%, 110%

	July	Aug	Sep	Oct	Nov	Dec	Jan	Feb	Mar	Apr	May	Jun	Total
Total Sales	27,963	31,896	37,035	32,805	42,534	157,401	12,060	28,215	45,765	51,093	62,163	71,703	600,633
Total Cost of Sales	21,005	24,239	28,523	25,058	33,138	128,216	7,920	21,263	35,838	40,282	49,467	57,387	472,335
Gross Profit	6,959	7,658	8,512	7,747	9,397	29,185	4,140	6,952	9,927	10,811	12,696	14,316	128,299
Accounting Fees													
Advertising	1,320	1,320	1,320	1,320	1,320	1,320	1,320	1,320	1,320	1,320	1,320	1,320	15,840
Bank Charges	110	110	110	110	110	110	110	110	110	110	110	110	1,320
Cleaning Expenses	238	238	238	238	238	238	238	238	238	238	238	238	2,860
Computer Consumables	165	165	165	165	165	165	165	165	165	165	165	165	1,980
Consultant Expenses	330	330	330	330	330	330	330	330	330	330	330	330	3,960
Couriers	88	88	88	88	88	88	88	88	88	88	88	88	1,056
Customer Consumables	66	66	66	66	66	66	66	66	66	66	66	66	792
Electricity	550			550			550			550			2,200
Hire Purchase Payments	715	715	715	715	715	715	715	715	715	715	715	715	8,580
Insurance										3,300			3,300
Interest Expense	572	572	572	572	572	572	572	572	572	572	572	572	6,864
Internet Fees	165			165			165			165			660
Lease Expenses	880	880	880	880	880	880	880	880	880	880	880	880	10,560
License Fees	770		550							550			1,320
Merchant Fees	352	352	352	352	352	352	352	352	352	352	352	352	4,224
Motor Vehicle rego & insurance							1,650		1,650				1,650
Motor Vehicle Fuel	381	381	381	381	381	381	381	381	381	381	381	381	4,576
Motor Vehicle Repairs & Maint	183	183	183	183	183	183	183	183	183	183	183	183	2,200
Motor Vehicle Tolls	334	334	334	334	334	334	334	334	334	334	334	334	4,004
Office Supplies	165	165	165	165	165	165	165	165	165	165	165	165	1,980
Subcontractor Expenses	572	572	572	572	572	572	572	572	572	572	572	572	6,864
Subscription and Dues	220		550					330		1,320			2,420
Telephone (inc mobile)	605	605	605	605	605	605	605	605	605	605	605	605	7,260
Travel Domestic	385	385	385	385	385	385	385	385	385	385	385	385	4,620
Travel Overseas									3,850				3,850
Wages and Salaries	4,052	4,052	4,052	4,052	4,052	4,052	4,052	4,052	4,052	4,052	4,052	4,052	48,620
Wages oncosts	405	405	405	405	405	405	405	405	405	405	405	405	4,852
Website expenses	935	935	935	935	935	935	935	935	935	935	935	935	11,220
Total Expenses	19,074	19,239	17,479	18,084	17,259	16,929	18,084	17,589	22,429	23,254	17,259	16,929	223,608
Net Profit	-12,116	-11,582	-8,967	-10,337	-7,863	12,256	-13,944	-10,637	-12,502	-12,443	-4,563	-2,613	95,310

12. **Play with the figures in the variation cells and see what happens.**

For example, if you change the percentage in the Sales Variation cell to '110%', projected sales go up by 10 per cent and you can see the impact 10 per cent can have. On a more gloomy note, change the percentage to '90%' and you can see how this change flows through.

The neat thing here is that you simply have to change a couple of figures and all your profit projections for the next 12 months update automatically.

13. **Now have a look at what would happen to your business profitability if sales were 90 per cent of your predictions, but cost of sales and expenses were 110 per cent.**

Here you have arrived at the crux of the matter. What does your profitability look like if sales were just a little worse than anticipated and expenses just a little higher? The results you see here will indicate susceptibility of your business plan to the winds of change.

I feel a little sheepish at introducing into this chapter something so technical as the preceding steps. After all, this is a business-planning book, not an Excel manual. However, I find scenario analysis a very powerful technique, and something that anyone responsible for creating financial forecasts should be aware of. The way that entering just one figure into one cell can update an entire Profit & Loss Projection can make modelling different scenarios super quick and super reliable.

What if the exchange rate changes?

If you're an importer or an exporter and you make transactions in any currency other than your own, one of the biggest unknowns for your business will be the exchange rate. I've seen perfectly profitable businesses crumble rapidly under a falling exchange rate that management failed to provide for.

You can use the scenario analysis I talk about in this chapter to see what impact changes in exchange rates could have on your business. For example, maybe you're importing from Europe and the exchange rate is 0.70 Euros to the dollar. If the Euro were to drop to 0.60, this represents a 17 per cent increase in your costs. You can simply plug 117 per cent into the Cost Variation cell of your scenario analysis to see the possible impact of this change on your overall Profit & Loss.

Chapter 9

Calculating Your Break-Even Point

- -

In This Chapter

▶ Figuring out the magic number where you make neither a profit, nor a loss

▶ Tweaking margins and adjusting expenses to stay on track

▶ Working out what needs to happen so you're still afloat in 12 months' time

- -

*U*nderstanding your break-even point is as essential to your business toolkit as food is to a teenage boy. (Three guesses as to who's in my family.)

Break-even calculations help you to decide prices, set sales budgets and assess the health of your business plan. You can figure out how far sales can drop before you start to make a loss, how much extra you have to sell before you turn a profit, how changing sales impact profits and how much you need to lift sales in order to compensate for an increase in costs.

Sounds handy? In this chapter, I explain how you can calculate the break-even point for your own business. So grab your calculator, hang a 'do not disturb' sign around your neck and get ready to go ...

Identifying Your Tipping Point

Your *break-even point* is the number of dollars you need to earn in any given period in order to cover your costs. Or, to put it differently, the total sales you have to make in order that you make neither a loss nor a profit.

Most business textbooks talk about your break-even point only in terms of *the business* breaking even. In other words, the break-even point is the point at which sales are high enough to cover the costs of your business. However, you can also think of your break-even point not only in terms of covering the costs of your business, but your living expenses too.

In real life, I find that people use the word *break-even* to refer to three totally different things:

- ✔ **Business break-even point:** When you calculate your business break-even point, you calculate the sales the business has to make in order to meet its business expenses. In other words, if the business breaks even, it neither makes a profit nor a loss. This calculation is most relevant for businesses with a company structure where directors' salaries (owner salaries) are factored into the fixed expenses of the company.

- ✔ **Business/personal break-even point:** When you calculate your business/personal break-even point, you calculate the sales the business has to make in order to meet business expenses and pay you — as the business owner — enough to cover your personal expenses.

  Most business plan books don't include any reference to personal expenses when calculating break-even, but I think that doing so is important for small businesses with single owner-operators or husband-and-wife teams. After all, even if your business does make a profit, this profit may not be enough if the business is your sole source of income and the profit generated isn't enough to cover your basic living expenses.

- ✔ **Cash break-even point:** When you calculate your cash break-even point, you calculate the sales you have to make in order for your cash out to match your cash in over a specified period of time (usually 12 months). In this scenario, cash out could include things like new equipment or business start-up costs, and cash in could include business loans or money that you have set aside in savings.

  Calculating your cash break-even point provides a simpler approach to doing a proper cashflow (a topic I cover in detail in Chapter 10). However, a cashflow is a more accurate and detailed approach and is preferable if your business offers credit to customers or has inventory.

In the first part of this chapter, I cover how to calculate business break-even, and business/personal break-even. I look at break-even from a cash perspective towards the end of this chapter (see the section 'Looking at Things from a Cash Perspective').

Calculating business break-even

The basic formula for calculating your business break-even point is easy:

Break-even point = Fixed expenses divided by gross profit margin

Imagine I have a friend (I'll call her Annie) who has a cafe on the main street. Her fixed expenses are $4,500 per week (one waitress, one kitchenhand, insurance, rent and so on). Overall, on average she makes a gross profit margin of about 60 per cent. (In other words, if she sells a focaccia for $10, the ingredients cost her $4; if she sells a coffee for $3, the ingredients cost $1.80.)

Annie's business break-even point is going to equal fixed expenses (that's $4,500 per week) divided by her gross profit margin (60 per cent) which is $7,500. In other words, she has to generate $7,500 in sales just to break even and cover her basic expenses. Figure 9-1 shows this principle in action.

Figure 9-1:
Calculating
business
break-even
point.

	A	B	C	D
1				
2	Average Gross Profit Margin	60%		Based on ingredients costing 40 cents for every dollar sold
3				
4	Fixed Expenses Business	$4,500.00		Staff, rent, insurance and so on
5				
6	Break-even Point	$7,500.00		Equals fixed expenses divided by gross profit margin
7				

Think this through to see how it works out. If Annie generates $7,500 in income, she'll have to pay out $3,000 in supplies (that's the cost of food at 40 cents in the dollar). This leaves $4,500 gross profit, which is exactly the amount she needs to cover her fixed expenses. This figure is Annie's business break-even point.

Factoring personal expenses into the equation

The break-even chat in the preceding section is all very well, but if your business has a sole trader or partnership structure, you probably need to do more than cover your business expenses, in that you'll need to generate enough income to cover personal expenses as well. (I'm assuming that if your business has a company structure, you already pay yourself a wage, and so your wage forms part of your fixed expenses.)

To bring personal expenses into the picture, you need to repeat the business break-even calculation, but this time include the amount of cash you need to generate to cover personal expenses.

Building on the example earlier in this chapter, what do you think break-even would be in the following situation?

- ✔ Annie has a cafe with fixed expenses of $4,500 per week. These expenses don't include any wages for herself.

- ✔ She needs to generate a minimum of $500 per week in order to cover her personal living expenses.

- ✔ She makes an average gross profit margin of 60 per cent.

The formula is the same; however, this time fixed expenses need to include not just business expenses but personal expenses also.

> Break-even point = Fixed expenses (including personal expenses) divided by gross profit margin

You could see how the sums pan out in Figure 9-2. Annie needs to earn an additional $833 per week (that's $8333 in total) in order for her business to break even and for her to generate enough to live on.

Figure 9-2: Calculating break-even point to cover both business and personal expenses.

	A	B	C	D
1				
2	Average Gross Profit Margin	60%		Based on ingredients costing 40 cents for every dollar sold
3				
4	Fixed Expenses Business	$4,500.00		Staff, rent, insurance and so on
5	Fixed Expenses Personal	$ 500.00		The minimum personal funds Annie needs to survive
6	Total Fixed Expenses	$5,000.00		
7				
8	Break-even Point	$8,333.33		Equals fixed expenses divided by gross profit margin
9				
10				

Calculating break-even for your business

Are you ready to calculate the break-even point for your own business? Just before I launch into a step-by-step explanation, I'm going to quickly recap the difference between variable costs and fixed expenses. (For more on this topic, scoot back to Chapter 6.)

- ✔ *Variable costs* (also sometimes called *direct costs* or *cost of goods sold*) are the costs that go up and down in direct relation to your sales, and typically include commissions, the cost of the goods you buy to resell to customers, raw materials, subcontract labour and so on.

✔ *Fixed expenses* are expenses that stay constant, regardless of whether your sales go up and down. Typical fixed expenses for your business may include accounting fees, bank fees, computer expenses, electricity, insurance, motor vehicles, rental, stationery and wages.

Got all that straight? Then here goes:

1. **Open a new worksheet in Excel (or any other spreadsheet software).**

   You can either start a whole new workbook or, if you have already created sales and profit projections, you can add a new worksheet to this workbook.

2. **Enter your gross profit margin on the first line, similar to Figure 9-2.**

   To calculate your gross profit margin, grab your average gross profit (per unit, product, service provided, month or per year), divide this by sales (again, per unit, product, service provided, month or per year) and multiply by 100. If you're not sure how to do this calculation, make your way back to Chapter 6, where I explain how to calculate your gross profit margin in lots of detail.

   If you are an owner-operated service business with no employees and no variable costs, your gross profit margin will be 100 per cent.

   Format your gross profit margin as a percentage. To do this, simply click the % button on the main toolbar.

3. **Add the fixed expenses for your business to the next line of the worksheet.**

   If you're not sure how much your fixed expenses are, Chapter 7 focuses on calculating the fixed expenses for your business. I usually like to calculate break-even and think of fixed expenses on a monthly basis, but you can choose any period of time that makes sense to you.

   If you have already created a worksheet for fixed expenses, similar to what I suggest in Chapter 7, you can link the fixed expenses cell on your break-even worksheet to your expenses worksheet. This way, whenever you update your expense projections, your break-even point will recalculate automatically.

4. **If your fixed expenses don't include any wages for yourself, add whatever you need for living expenses to the next line of the worksheet.**

   Again, Chapter 7 has lots of tips about building a personal budget so that you're realistic about how much you need to survive.

5. **Total up your business and personal fixed expenses.**

   Figure 9-2 shows the general idea.

6. Add a row that calculates break-even point, dividing total fixed expenses by the average gross profit margin.

In Figure 9-2, the formula for the break-even point is =**B6/B2**. Simple. You now know what you have to achieve in sales in order to meet your business expenses.

If it suits, you can express the break-even point in a different time period. In Step 3 in the preceding steps, if you express your fixed expenses as total expenses for a month, consequently your break-even point calculates what you need to achieve in sales per month. However, maybe it makes more sense to you to look at your break-even point per day, per week or per year. Another option (again, if relevant to your business), is to express the break-even point in units sold, or the number of services provided, rather than dollars. For example, if your break-even point is $10,000 a week and you're selling custom-built handmade guitars at $5,000 a pop, you know you have to sell two guitars a week to break even. Or if your break-even point is $4,000 a month and you're mowing lawns at an average of $50 a lawn, you know you have to mow 80 lawns a month to break even.

Calculating a break-even point using the method shown in the preceding steps gives you a general indication of how much income your business needs to generate in order to make neither a profit nor a loss over a sustained period of time. However, this calculation doesn't take into account the cash requirements for a business. A business can make a profit but still have negative cashflow (and vice versa), because of factors such as start-up costs, extending customer credit or building inventory. For a more detailed explanation of cashflow management, see Chapter 10.

Changing Your Break-Even Point

If you find that your business is trading unprofitably, and despite your best efforts you can't get your sales high enough to meet your break-even point, your only option may be to change your break-even point.

Using the principles of break-even calculations, you have three possible solutions:

✔ Raise your prices (which is often not an option if you're finding it hard to make enough sales)

✔ Cut your variable costs (that is, the costs of production or providing your service)

✔ Cut your fixed costs

For example, if I go back to the cafe owner whose calculations are shown in Figure 9-2, I can see that Annie needs to generate $8,333 per week just to pay expenses. Imagine that the local council is planning major road works and Annie knows that her turnover is going to be affected. She reckons she'll probably generate only about $6,000 a week while the work is going on.

Annie goes to the worksheet where she calculated her break-even and experiments with the different scenarios, shown in Figure 9-3.

- ✔ In Strategy One, Annie can see that she'd have to increase gross profit margin to 83.5 per cent in order to break even if sales dropped to $6,000 per week. She knows she can't cut food costs or increase prices this much, so this strategy doesn't seem practical.

- ✔ In Strategy Two, she keeps her margins the same but cuts her expenses by $1,400 a week. This seems to work, but she doesn't know if she can cut expenses by this much and still stay open.

- ✔ In Strategy Three, Annie increases her margin by 5 per cent and cuts her expenses by $1,000 a week. She can see that this will work, and thinks that cutting her expenses by this much is probably possible, especially if her landlord agrees to a temporary reduction in rent.

Figure 9-3: Understanding break-even enables you to plan ahead for changes in trading conditions.

	A	B	C	D	E
1	CURRENT BREAK-EVEN POINT			STRATEGY ONE	
2	Average Gross Profit Margin	60%		Average Gross Profit Margin	83.5%
3					
4	Fixed Expenses Business	$ 4,500.00		Fixed Expenses Business	$ 4,500.00
5	Fixed Expenses Personal	$ 500.00		Fixed Expenses Personal	$ 500.00
6	Total Fixed Expenses	$ 5,000.00		Total Fixed Expenses	$ 5,000.00
7					
8	Break-even Point	$ 8,333.33		Break-even Point	$ 5,988.02
9					
10	STRATEGY TWO			STRATEGY THREE	
11	Average Gross Profit Margin	60%		Average Gross Profit Margin	65%
12					
13	Fixed Expenses Business	$ 3,100.00		Fixed Expenses Business	$ 3,500.00
14	Fixed Expenses Personal	$ 500.00		Fixed Expenses Personal	$ 400.00
15	Total Fixed Expenses	$ 3,600.00		Total Fixed Expenses	$ 3,900.00
16					
17	Break-even Point	$ 6,000.00		Break-even Point	$ 6,000.00

The handy thing about understanding your break-even point in this kind of detail is that you can take pre-emptive action if you know that costs are going to increase or sales are going to decrease.

What does something really cost?

One of the things that can do your head in when working with costings is the question of how to apportion the fixed costs of your business across every item sold or every service provided.

Think of a business selling homemade fudge. The cost of ingredients for fudge stays the same for every packet sold, but the fixed costs (premises rental, equipment rental, insurance and so on) per packet go up or down depending on the number of packets of fudge made.

If the fixed costs are $700 a week and the business makes 700 packets of fudge that week, the fixed costs are $1 per packet. But if the business makes 1,400 packets of fudge, the fixed costs are only 50 cents per packet.

For this reason, it can sometimes be hard to arrive at the 'true' cost of an item. For you as a business owner, the challenge in this respect is twofold: First, be ever vigilant about controlling your fixed costs; second, always try to maximise production to make as full use of resources as you can. This may mean making full use of rented premises, keeping staff productive and, of course, ensuring that sales are as high as they can possibly be given this level of expenses. By maximising resources in this way, you keep the fixed costs per unit as low as possible.

Looking at Things from a Cash Perspective

When I was teaching at our local business college, one of the exercises teachers were asked to do with the students (all of whom were planning their new businesses) was to do a break-even analysis from a cash perspective for the first 12 months of trading.

At first I was a bit sceptical of this somewhat simplistic approach, because the only way to be really sure how things stand from a cash perspective is to do a proper cashflow, a topic I cover in Chapter 10. However, if you don't offer credit to customers and you don't carry inventory, this cash break-even analysis can be a very powerful and relatively simple-to-use technique.

The idea is that you don't look simply at business profitability, but also at how much cash you have in the bank to begin with, how much cash you intend to spend on setting up and how much money (if any) you intend to borrow.

You can see how this analysis looks in Figure 9-4, where I take the figures for Annie's cafe business (the example I use earlier in this chapter), but imagine that she's in her first 12 months of trading. You can see that when I factor in her existing savings and the fact that she's borrowing slightly more than she needs to spend for the start-up, her break-even point drops from $8,333 to $7,467. What this means, in practical terms, is that although in the long-term Annie does need to generate $8,333 in sales every week in order to break-even, she only has to average $7,371 in the first 12 months. This is probably a good thing, because most businesses need some time to build up trading.

Doing a cash break-even analysis in this way takes only ten minutes or so of your time (assuming you download the template that I provide), so I recommend you see what this technique reveals.

To help you with your cash break-even analysis, do the following:

1. **Go to www.dummies.com/go/creatingbusinessplan and download the 12-Month Break-Even worksheet template and open it up in Excel.**

   You'll see something pretty similar to Figure 9-4.

Figure 9-4:
Calculating what you need to do in order to break even in the first 12 months.

	A	B	C	D
1	Calculating Your 'Cash' Break-Even Point for the First 12 Months of a New Business			
2	only enter figures in the cells highlighted in grey			
3				
4	Average Gross Profit Margin	60%		For more about calculating your gross profit margin, refer to Chapter 6
5				
6	Savings available	-$ 20,000.00		Enter your total savings as a minus amount
7	Other sources of income for the first 12 months	$ 5,000.00		Enter any other non-business sources of income as a minus amount
8	Proceeds from business loan	-$ 80,000.00		Enter any loan finance as a minus amount
9	Money required for setup expenses	$ 75,000.00		For more about creating a startup budget, refer to Chapter 4
10	Total fixed expenses (business) for the first 12 months	$ 234,000.00		Don't include variable costs or wages paid to yourself, but do include loan repayments
11	Total personal expenses for the first 12 months	$ 26,000.00		Enter the minimum amount you need to live on, before tax
12	What you need to have as a balance in the bank in 12 months	$ 3,000.00		Enter the minimum amount you need to have in the bank so you can sleep at night
13	Total	$ 233,000.00		
14				
15	Break-even point over 12 months	$ 388,333.33		Level of sales required to break even, from a cash perspective, over the next 12 months
16	Monthly break-even point	$ 32,361.11		
17	Weekly break-even point	$ 7,467.95		
18				

2. **Follow the instructions against each row of the worksheet, referring to your previous workings where relevant.**

   You'll notice that this worksheet is a bit different from a regular break-even analysis in that it includes loan finance, start-up costs and other sources of income. I've entered some figures into the template so you can get the general idea of how everything works; you need to override these figures with your own.

3. **Look at the break-even point and see how this compares to your projected sales for the first 12 months.**

   If your break-even point is greater than what you've forecasted in sales, you almost certainly have a problem. You need to reduce start-up expenses, increase finance, reduce costs or stop eating.

   If your break-even point is less than what you've forecasted in sales, things are looking good. (Although if you offer customers credit or have stock on hand, I still recommend that you work through a more detailed cashflow, as explained in Chapter 10.)

Chapter 10

Creating Cashflows and Building Budgets

. . . .

In This Chapter

▶ Ruminating on the many reasons cash is different from profit

▶ Looking at a Cashflow Projection report and how it's different from a Profit &
Loss Projection

▶ Analysing how much money is going to flow in and out the door

▶ Creating your all-singing, all-dancing Cashflow Projection report

▶ Designing a budget that works hand-in-hand with cash demands

▶ Working on a Balance Sheet Projection

. . . .

Did you know that your business can make a profit yet can run out
of cash? Of all the perils of business, one of the most disheartening
has to be a promising enterprise that grows so fast that it starves itself of
funds. However, if you have an eye to the future, not to mention the ability
to create a Cashflow Projection report, you should be able to predict when
a cash crunch is going to occur. You can then plan accordingly, maybe
approaching the bank for additional finance, timing expenses differently or
consciously slowing growth.

In this chapter, I show you how to create a Cashflow Projection report for
your business, and I explain the many reasons cash in the bank can be so
different from profit. I also explore the need to create ongoing budgets.
Budgets enable you to set goals for income and limits on expenses, imposing
a gentle discipline on the day-to-day running of your business that helps
you meet the predictions of your Cashflow Projections and ensure that
everything stays on track.

Understanding Why Cash Is Different from Profit

I wish I had a dollar for every time a client asks, 'Veechi, my reports say I'm making fistfuls of cash, but how come I have nothing in the bank?' Similarly, I occasionally witness clients who are wallowing in cash and living the high life, even though their Profit & Loss reports are decidedly gloomy.

In the first part of this chapter, I explain why profit doesn't always equal cash and why cash doesn't always equal profit.

Five reasons your projections may look rosy, but cash could be tight

Even if your Profit & Loss Projection for the next 12 months looks rosy as can be, you may still find yourself short of cash during this period. Here are a few of the reasons:

- ✔ **You need to pay tax:** A tricky habit to avoid (do tell me if you discover how), but the truth is that as soon as you make any profit, you have to pay tax. Unless your business has a company structure, tax isn't usually shown in your Profit & Loss Projection, hence why tax payments can result in a cashflow squeeze, despite profitable results.

- ✔ **You buy new equipment or have major start-up costs:** As I explain in Chapters 4 and 7, start-up costs for your business aren't usually shown as an expense in your Profit & Loss Projections. You need to allow for these costs separately.

- ✔ **You make loan repayments:** If you only show interest expense on your Profit & Loss Projection (rather than the whole value of each loan repayment), then your actual cash out will be more than your projected expenses.

- ✔ **You offer customer credit:** If you bill a customer in April, your Profit & Loss Projection will show this income in April, even though you may not actually receive the cash until weeks or months later. Therefore, any increase in what customers owe you will chew up your cash.

- ✔ **You increase inventory levels:** If you buy or manufacture goods for resale, as your business grows, your stock levels will increase, quickly using up cash.

In this chapter, I show you how to allow for all of these things (tax, new equipment, customer credit, loans and inventory) using a Cashflow Projection report, so that you can plan not just for profit, but for cash also.

Many a business has floundered due to lack of cash, even though it has been trading profitably. This is the reason creating a Cashflow Projection in addition to a Profit & Loss Projection is so crucial.

Five reasons your projections may look grim, but cash could be flowing

It may be easy to grasp why a business may not have any cash even though it's turning a profit. However, what about the opposite scenario, where the Profit & Loss Projection looks pretty gloomy but you still have ready cash on hand? Here are some reasons this situation can occur:

✔ **You receive a loan:** Your Profit & Loss Projection shows only income from trading, and doesn't include money received from loans. (Loans are both a blessing and a curse. When you receive a loan, the sudden influx of cash can burn a hole in the thickest of pockets.)

✔ **Your receive credit from creditors:** In the short-term, you can keep your bank account stable while making a loss simply by receiving credit from creditors.

✔ **You reduce the value of inventory:** If your stock levels go down, you will have more cash available. Simple as that.

✔ **You reduce customer credit:** If customers are likely to owe you less at the end of this 12-month period than they do at the beginning, this will be a source of cash.

✔ **You haven't yet paid taxes to the government:** If you charge consumer tax to customers (GST, VAT or sales tax) or pay consumer tax on expenses, and you have to pay the difference between tax collected and tax paid to the government, then your Profit & Loss Projection should show all income and expenses not including this tax. However, if you only submit a return to the government every three or six months, you may end up with additional funds in your bank account as the due date for lodging this return approaches.

Having cash in the bank when a business is trading unprofitably can be quite dangerous, because the availability of cash can lull you into a false sense of security, and encourage you to spend beyond your means.

Summarising what's Different about a Cashflow Report

A Cashflow Projection is very similar to a Profit & Loss Projection, but with a few notable differences. I summarise these differences in Table 10-1.

Table 10-1	**Differences between a Profit & Loss Projection and a Cashflow Projection**
A Profit & Loss Projection . . .	*A Cashflow Projection . . .*
Shows sales in the month that they're made	Provides additional detail to show sales in the month that payment is received
Doesn't include incoming funds from loans or other sources of finance	Includes additional detail showing all sources of funds, including loans and capital contributions
Doesn't include consumer taxes (GST, VAT or sales tax) but shows all figures net of tax	More complex Cashflow Projections may show figures including tax, and then show tax payments separately
Shows only the interest on loan repayments, not the full value of the loan repayments	Shows the full value of loan repayments
Shows cost of sales (the cost of materials and so on) at the time a sale is made, regardless of when materials where purchased	Provides additional detail to show the purchase of materials in the month payment is made
Doesn't include capital expenditure or start-up costs	Includes all cash outflows, including capital expenditure and start-up costs
Doesn't include owner drawings	Includes a row to show owner drawings on projections for sole traders and partnerships
Includes no information regarding likely cash available	Calculates the closing bank balance for the end of each month

To see how these differences play out, have a look at the Cashflow Projection in Figure 10-1. Can you see how the first half of the report mirrors the format of a Profit & Loss Projection? (Except for the fact that I've hidden the detail of the expense rows, so that everything can fit on this page.) Cash inflows reflect cash collected from sales (as opposed to actual sales generated) as well as incoming funds from loans. Cash outflows include the purchase of new equipment, purchase of stock (as opposed to the actual cost of goods sold), expenses and loan repayments.

Figure 10-1:
A Cashflow Projection predicts the closing balance of your bank account.

	Jun	Jul	Aug	Sep	Oct	Nov	Dec	Jan	Feb	Mar	Apr	May	Jun	Total
Total Sales		31,070	35,440	41,150	36,450	47,260	174,890	13,400	31,350	50,850	56,770	69,070	79,670	667,370
Cash Collected		25,000	31,070	35,440	41,150	36,450	47,260	174,890	13,400	31,350	50,850	56,770	69,070	
Debtors at Month End	25000	31,070	35,440	41,150	36,450	47,260	174,890	13,400	31,350	50,850	56,770	69,070	79,670	
Total Cost of Sales		19,095	22,035	25,930	22,780	30,125	116,560	7,200	19,330	32,580	36,620	44,970	52,170	429,395
Stock Purchases (Paid Cash on Delivery)		24,000	26,000	23,000	29,000	110,000	24,000	15,000	34,000	37,000	43,000	50,000	50,000	465,000
Inventory at Month End	25000	29,905	33,870	30,940	37,160	117,035	24,475	32,275	46,945	51,365	57,745	62,775	60,605	
Gross Profit		11,975	13,405	15,220	13,670	17,135	58,330	6,200	12,020	18,270	20,150	24,100	27,500	237,975
Total Expenses		18,857	19,007	17,407	17,957	17,207	16,907	17,957	17,507	21,907	24,157	17,207	16,907	222,980
Net Profit		- 6,882	- 5,602	- 2,187	- 4,287	72	41,423	- 11,757	- 5,487	- 3,637	- 4,007	6,893	10,593	14,995
CASH INFLOWS														
Cash Collected From Sales		25,000	31,070	35,440	41,150	36,450	47,260	174,890	13,400	31,350	50,850	56,770	69,070	612,700
Loan Finance		120,000												120,000
Total Cash Inflows		145,000	31,070	35,440	41,150	36,450	47,260	174,890	13,400	31,350	50,850	56,770	69,070	732,700
CASH OUTFLOWS														
Purchase of New Equipment		12,000		25,000				12,000				5,000		54,000
Purchases of Stock		24,000	26,000	23,000	29,000	110,000	24,000	15,000	34,000	37,000	43,000	50,000	50,000	465,000
Expenses		18,857	19,007	17,407	17,957	17,207	16,907	17,957	17,507	21,907	24,157	17,207	16,907	222,980
Company Tax					2,000			2,000			2,000			6,000
Loan Repayments		2,500	2,500	2,500	2,500	2,500	2,500	2,500	2,500	2,500	2,500	2,500	2,500	30,000
		57,357	47,507	67,907	51,457	129,707	43,407	49,457	54,007	61,407	71,657	74,707	69,407	777,980
Opening Cash		1,000	88,643	72,207	39,740	29,433	63,823	59,970	65,463	24,857	5,200	26,007	43,943	
Cash Inflow less Cash Outflow		87,643	- 16,437	- 32,467	- 10,307	- 93,257	3,853	125,433	- 40,607	- 30,057	- 20,807	- 17,937	337	
Closing Cash		88,643	72,207	39,740	29,433	- 63,823	59,970	65,463	24,857	5,200	26,007	43,943	44,280	

In Figure 10-1, you can see how the cash situation for this business is fairly dire, resulting in a negative balance of $44,280 at the end of 12 months, even though the total profit over this same period is reasonably stable at $14,995. The summary of Cash Inflows and Cash Outflows explain why, and provide some insight into how this business might be able to manage its cash situation.

Looking at Cash Coming In

If your business sells to other businesses (as opposed to direct to the consumer), you will almost certainly be expected to offer credit to your customers. The amount of credit depends very much on whom you're selling to and the industry you're in. Some industries are lucky enough to have 7-day accounts as standard, but most industries expect at least 30 days from date of invoice, if not 30 days from end of month. (Invoices paid 30 days from end of month means that all April invoices will be paid by 30 May, all May invoices by 30 June, and so on. With these terms, an invoice dated 1 April doesn't fall due for payment until 30 May, meaning the customer effectively receives 59 days credit on this invoice.) Some large supermarket chains and department stores may even negotiate for special payment terms of up to 120 days.

Customer credit is a brutal drain on cashflow, especially for growing businesses. If your business is growing, more customers will demand credit, and this will require cash. For example, if I offer credit terms that are 30 days from date of invoice, and my sales average $25,000 a month, I will always be owed $25,000 or so (probably more actually, given that many customers try to extend credit terms beyond the due date). If my business grows and in 12 months' time I average $40,000 sales per month, I need an additional $15,000 in funding or excess profits in order to keep my head above water.

When creating a Cashflow Projection, you not only need to look at money collected from sales, but also at any other sources of funds, such as loan finance or capital contributions from the owners.

Calculating cash collected versus sales made

If you offer credit to your customers, creating a Cashflow Projection in addition to a Profit & Loss Projection is important if either one of the following situations apply:

- ✔ Your business is growing and your sales are increasing each month.
- ✔ You have seasonal variations with bumper months and lean months.

In Figure 10-2, can you see how the first row under Cash Inflows on my Cashflow Projection shows a row called Cash Collected from Sales? In this row, I show when I think I'm likely to receive the cash from sales. Can you see how in December the cash received is likely to be only $47,260 (which is the amount of sales for November), even though December is actually a huge month for sales at $174,890?

In this example, you can see that this business has major seasonal variations with sales, and for this reason planning for cashflow is crucial. However, even for a business that doesn't have seasonal variations, if this business is growing, this growth translates to a demand for cash.

	A	C	D	E	F	G	H
1		Jul	Aug	Sep	Oct	Nov	Dec
2	Total Sales	31,070	35,440	41,150	36,450	47,260	174,890
4							
5	Total Cost of Sales	19,095	22,035	25,930	22,780	30,125	116,560
8							
9	Gross Profit	11,975	13,405	15,220	13,670	17,135	58,330
10							
52	Total Expenses	18,857	19,007	17,407	17,957	17,207	16,907
53							
54	Net Profit	- 6,882 -	5,602 -	2,187 -	4,287 -	72	41,423
55							
56	CASH INFLOWS						
57	Cash Collected From Sales	25,000	31,070	35,440	41,150	36,450	47,260
58	Loan Finance	120,000					
59	Total Cash Inflows	145,000	31,070	35,440	41,150	36,450	47,260

Figure 10-2: Looking at cash collections.

When adding a Cash Collected row to your Cashflow Projection, don't forget to include the value of cash you will receive from customers who currently owe you money. In Figure 10-2, the Cash Collected amount for July is $25,000, which is the value of debtors outstanding as at the end of June.

Thinking about loans and other sources of funds

Bank loans or any other source of finance also make a big impact on cashflow. When you receive a loan, your Cashflow Projection will show the full amount of this loan, yet your Profit & Loss Projection won't show a cent. (Why? Because a loan isn't income, and your Profit & Loss Projection only shows actual business income.)

You generally show loan finance at the bottom of your Cashflow Projection report, in the section that summarises all cash inflows. In Figure 10-2, you can see $120,000 in loan finance coming in during July.

Your Cashflow Projection is also the spot to record any other sources of funds, such as personal funds you or your business partner plan to contribute. Again, personal contributions of funds don't count as business income (which is why you don't show these contributions on your Profit & Loss Projection) but they certainly do count as incoming cash (which is why these contributions show on your Cashflow Projection).

Thinking about Cash Flowing Out

The four biggest things that chew up cash in a new business, yet don't actually count as an expense, are the purchase of new equipment, the purchase of stock, the payment of tax bills and the repayment of loans. You need to consider all of these factors when summarising the Cash Outflows in your Cashflow Projection.

Allowing for the purchase of new equipment (or other start-up items)

In Chapter 4, I go into a whole load of detail about creating a budget for your new business, talking about start-up costs such as new equipment, vehicles, computers and rental bonds. I also explain how these start-up costs aren't really expenses in terms of your Profit & Loss. For example, if you spend $50,000 in setting up a new business and in the first month of trading you make $1,000 worth of sales and you have $500 of expenses, you've still made $500 profit in your first month, not a $49,500 loss.

So, having explained that you don't include start-up costs in your Profit & Loss Projections, you may have been wondering where it is that you *do* show your start-up costs. The answer is in your Cashflow Projection report.

Back in Figure 10-1, check out how Purchase of New Equipment shows as the first row under the Cash Outflows heading. Of course, you can change this heading to whatever is most relevant for you (labelling this row as New Vehicle, Start-up Costs, Shop Fit-out Costs or whatever).

Looking at payment for stock versus cost of sales

If you buy or manufacture goods for resale, you almost certainly carry stock. (Possible exceptions would be if you make custom one-off items, or if you make fresh goods, all of which you sell each day.)

If you carry stock, creating a Cashflow Projection in addition to a Profit & Loss Projection is important if the value of the stock that you carry is likely to exceed the value of credit you can obtain from creditors. (For example, if you need to carry only four weeks' worth of stock at any one time, and your creditors offer you four weeks' credit, the two cancel one another out. However, most businesses need to carry up to six months' worth of stock at any one time, especially if importing goods from overseas where the lead time between placing an order and receiving goods is long.) What this means is that as your business grows, you need to finance the increase in the value of stock you have to carry.

A Cashflow Projection is also helpful if you need to order minimum quantities. For example, maybe you can only secure decent volume discounts if you order 1,000 units or more of something at a time. This may mean you need to order only once every three months or so, but you need to budget accordingly so that you can finance three months' worth of stock with each order.

In Figure 10-3, I've used my Profit & Loss Projection as a starting point, and then modified the cost of sales section to include additional information about when I need to pay for stock. The row called Inventory at Month End calculates automatically, based on the value of inventory at the end of the previous month plus Purchase of Stock less Cost of Sales. I enter the figures against Purchases of Stock manually, ensuring that the order is timed so that I always have at least one month's worth of stock on hand at any one time. You can see, for example, that my purchases are particularly high during November, because I have to allow for December being a huge sales month.

Adding a row to your Cashflow Projection that predicts your stock levels at the end of each month is a great way to keep yourself 'honest' and test how realistic your stock purchase figures really are.

Figure 10-3:
Calculating
inventory
and
estimating
when you
will have
pay for it.

	A	B	C	D	E	F	G	H	I
1			Jun	Jul	Aug	Sep	Oct	Nov	Dec	Jan
2	Total Sales			31,070	35,440	41,150	36,450	47,260	174,890	13,400
3	Cash Collected			25,000	31,070	35,440	41,150	36,450	47,260	174,890
4										
5	Total Cost of Sales			19,095	22,035	25,930	22,780	30,125	116,560	7,200
6	Purchase of Stock			24,000	26,000	23,000	29,000	110,000	24,000	15,000
7	Inventory at Month End		25000	29,905	33,870	30,940	37,160	117,035	24,475	32,275

Deciding where to show tax payments

One of the questions people often ask is whether to include personal or company tax in their Cashflow Projection. The answer depends on whether your business is structured as a sole trader, partnership or company:

- **If you're a sole trader or partnership:** The amount of personal tax you pay depends on many factors, including whether you have any additional sources of income other than the business. For this reason, I suggest that you don't include personal income tax as an expense on your Cashflow Projection, but that you do make an allowance for personal drawings in the Cash Outflows section of your Cashflow Projection, and that this allowance is enough to cover any personal tax you may have to pay.

If you have a sole trader or partnership structure, you may still need to pay tax on profits made even if you don't draw any funds from the business. For example, maybe your business has made a $30,000 profit and you've used this profit to buy new equipment (which you can't claim as an outright tax deduction, but must instead claim back over several years). Even if you haven't drawn a cent out of the business, you still need to pay tax on this $30,000 profit.

- **If your business has a company structure:** You need to include company tax expense on your Profit & Loss Projection. I explain how to do this in Chapter 8, where you make a monthly allowance for company tax based on profits made. However, if you only pay company tax once a year, you may want to adjust your Cashflow Projection to remove the monthly allowance for company tax and instead only show tax in the month in which it's due.

✔ **If your business is subject to any kind of value-added tax (known, for example, as VAT in Canada and the UK, or GST in Australia and New Zealand):** You don't include this tax in any of your expenses. Instead, you show the value of each expense before tax is applied. (Why? Because this kind of tax applies only to the final sale to the consumer — as a business, you're entitled to claim back any tax of this nature that you pay.)

✔ **If your business pays a sales tax on purchases (something that applies in almost every state within the United States):** You should include sales tax in your expenses, showing the value of each expense inclusive of the tax that you pay. (Why? Because this tax forms part of the cost of this expense — you can't claim this tax back from the government.)

Factoring in loan repayments

As I explain in Chapter 7, loan repayments and loan interest are two entirely different things. For example, if you have a bank loan with repayments of $1,000 per week, but you have only $15,000 outstanding on this loan, the interest on this loan will be only about $15 per week. In terms of the profit of your business, the only expense that you can claim is the interest.

If you decide to include both a Profit & Loss Projection and a Cashflow Projection in your business plan, you should show the value of the interest expense in your Profit & Loss Projection, and the value of the loan repayment in your Cashflow Projection. You show this amount as a separate row under Cash Outflows, as per Figure 10-1.

What about supplier credit?

In the same way as you may receive cash from sales several weeks after the sale is made, you may also not have to pay suppliers until several weeks after you receive the goods you purchase. In terms of Cashflow Projections, adjusting expenses to allow for supplier credit can get quite tricky, especially given that only some expenses will be subject to credit. (For example, most advertising accounts probably offer you 30 days credit, but your staff wages need to be paid weekly, with no credit terms.)

I've created lots of Cashflow Projections for different businesses over the years, many of which have been hideously (and probably unnecessarily) complex. I now try to keep Cashflow Projections as simple as possible. For this reason, unless a business is importing goods and operates on extended credit terms of 90 or 120 days, I take a financially conservative approach and don't usually adjust figures to allow for supplier credit.

Predicting the Bottom Line

In the earlier sections in this chapter, I talk about why profit is different from cash, and I explore how to calculate likely cash in and cash out for your business. The final step is to predict how much cash you're likely to have in the bank at the end of each month.

The easiest way to create a Cashflow Projection is to use a spreadsheet (have a look at the earlier figures in this chapter for some examples). The most straightforward approach is usually to start with your Profit & Loss Projection, save it under a different name, and then make all the necessary changes, adding several lines to modify the Profit & Loss Projection so it becomes a Cashflow Projection.

Setting up a worksheet in Excel

Although creating a Cashflow Projection can be quite complex, please don't be discouraged: A simple cashflow is relatively easy to create and once you learn how to do it, can be an enormously powerful tool.

To help make this process as straightforward as possible, I explain how to create a Cashflow Projection in three different ways:

✔ You can follow the step-by-step guide here in this chapter.

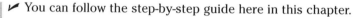
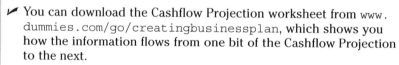

✔ You can download the Cashflow Projection worksheet from www. dummies.com/go/creatingbusinessplan, which shows you how the information flows from one bit of the Cashflow Projection to the next.

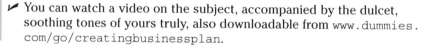

✔ You can watch a video on the subject, accompanied by the dulcet, soothing tones of yours truly, also downloadable from www.dummies. com/go/creatingbusinessplan.

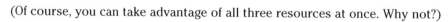

(Of course, you can take advantage of all three resources at once. Why not?)

Meanwhile, here's the step-by-step guide:

1. Make a copy of your Profit & Loss Projection.

I'm assuming here that you have already created a Profit & Loss Projection. If not, skedaddle back to Chapter 8.

Incidentally, Chapter 8 also explains how you can copy and paste links to data, rather than just copying the data. If you're comfortable with these technicalities, you can create a new worksheet that links back to your Profit & Loss worksheet, meaning that if you update a figure in your Profit & Loss, it will automatically update your cashflow.

2. **Set up Cash Inflows and Outflows to match the headings in Figure 10-1.**

   If any of these headings aren't relevant to your business (maybe you don't offer customers credit or you're not planning to take out a loan), skip this information.

   If your business has a sole trader or partnership structure, you also need to allow for any drawings that you plan to take out of the business. In this scenario, include an additional row for Owner's Drawings.

3. **Complete the detail required in order to get an accurate picture of Cash Inflows and Outflows.**

   I explain how to show cash collected from sales, loan finance, new equipment, payment for stock, tax bills and loan repayments earlier in this chapter (refer to 'Looking at Cash Coming In' and 'Thinking about Cash Flowing Out' for more details).

4. **Add rows for Opening and Closing Cash.**

   Again, check out the format of Figure 10-1 for how this looks.

5. **Enter the balance of Opening Cash in the first column.**

   In Figure 10-1, my Cashflow Projection starts in July. Therefore, in the July column next to Opening Cash, I enter the opening balance of my bank account (or what I think the opening balance is likely to be). For simplicity's sake, if I have more than one bank account (maybe I have both a savings and a cheque account) I combine the balance of all my accounts.

6. **Calculate Closing Cash.**

   Nice and easy. The balance of Closing Cash is equal to the balance of Opening Cash plus Cash Inflows less Cash Outflows. Type in a formula to this effect. For example, the formula in Figure 10-1 for July would be = **C70** + **C71**.

7. **Review the predicted Closing Cash balance for each month.**

   Look at the predicted Closing Cash balance for each month and ponder whether any problems are looming. If necessary, you may need to time expenses differently or secure additional finance. (Read on to find out more.)

Making a pre-emptive strike

So what should you do if your Profit & Loss Projection looks hunky dory, and you're happy with the whole concept of your business model and strategy, but your Cashflow Projection shows you don't have enough funds, or that you're going to hit a few months of cash difficulties?

The good thing about being able to predict a cashflow squeeze is that you'll have more options than if you wait until creditors are pounding at the door and you can't supply customers because you have no stock. Here are some ideas:

✔ If your business is profitable, you may well be able to secure a business loan or a short-term overdraft. (The loans manager is going to be much more amenable if you ask for finance before you hit troubled times.)

✔ If the profitability of your business is really marginal, you may want to revisit your whole business model, review your pricing and look at what you can do to reduce costs.

✔ If you'd planned to buy any equipment outright, think about leasing instead, so that you preserve your precious funds for working capital.

✔ If you have control over the timing of your expenses and the predicted cash shortfall is only temporary, see if you can shift some expenses to later months.

The example in Figure 10-1 is interesting in terms of cashflow requirements and the need for forward planning. You can see that although the business is profitable over the first 12 months, generating total profits of $14,995, by the end of 12 months the bank account is in the red by $44,280, and indeed peaks in the month of November with a predicted overdrawn balance of $63,283. This cashflow not only shows a business in need of additional finance to see it through the next 12 months of trading, but also a business that may want to delay expenses if at all possible in the months of October through to December.

Calculating sustainable growth

One of the paradoxical things about being in business is that if you get too successful too quickly, you can actually send yourself down the gurgler. Just in case you think I'm talking out of my ear, here's my logic.

As your business grows, you need more cash, more furniture, more computers and so on. These new assets take up cash and, in order to pay for them, you need to first make a profit and then invest this profit back into the business. However, if you grow too fast, you need new assets faster than you can make and invest your profit.

This concept of growing faster than you can make and invest your profit is often called *the limit of sustainable growth*. Without delving too much into the mathematics, as your business grows your assets have to grow with it. You can either finance these assets by re-investing profits or you can finance them by taking out a loan. For example, if you can invest enough profit to increase cash, debtors, equipment and so on by 10 per cent a year, your business can comfortably grow at 10 per cent a year.

Stay away from cash gobblers

Be canny about how you use up your cash. In particular, don't spend big lumps of cash unless you have to. For example, unless you have an enormous cash cushion behind you, don't even consider paying outright for equipment or motor vehicles that you can otherwise lease or hire purchase. Similarly, don't pay off loans in advance of your repayment schedule unless you can redraw on funds whenever you want.

Imagine that your business turns over $250,000 a year and you have around $50,000 tied up in stock, computer equipment and outstanding customer accounts. If you made a profit this year of $40,000 and you had personal drawings of $35,000, this result means you have put back only $5,000 into the business.

The $5,000 you have available to reinvest divided by $50,000 (which is the total value of cash plus debtors plus equipment) equals 10 per cent. This year's turnover of $250,000 plus 10 per cent equals $275,000, meaning this amount is the maximum you can grow your business in the next year without having to seek extra finance.

The pace at which a business can comfortably grow *is* limited: To be very successful, too quickly, runs the risk of putting such a strain on your cashflow that, unless you can secure additional finance, your business may not survive.

Building Your First Budget

You may be feeling as if you've spent days or weeks assembling financial forecasts and surely, when complete, these figures form a budget. In some ways that's true, but the difference between a budget and a Profit & Loss Projection (or a Cashflow Projection for that matter) lies in the psychology of how you use the information.

An analogy using home finances may help clarify how budgets differ from projections. Imagine you're forever having problems managing your home finances, and you struggle to meet mortgage payments or repay credit card debts. So you sit down and look at the situation. You think about your income, you list your expenses and you try to figure out how to make ends meet. When you write everything down you can see how tight things are, and so you have to adjust your figures. Maybe you plan to earn a little more income by working some overtime; maybe you plan to reduce your spending by eating out less often or cutting back holidays. This process of balancing likely money in against likely money out is effectively your personal Profit & Loss Projection.

After you complete this process, the figures in this projection become your *budget*. Income budgets in turn become goals, and expense budgets become limits. Your job is to meet these goals and live within these limits. In this way, a budget is the tool that (hopefully) enables you to fulfil your plan.

In the context of your business, a *projection* looks to the future, usually extending at least 12 months ahead. As part of creating a projection, you experiment with different scenarios (what if sales decrease or expenses rise?) until you arrive at a Profit & Loss Projection that fits with your business plan and that you think you can achieve.

From this projection, you create your *budget*, which then sets the sales goals and expense limits that you intend to live or die by. If you're in an organisation with several employees, responsibility for meeting this budget is usually shared. For example, the sales manager is responsible for meeting the sales budget, while the marketing manager is responsible for staying within the marketing budget.

Allocating budgets in detail

Sometimes you need to split budget figures into more detail in order to ensure the figures are achieved. For example, your Profit & Loss or Cashflow Projection may have just a single figure for sales, but your budget may split this figure into individual sales budgets for each salesperson, region or division. Similarly, your Profit & Loss or Cashflow Projection may have just a single figure for advertising, but your budget splits this figure into online ads, printed ads, trade shows and so on.

One of the trickier aspects of budget management can be managing the psychology of sales budgets. On the one hand, if you make sales budgets too low, your sales team may become complacent. On the other hand, if you make sales budgets too high and you don't achieve these sales, you may find that you have overspent on business expenses and your business is unprofitable. A slightly sneaky solution is to keep two sets of sales budgets: One for sales staff and another for yourself or your finance manager. The lower set of sales budgets are what you use in order to set your expense budgets for the year, and provide a good, conservative base for financial management. The higher set of budgets is what you provide to your sales team, and which hopefully acts as a motivator.

Comparing budgets against actuals

The essence of a budget is control. For example, imagine you have a set budget for travel expenses for the year. If you compare your actual spending against your budget as the year progresses, you can take action ahead of time if it seems as if you're likely to exceed this budget.

The best way to monitor budgets is by entering monthly budgets into your accounting software and then, every month (come hail, rain or shine), comparing your budgets against actual results. Figure 10-4 shows an example comparison.

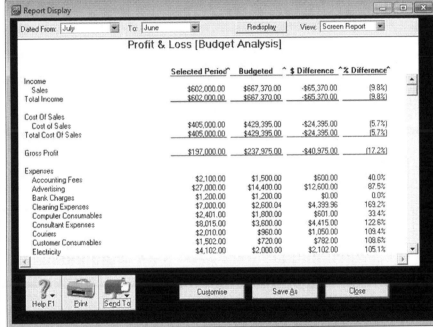

Figure 10-4: Comparing budgets against actuals is easy using accounting software.

Report Display

Dated From: July   To: June   Redisplay   View: Screen Report

Profit & Loss [Budget Analysis]

	Selected Period	Budgeted	$ Difference	% Difference
Income				
Sales	$602,000.00	$667,370.00	-$65,370.00	(9.8%)
Total Income	$602,000.00	$667,370.00	-$65,370.00	(9.8%)
Cost Of Sales				
Cost of Sales	$405,000.00	$429,395.00	-$24,395.00	(5.7%)
Total Cost Of Sales	$405,000.00	$429,395.00	-$24,395.00	(5.7%)
Gross Profit	$197,000.00	$237,975.00	-$40,975.00	(17.2%)
Expenses				
Accounting Fees	$2,100.00	$1,500.00	$600.00	40.0%
Advertising	$27,000.00	$14,400.00	$12,600.00	87.5%
Bank Charges	$1,200.00	$1,200.00	$0.00	0.0%
Cleaning Expenses	$7,000.00	$2,600.04	$4,399.96	169.2%
Computer Consumables	$2,401.00	$1,800.00	$601.00	33.4%
Consultant Expenses	$8,015.00	$3,600.00	$4,415.00	122.6%
Couriers	$2,010.00	$960.00	$1,050.00	109.4%
Customer Consumables	$1,502.00	$720.00	$782.00	108.6%
Electricity	$4,102.00	$2,000.00	$2,102.00	105.1%

Help F1   Print   Send To   Customise   Save As   Close

You can always cut more

For many years, I worked as a consultant to a family company in a sector of the manufacturing industry that was in decline (due to cheap imports). Money was tight, and I admired the way the family were tough on spending and kept expenses lean. Then disaster hit, in a triple whammy of plummeting exchange rates, an insurance claim gone wrong and a major customer who went elsewhere. Suddenly the company needed to cut expenses by 25 per cent almost overnight in order to keep trading and prevent the family members from losing their homes.

I didn't know how expenses could be cut any more, but necessity is the mother of invention. The second warehouse was closed, staff were cut, vehicles traded in, leased equipment returned and marketing budgets slashed. The result? Sales did decline (you usually can't maintain sales on a skeleton staff with little marketing) but the reduction in expenses more than compensated. The company survived.

This lesson taught me that a business, especially one that has been established for a while, almost always has areas in which it can save money. The intent and commitment just has to be there. For this reason, setting a budget and then sticking to it makes complete sense. A budget provides an imperative, a discipline, that no business with clear goals can really afford to be without.

Creating Balance Sheet Projections

One of the reports that most business planning books suggest you include in the financial section of your plan is a Balance Sheet Projection. (Wondering what this is? A *Balance Sheet* is a report that provides a snapshot of your assets and liabilities at a single point in time. A *Balance Sheet Projection* is the same thing, but provides a forecast for some time in the future as to what you think your assets and liabilities will be.)

I'm hesitant about insisting on a Balance Sheet Projection as part of a business plan simply because this report requires a high level of accounting expertise. Unless you're using business-planning software, a Balance Sheet Projection will probably require that you get help from your accountant, which could be an additional expense you can ill afford.

However, I'd be very slack if I didn't explain how this report works so that you can decide for yourself.

Figure 10-5 shows a simple Balance Sheet Projection that corresponds to the Cashflow Projection earlier in this chapter (see Figures 10-1 to 10-3). I don't really have scope in this book to cover how to construct a Balance Sheet from scratch, but the key concept of a Balance Sheet — and, indeed, of bookkeeping theory — is that Total Assets always equal the combined sum of Total Liabilities and Total Equity. Therefore, if the balance of an asset account changes, the balance of a liability or equity account must also change.

To construct a Balance Sheet Projection, you start with your Balance Sheet as it is right now. If your business hasn't started yet, chances are your Balance Sheet is a series of nil balances; if you've been trading for a while, use your accounting software to generate this report. You can see how this works in Figure 10-5, where the first column shows the actual Balance Sheet as at June 30.

Can you see how the Cashflow Projection in Figure 10-1 starts from July and runs through to June the following year? For this reason, the second column in Figure 10-5 shows the Balance Sheet Projection at this same point, 12 months into the future.

I calculated the figures for this Balance Sheet Projection by looking at the balances for key accounts (cash, debtors, inventory, equipment and loans) on the Cashflow Projection, and entering these balances in the second column of my Balance Sheet Projection. I left other accounts such as Petty Cash and Credit Cards Outstanding unchanged. After a bit of muttering and cussing, not to mention a solid hour of brain-scratching, I got my projection to balance. An hour isn't very long, I admit, but I do have a degree in accounting *and* I've done many Cashflow Projections in my time *and* this is a very simple example. (A real-life Balance Sheet is normally much more complicated.)

You may think I'm not sounding very positive, but I like to think I'm a realist. In summary, if you're wondering whether to include a Balance Sheet Projection as part of your business plan, my answer is 'yes' if you have a method by which you can create this report quickly and easily (maybe you have a financial expert in-house or you're using business planning software). Otherwise, your time is probably better spent focusing on other tasks.

Balance Sheet Projection

Current Assets	June 30 This Year	June 30 Next Year	Difference
Cash at Bank	$1,000	-$44,280	$45,280
Petty Cash	$200	$200	$0
Accounts Receivable	$25,000	$79,670	-$54,670
Inventory	$25,000	$60,605	-$35,605
Non-Current Assets			
Computer Equipment	$22,000	$22,000	$0
Specialist Equipment		$54,000	-$54,000
Tools	$12,050	$12,050	$0
TOTAL ASSETS	**$85,250**	**$184,245**	**-$98,995**
Current Liabilities			
Accounts Payable	$0	$0	$0
Credit Card Outstanding	$3,200	$3,200	$0
Employee Deductions Owing	$5,500	$5,500	$0
Non-Current Liabilities			
Bank Loans	$0	$90,000	-$90,000
TOTAL LIABILITIES	**$8,700**	**$98,700**	**-$90,000**
Current Year Profits (after Tax)	$0	$8,995	-$8,995
Retained Profits	$76,550	$76,550	$0
TOTAL EQUITY	**$76,550**	**$85,545**	**-$8,995**
ASSETS LESS LIABILITIES	**$76,550**	**$85,545**	**-$8,995**

Figure 10-5:
Creating
a Balance
Sheet
Projection.

Part IV
Transforming Your Idea into Reality

Five Qualities Your Goals Must Have

In order for a goal to count as a goal, it must be SMART:

- ✔ **Specific:** When talking about a goal, are you being really precise about what you hope to achieve?

- ✔ **Measurable:** Can you measure this goal in some way? (Dollars sold, units sold, new customers gained, email enquiries received, hits on the website.)

- ✔ **Achievable:** Can you reasonably achieve this goal, or are you talking about Mission Impossible? Setting goals is pointless unless you can reasonably achieve them.

- ✔ **Realistic:** Even if a goal is potentially achievable, is it realistic? Do you definitely have enough time and enough funds to ensure the goal can be met?

- ✔ **Time specific:** Any goal needs a time frame. By when do you plan to reach this goal?

Read more about the psychology of setting goals (and achieving them) at
www.dummies.com/extras/creatingbusinessplan.

In this part . . .

- ✔ Discover how to build a business that thrives independently of you. Develop a people plan and get help to expand your business.

- ✔ Learn how to create a marketing plan that helps you to grow sales and attract the customers you want.

- ✔ Don't be on the back foot. Instead, find out how to stay one step ahead of change, grabbing opportunities before they pass you by.

- ✔ Catch that poisoned arrow before it hits your Achilles heel. Take pre-emptive action to guard against your weaknesses, and plan wisely so that you can minimise risk and protect your personal assets.

- ✔ Present a well-structured polished business plan that can't fail to impress yourself, your colleagues and potential investors.

Chapter 11

Separating Yourself from Your Business

In This Chapter

▶ Working out where you're headed: Cottage industry or multi-million dollar enterprise?

▶ Playing with the different roles needed to make a business work

▶ Creating a business that's independent from you

▶ Understanding that some businesses are harder to grow than others

▶ Building the people part of your business plan

Many years ago, I did some consulting work for a guy who'd started his own industrial welding business. The reporting systems for this business were a complete nightmare. As I trawled through the accounts, trying to make sense of it all, my client looked across the room at me and announced, in a somewhat apologetic tone, 'You know something? I'm a really good welder.'

For me, this brief interchange summarises the dilemma many business owners face. People start out in their business doing what they're good at, and what they love to do (whether this is welding, performing music or face-painting at kids' parties). But before long, they find they spend more and more time doing stuff they're not naturally good at, such as bookkeeping, looking through contracts, hiring employees or managing websites. Sometimes this extra work becomes such a burden that the joy of being in business is lost. Or sometimes the business owner rises to the challenge, thriving on these extra demands and enjoying the reprieve from day-to-day tasks.

In this chapter, I explore the questions of what *you* want to achieve with your business. Do you plan to take on employees and grow your business? Do you have a unique concept that means you could potentially sell your business for a substantial profit in five or ten years' time? Or are you happy tinkering away in your home office, earning a modest income with little stress and few demands?

No answer is right, no answer is wrong. However, the process of creating a business plan provides an ideal opportunity for you to decide the direction in which you wish to head.

Deciding What Path You Want to Take

Generally, business-planning books assume that you want to grow your business, take on employees, maybe even develop a franchise or expand internationally. (After all, the very expression 'business planning' implies an intention to expand and develop.)

However, in the first part of this chapter, I want to spend a bit of time exploring whether you feel this desire for expansion. Maybe you're quite content pursuing a small home-based part-time business, or maybe you don't want the stress of taking on employees.

Taking a step back and thinking of all the self-employed people I know or have worked with, I can see that most people follow one out of three different paths (or occasionally all three paths, but one after the other):

- A simple owner-operated business with no employees.
- A business where the owner focuses on providing the service but employs others to help run administrative functions of the business.
- A business built by the owner that then has a life of its own, where employees provide the services or manufacture products and the owner is in a management role. Ultimately, the owner may even seek to create a franchise.

The question you need to answer is which path do you want to take? Even though most business books imply that if you're serious about being in business, the third path is the only way forward, this isn't necessarily true. Small owner-operated businesses may have less opportunity for profit, but profit is only one of the many motivators for being in business.

Doing the thing you love to do

A starting point for many small businesses is that a person starts a business doing the thing that they have experience doing, or possibly the thing that they've just completed studying. So the person who was working as a high-school teacher starts a business tutoring high-school students, the physiotherapist who was working at her local hospital opens her own practice, or the newly qualified chef opens a restaurant.

The upside of running a business in this way is that you get to do what you love to do, and usually what you're good at. You also have the perks of self-employment (choosing your own hours, possibly charging more for your services and being your own boss).

The downside of being a solo owner-operator is often long hours, with no income when you're on holidays or if you're sick. The experience of being cleaner, shop assistant, bookkeeper, marketing manager and finance manager all within the course of a single day can be relentless, and you may end up feeling that you're a jack-of-all-trades but a master of none. Your business is utterly dependent on you; if you don't turn up, you don't get paid. In addition, the amount of money you can make from your business is always limited by the number of hours you're able to work.

Some people would argue that the kind of work involved with an owner-operator business, where it's just you and you do your own thing, defeats the purpose of going into business. They would argue that unless you want to conceive of a business that has a life of its own beyond yourself, you're better just to keep working for someone else. Otherwise, you're not really creating a business; rather, you're creating a job with a pile of overheads.

I disagree. Although I acknowledge that this small-scale kind of operation has its drawbacks, I've lived in a regional area and been self-employed for too long to be that naïve. Sometimes no jobs are available and the only option is to be self-employed. Sometimes you may have such substantial family commitments that your business becomes a relatively peripheral part of your life, and the income it generates is just a bonus, not the core. Sometimes the way you generate income is so personal, so idiosyncratic (maybe you're an artist, a faith healer or an inventor) that you can't conceive of a way that this business can be grown beyond yourself. All of these reasons are perfectly valid reasons for being in business, yet staying small.

Even though you may have perfectly valid reasons for staying small, if you're currently self-employed and you have no employees — or you're planning to start a new business with this structure — do pause to consider what your options might be. Conceiving a way to run your business so that it can operate without you can be challenging, but is the only way forward if you want to generate profits that aren't directly dependent on the hours that you work.

Getting help and delegating what you can

If you're not content to be an owner-operator doing everything yourself, the first and most natural stage of expansion is usually to employ some assistance. Maybe you hire a bookkeeper, employ a casual labourer, or get assistance with marketing or website design.

Many experts and professionals end up with this kind of model. For example, our local orthodontist hires several employees (two receptionists, a dental hygienist and an office manager) but he is the only guy doing the actual work (you know, the multi-colour braces and general teenage torture). Sure, he could probably hire another orthodontist to work for him, but he has a great deal invested in his reputation and, for whatever reason, feels he can't trust another person to provide the same quality of service.

In a way, the part of my business income that I generate writing books is similar. I employ a bookkeeper and office admin person, and occasionally get help researching topics, but at the end of day (and I confess that it's truly the end of the day as I write this), the only ones left standing are me and my cute little silver laptop.

This way of working is what many people choose. You get to do the thing you love and you can choose your own hours, be your own boss and usually make a decent living. And, unlike single owner-operators who do everything themselves, you can hire others to help with day-to-day business operations, so that you can focus on doing the thing that you're good at.

The downside, of course, is that you're still 'it' as far as the business is concerned. You are your business, and your business is you. Your income is always limited by the number of hours you're able to work, and if you're on holiday or sick, the business doesn't generate income.

If your business has this kind of structure, you may find it hard to imagine how you can expand your business so that employees could provide the same services as you currently do. However, nobody is indispensable, and no matter how smart or talented you are, chances are someone's out there who can do all the things you do.

One of the tricks to making the leap to hiring others to provide the services you currently provide is to imagine a little person is sitting on your shoulder, watching everything you do and documenting your activities in a 'how-to manual'. This is the first step towards separating yourself from your business, so that you can describe to others the attitudes, skills and standards that you expect. (For more on this topic, see the section 'Documenting and building systems', later in this chapter.)

Building a business that's separate from you

The third path that you can take (refer to the preceding sections for an outline of the other two paths) is to create a business where employees are the ones providing your service or manufacturing your products. If you look around you, most medium-sized businesses fall into this category. For example:

- Our local plumbing company has a team of plumbers, each with their own van and apprentice, providing plumbing services. The owner occasionally helps out on tricky jobs, but mostly focuses on management and marketing.

- The place where my son learns piano is a music school, with lots of different tutors teaching different instruments. The owners teach sometimes, but other teachers run most of the classes.

- My neighbour runs a small chain of three cafes. He rarely cooks or serves tables any more, but focuses on the finances and management.

- A girlfriend of mine has a business selling baby sleeping bags. She still does the design and marketing, but she has moved production offshore and uses a distributor for sales.

Can you see that for each of these examples, the business owners have made a leap in how they think of their businesses? The plumber is now the manager of a plumbing services company; the music tutors started their own music school; the barista opened a chain of cafes; the seamstress runs a manufacturing company. In all of these examples, the owner no longer unblocks pipes, teaches violin, serves coffee or stitches fabric. In return, the potential for each of these businesses is that the owners can have more freedom and earn more money than they otherwise would have done.

For me, this transition from owner to entrepreneur is really exciting. Freedom from the shackles of the daily grind provides an opportunity to do the other things in life that have only been dreams up until now.

If you haven't made this transition, and your business is still dependent on you for pretty much every cent of income, my question to you is this: Have you ever consciously made the decision *not* to be entrepreneurial? Or have you never really let yourself imagine how you could do things differently?

If not, do try to give the visionary in you some room to breathe. Spend time thinking about how you can grow your business and create something that has a life of its own.

In Chapter 10, I make a distinction between budgets and Profit & Loss Projection reports, explaining that a budget sets sales goals and spending limits that you must try to stick to, whereas a Profit & Loss Projection answers the 'what if' questions, and enables you to model different scenarios. Even if you're just starting out in business, I suggest you spend some time experimenting with what your Profit & Loss Projection might look like in a few years' time, if you were to have a team of employees and possibly multiple locations or a much-increased product range.

Creating a way of doing business

The queen diva of all business models is, of course, the franchise. A *franchise* is where you figure out such a neat and unique way of doing business that this concept itself becomes something you can sell. A franchise embodies the whole way you do business, including buying policies, logos, marketing techniques, pricing, uniforms and more. Table 11-1 outlines various business models, and how specific owner-operator businesses could move into the franchise or international model.

Note: I'm not talking about you purchasing a franchise here; rather, I'm talking about you building such a successful way of doing business that you create your own franchise.

Table 11-1	Moving from a Small Business to a Big Business	
Owner-Operator	*Business with Employees*	*Franchise/International Model*
Yoga teacher	Yoga school	Patented method of teaching and streaming online yoga classes
Plumber	Plumbing business with a team of ten employees	National plumbing franchise
eBay book sales	eBay business with three employees	eBay model for buying and selling books
A farmer selling homemade chilli sauce and pickles	A chilli sauce company with a recognised brand and national distribution	A method of manufacturing and distributing sauces/pickles that can be replicated worldwide
A corner cafe in the local town	A couple of cafes with several employees	A franchise restaurant chain
A fashion blogger selling clothes online	An online clothing store with 50 brands and national distribution	An innovative system (including software) for selling clothes online that can be replicated in other countries
Your business	.... (fill in the blanks)	.... (fill in the blanks)

Creating your own franchise takes the requirement that you separate yourself from your business to a whole new level. To use the example of the plumbing company I refer to in the preceding section: When the owners (a husband-and-wife team) employed a team of plumbers to do the plumbing work, they entrusted others to provide the core service of the business on their behalf and, to do this, they had to provide a certain level of supervision and training. However, what if this plumbing company does really well and the owners decide to create a franchise? At this point, the owners need to analyse what it is that makes their business different. They need to quantify these differences and create systems so that others can copy these differences.

The upside of expanding to become a franchise is the opportunity to make very healthy profits. In many ways, a franchise is the ultimate realisation of the entrepreneur's dream.

Wearing Different Hats

Have you heard of a book called *The E-Myth* or *The E-Myth Revisited* (written by Michael Gerber and published by HarperBusiness)? This book has sold over 3 million copies, and the terminology that Gerber uses to describe the roles owners play in their businesses has become almost standard in some circles.

Gerber likes to describe the roles of a business owner as being technician, manager or entrepreneur. I may not describe these roles here exactly as Gerber might, but here's the general idea:

- **Technician:** These are people who work in their business, not on their business — the plumber who unblocks drains, the cafe owner who serves coffee, or the freelance consultant who goes out to meet clients.

- **Manager:** A manager is someone who organises the day-to-day running of a business, ordering stock, looking at profit margins, paying the bills and replying to customers.

- **Entrepreneur:** An entrepreneur is the visionary, the person who's thinking of the business as a thing that's separate to the service it provides or the product it sells, and who is looking for ways to build the business and expand.

I really like this way of thinking of the roles in a business, because it goes a long way to explaining that feeling I've felt so often as a business owner, of having all these balls in the air that I have to juggle. The idea is that if it's just you in your business (which it is for most people when they start out), you need to balance out these roles. The idea sounds simple, but is tricky to do.

These roles correspond to some degree with what I talk about earlier in this chapter. Someone who is happiest being a 'technician' often ends up not expanding their business, and instead typically provides services or makes products themselves (refer to 'Doing the thing you love to do' earlier in this chapter). A person whose 'manager' side wins out typically ends up organising others. This person is content to get employees to assist in running the business and is good at monitoring costs and ensuring efficient operations (refer to 'Getting help and delegating what you can'). The 'entrepreneur' personality is the one who's always looking for the winning idea, and is keenest to create a business with a life of its own (refer to 'Building a business that's separate from you' or 'Creating a way of doing business').

If your business is still pretty small, letting any one of the three roles of technician, manager or entrepreneur dominate at the expense of the others can be a problem. The technician will probably fail to grow the business, the manager may well fail to look to the future and plan for change, and the entrepreneur, if left to his or her own devices, may burn through a whole load of money very fast pursuing one idea after another.

What I think is so clever about the way Gerber identifies these roles is that you can apply this thinking to yourself and your own business. For example:

✔ Most people find that the technician role (doing the thing that they're good at, such as fixing pipes, teaching music or making a mean espresso coffee) feels comfortable and safe.

✔ The role of manager fits well with some people but not with others (many businesspeople hate having to think about money, tax, legals, schedules and so on, but others are relatively okay with this role).

✔ The role of entrepreneur is the role that comes hardest to most people. If you're inherently a bit conservative (as I confess to being myself), what happens is whenever the entrepreneur voice pipes up with a good idea, the conservative manager voice calls out 'Oh no, that's way too scary'. The entrepreneur and manager are so busy tussling away that the only person left to do anything is the technician, who continues to get on with the job. And then nothing changes.

The way to move on from this situation, and give all three roles a part to play, is to build a business that has a life of its own. Which just happens to be the next topic in this chapter ...

Building a Business with a Life of its Own

In the preceding sections in this chapter, I talk about why creating a business with a life of its own is generally the best way to gain more freedom and flexibility, and hopefully more profits to boot. I also talk about the different roles or 'hats' people typically wear in business, and how important it is to balance these roles, especially when you're just getting started and you have only you in the business.

However, the transition to creating a business with its own identity, separate from you, isn't always easy. In the following sections, I provide some guidelines as to how you may be able to make this happen.

Defining your difference

The first step in giving your business some of its own life force is to be clear about what it is that makes you different. I spend a heap of time deliberating on this very topic back in Chapter 2, so I won't repeat myself here. Suffice to say that you must identify what makes your business different, and this difference must relate to the identity of your business, and not you personally.

Some examples may help to set this in context:

- ✔ A dry-cleaning company uses alternative chemical processing, arguably better for the environment and for those with sensitive skin.
- ✔ An online clothes store offers multiple views of each item of clothing, and provides recommendations as to the body types each garment is best suited for.
- ✔ A mechanic workshop offers a free home drop-off and pick-up service, and routinely details all vehicles as part of any service or repair work.

None of the preceding ideas are particularly revolutionary but, if executed well and combined with a cohesive marketing strategy and company commitment, they have the potential to make these businesses stand apart from others.

I find that business owners can be very vague regarding what it is that makes their business successful, especially with smaller businesses where the owner is still very much hands-on. To use the mechanic workshop example from the preceding list, this mechanic may offer free home drop-offs and detailing, but is this really the reason for the workshop's success? Or is it that the head mechanic is such a lovely guy that customers instantly warm to him? Or that this workshop is the only repair service within a 10-kilometre radius?

Without an understanding of what makes this business successful, the owner is vulnerable. If the drawcard is the gorgeous mechanic, what might happen to the business if he leaves? If the lack of competition in a

10-kilometre radius is the reason for steady business, what might happen if another mechanic opens up shop nearby?

You can try to deduce the reasons for your success using a few techniques:

- ✔ If your business operates in more than one location, experiment by trialling specific services or marketing techniques in one location but not the other, and see what happens.

- ✔ Return to the competitive analysis you did in Chapter 3 (or if you haven't already done it, do it now). This objective comparative process is a good way to get a sense of why your customers come to you.

- ✔ Ask your customers why they love you! (And if they say it's because of your good-looking head mechanic, sigh long and loud.) You can ask customers face to face, run surveys, put up quick questions on Facebook, or do whatever fits your customer base best.

- ✔ Try opening a new location and trying to replicate your success from the first location. If the new location performs differently, try to get to the bottom of why.

- ✔ If you think that part of your success is due to something relatively simple (I think of my local butcher who, after each interaction, looks at me with a smile and says 'Can I get you anything else today?' — even if a queue of people is waiting behind me), then try measuring sales when you employ this technique or strategy for a week, and compare sales to another week where you don't do this.

If you can figure out why you're successful, and measure how much difference this strategy, product or technique makes to your business, you're well on the way to being able to replicate your success and grow your business.

Documenting and building systems

One of the things that a franchise offers, in contrast to other businesses of a similar type, is consistency. As my husband likes to say in a satisfied voice regarding the coffee he buys from a certain fast-food chain, 'this bunch make the best worst coffee in the world'. In other words, he knows the coffee is going to be average, he knows it won't be that hot, but still it hits the spot and it's the same every time, wherever we are in the country.

This consistency is one of the secrets to expanding a business beyond one location, building a brand or even preparing your business to become a franchise in its own right. Take the example of my aunt, who ran a guesthouse in the wilds of northern Scotland for 30 years or more. She was a wonderful hostess, but occasionally she'd be away for the weekend or even for a week or two. How could she guarantee that her guests would get exactly the same quality of experience when she was away as when she was there?

A happy customer may share the love with one or two people, but unhappy customers share their disgruntlement with ten. If you can get rid of the hit-and-miss element that plagues so many businesses, positive word-of-mouth recommendations may be almost all the marketing you need.

So how do you guarantee consistency, particularly as your business grows and you're not around to serve each customer or supervise each employee? The answer is in procedures and documentation. First, you figure out what it is that your business does well (which I refer to in the preceding section); next, you articulate this difference in words in a way that employees can follow.

Here are some examples of how to provide a consistent experience for customers:

- ✔ **Checklists:** For any complex activities, where employees need to fulfil several tasks in a specific sequence, create a checklist. For example, if your business is such that a customer order can be quite complex (maybe you need to check quantities, availability, delivery dates, payment methods and more), a checklist ensures nothing gets forgotten.

- ✔ **Complaints procedures:** Do you know that one of the ways to make customers happiest is to do everything you can to fix something when they complain? However, the gentle art of responding well to a grumpy customer isn't something that comes naturally to most people, and so procedures for dealing with complaints are essential.

- ✔ **Customer service procedures:** Ideally, you need a procedure for any customer interaction that happens on a regular basis, whether this be a customer enquiry, order or sale.

- ✔ **Manufacturing procedures:** If you're a manufacturer, even if you're operating on a relatively small scale making things to sell locally or at markets, the quality of your product needs to be the same each time. Sounds simple, but imagine you're making homemade jams, and the quality of produce available varies according to the time of year. In this scenario, you may need to limit production to certain times of year in order to guarantee consistency.

  Similarly, if you've been manufacturing products yourself and you're now ready to delegate this process, you need to document exactly what you do, using precise quantities, times, production methods and so on.

- ✔ **Phone scripts and email templates:** I can feel you wincing a little here, as you wonder if you're really so dictatorial that you can bear writing out scripts for employees to follow when they answer the phone, or templates for when they reply to emails. Remember two things, however: Firstly, what you're trying to achieve is consistency for the customer; secondly, if you have spent time figuring out the ingredients that have made your business successful and you know that how you answer the phone or reply to emails is part of this success, then, of course, you want to be able to repeat this formula, time and time again.

✔ **Presentation:** As someone who hates uniform in almost any shape or form, I squirm a little as I write this. But businesses love uniforms for the reason that they provide consistency for the customer and reinforce the company's image. Even something as simple as a polo shirt with your company logo monogrammed on the front can make a difference to how customers perceive you.

✔ **Rates and pricing:** Standardised rates and pricing are a must. So if you tend to quote on a somewhat intuitive basis for jobs, you need to spend time figuring out a method for pricing and stick to that instead.

If you're still small and you're thinking about how to expand your business, one great source of inspiration (if available) is to look at franchises that offer a similar service or product to your own. For example, if you're starting a lawn mowing business, take a look at how the lawn mowing franchises approach their branding, marketing and customer service. If you're starting a bookkeeping business, look at the bookkeeping franchises and how they organise their pricing and services. I'm not suggesting you steal intellectual property here or that you try to copy the systems of a franchise without paying to belong — more that you take a look at the general approach of this franchise and use this as inspiration. (Or, of course, you may even consider becoming a franchisee.)

Setting goals for you and your business

I've worked as a business consultant for more than ten years now, and I've noticed a certain quality in the handful of very successful businesspeople I've encountered during this time. Each of these people have had a very specific goal in mind, and they've been possessed by an inner drive to meet this goal.

Interestingly enough, these goals have been ultimately personal, rather than business-orientated, such as the desire to be able to retire by the age of 50 on a guaranteed income for life, or the dream to be able to buy a house for each one of the children, or to be able to work only 20 hours a week and still be financially secure.

If you're trying to create a business that grows and is ultimately independent of you, ask yourself what you want to achieve from this growth. Do you have a specific financial goal or a certain time frame? If not, spend some time thinking what this goal might be, and then building your business plan around this goal.

Timothy Ferriss (author of *The 4-Hour Workweek*, published by Crown) has interesting perspectives on long-term goal setting. One of his appealing arguments is that someone who works 8 hours a week and earns $50,000 a year is actually much richer than someone who works 60 hours a week and earns $200,000 a year. He argues that income is relative, and profit not the only performance measure.

While setting goals is an important part of business success, just wanting to be a millionaire isn't enough. You need to ensure that your business has some kind of competitive edge or winning strategy (refer to Chapters 2 and 3 for more on this topic) and you need to understand how to build on this strategy with good systems. Unless you have these elements in place, ambitious plans to open a new shop every six months or become an internationally recognised brand are just pie-in-the-sky.

Planning for a graceful exit

One of the best ways to get yourself into the mindset of thinking of your business as independent from you is to imagine selling it.

Always try to have an exit plan simmering away, even if you don't plan to sell any time in the immediate future. Ask yourself the following questions: If I were to sell this business today, what could I get for it? Can this business run independently of me? What assets or business systems do I have to sell? How can I maximise the price I can get for this business?

Appreciating the Limitations of Your Business

In the preceding sections in this chapter, I talk about the idea of creating a business that has a life of its own, separate from you. I also mention early in this chapter that not everyone wants to go down this path, and I talk about the pros and cons of operating your business in different ways.

When thinking on these topics, you also have to keep in mind that some businesses are much harder than others to expand. Here are some of the kinds of businesses that can be hard to grow, along with why:

> ✓ **Businesses limited by physical constraints or high start-up costs that require substantial capital:** Farmers are an obvious example here, limited by the amount of land they have, and lacking capital to expand. Other examples could be a professional truck driver limited by the high

capital cost of additional trucks, or the capacity of a guesthouse owner to expand due to the high cost of purchasing real estate.

- ✔ **Businesses based on the artistic skills of the owner:** Examples include a classical pianist performing around the country, a stand-up comedian or a theatre producer. Sure, you could team up with other artists in a similar field, but the actual core of what you do (such as playing virtuosic piano) is almost impossible to delegate.

- ✔ **Businesses making products that require very specific skills, particularly those of an artistic nature:** For example, glass blowing, fine-art painting and pottery. Custom manufacturing of one-off goods also falls into this category, where the craftsperson (such as a cabinet-maker) builds a reputation that is very much linked to that person as an individual, rather than to the business.

- ✔ **Businesses with expert services where the service provided is very much associated with the individual providing the service:** Think specialist medical professionals (acupuncturist, paediatrician, orthodontist) or specialist consultants (business mentors, human resources consultants).

- ✔ **Businesses servicing a rural location where the owner provides the services and expansion involves too much travel:** Our local horse dentist (yes, there is such a thing as a horse dentist!) springs to mind.

The more entrepreneurial personalities may be reading the preceding list thinking that I'm lacking imagination, and that the businesses in the list could be expanded in plenty of ways. The artist could commercialise her images as cushions, postcards or wallpaper; the horse dentist could set up an online consultancy; the cabinet-maker could spend oodles on high-end marketing and build up an international reputation. In my defence, I'm not saying that these businesses are impossible to grow — I'm just saying they're harder to grow than others. (And besides, the artist may not want to design wallpaper, and online horse dentistry may prove massively impractical.)

If your business falls into one of the categories outlined in the preceding list and you're having problems imagining how you separate yourself from your business, hop onto the internet and search worldwide for the product you sell or the service you provide. Look for examples of others similar to you and how they have grown their business to be something bigger.

Although businesses with expert services can be hard to expand, for those who manage to do so and build a network of professionals who provide a high consistency of service, the rewards can be substantial.

Planning for People

If you're creating a written business plan (and given the title of this book I guess that many of you are) and have read the earlier sections in this chapter, you may be wondering how this chapter relates to what you include in your plan.

In truth, what I've written in this chapter up until this point is more about creating a mindset for your business, setting goals for what you want to achieve, and planning for how you will employ others to help you realise these goals. In terms of your plan, the main information you need to include is how you plan to structure your business, what your ultimate goal is, who you have on your team, the skills that your team have, and who is going to do what.

Planning for help

Even if you're a solo owner-operator, or you have a single business partner, think about the skills involved in running your business and the different roles involved. If more than one of you is in the business, divvy up these roles and be clear about who does what; if you're by yourself, have a think about your areas of weakness, and where it may be best to seek help (this help may be from a casual employee, a part-timer, a consultant or an outside professional).

For each of the tasks in Table 11-2, detail the skills required and whether you plan to do this task yourself, your business partner plans to do it, or you plan to use an employee or an outside professional.

If you're not much of a typist, go to www.dummies.com/go/creatingbusinessplan to download the Task Allocation template shown in Table 11-2.

You probably won't choose to put a table in this format in your business plan. Instead, I suggest that your plan simply includes a descriptive section about the people involved in the business and who's responsible for doing what. For each key person, write a short description of that person's role, including relevant work experience and qualifications.

If your plan is going to be read by outsiders (that is, the plan isn't just for your own use) don't hesitate to blow your own trumpet (or your employees' trumpets for that matter) to emphasise the skills and qualifications that you have.

Table 11-2	Planning for Task Allocation	
Task	*Skills/Qualifications Required*	*Who Will Do This in Your Business?*
Accountancy and tax		
Administration/Secretarial		
Bookkeeping		
Human resources		
Legal		
Marketing		

The ability to seek out the best possible people and glue them on is a common attribute I've observed in successful businesspeople. Don't worry if you can't hire someone as an employee; a day a week or a day a month consulting may be all that you require. For example, if you need help with your bookkeeping, going hunting for a bookkeeper with excellent qualifications and a great reputation is infinitely better than employing your sister's daughter or your best friend's aunty (unless that person also comes with excellent qualifications and a great reputation).

Deciding whether to make someone an employee, or not

One of the practical considerations when getting help is whether to use contractors or professionals, casual employees or permanent employees. Here are some things to bear in mind:

- **Cheaper rates:** An employee is generally cheaper on an hourly basis than a contractor. However, when comparing rates, ensure that you include all relevant employee on-costs (see the following section to find out more).

- **Flexibility during quiet times:** If your business is seasonal or experiences highs and lows in demand, permanent employees can prove expensive because you have to pay them all year round, regardless of requirements. In this scenario, casual employees or contractors are a better bet.

✔ **Reliability and commitment:** If you find someone who has just the skills that you're looking for and you feel that this person would be a real asset for your business, rusting this person on by offering a permanent job, if you can afford to do so, is going to be preferable to hiring this person as a contractor.

✔ **Securing skills for your business:** If your business requires very specific skills and these skills are in high demand, putting a skilled person on the payroll (rather than hiring a contractor) means that this person cannot also work for your competition.

Calculating the costs of labour

Employee wages are likely to make up a large percentage of your ongoing expenses. Yet one thing that I've found, from years of working with clients, is that most business owners don't take the time to calculate the true cost of labour expenses.

Some of the direct costs (depending on where you are in the world) include health insurance, workers compensation insurance and superannuation/retirement/pension payments. Indirect costs include things such as uniforms or providing computers, mobile phones and vehicles. In addition, while you may have a feel for how many hours a week an employee works, do you know how many hours this employee really works in practice, after allowing for holiday leave, sick leave, training leave, public holidays and so on?

Figure 11-1 shows my calculations regarding the true cost of labour for a shop assistant. In this example, can you see how if I pay this assistant $20/hour, the true hourly cost (when averaged over time) works out at $27.15/hour?

To do your own calculations similar to those shown in Figure 11-1, go to www.dummies.com/go/creatingbusinessplan and look for the Calculating the True Cost of Labour template relevant to you. (You can find different templates for the UK, US, Canada and Australia, because each country has slightly different workplace regulations.)

An important part of the business planning process is for you to be right across the minimum pay and the statutory obligations of being an employer. See Chapter 14 for more about managing risk and complying with regulations.

The True Cost of Labour

Edit the cells shaded in blue to get an indication of the true hourly cost of labour for your business

			Hourly rate			
			$ 15	$ 20	$ 25	$ 30
LEAVE						
Annual leave	20 days per year	7.69%	$ 1.15	$ 1.54	$ 1.92	$ 2.31
Leave Loading	17.5% per cent of hols	1.35%	$ 0.20	$ 0.27	$ 0.34	$ 0.40
Sick leave	10 days per year	3.85%	$ 0.58	$ 0.77	$ 0.96	$ 1.15
Public holidays	10 days per year	3.85%	$ 0.58	$ 0.77	$ 0.96	$ 1.15
Other types of leave	2 days per year	0.77%	$ 0.12	$ 0.15	$ 0.19	$ 0.23
EXPENSES						
Superannuation	9.25 per cent	9.25%	$ 1.39	$ 1.85	$ 2.31	$ 2.78
Workers compensation	4 per cent	4.00%	$ 0.01	$ 0.01	$ 0.01	$ 0.02
Payroll tax (if applicable)	6 per cent	6.00%	$ 0.90	$ 1.20	$ 1.50	$ 1.80
OTHER						
Paid breaks	10 minutes per day	2.19%	$ 0.33	$ 0.44	$ 0.55	$ 0.66
Training cost	2 days per year	0.77%	$ 0.12	$ 0.15	$ 0.19	$ 0.23
True Hourly Cost			$ 20.36	$ 27.15	$ 33.94	$ 40.73

Figure 11-1: Calculating the true cost of labour is an important part of the business planning process.

Keep hold of those reins

One of the things that you may experience when you hire your first employees is a feeling of relief so strong that you declare, 'Here you are. I trust you. Please feel free to organise me, my business and my life.'

Don't kid yourself that this letting go is you being a hands-off manager or a good delegator. Handing over the reins to someone else in this way is bound to end in tears: If an employee takes over and does everything well, you'll be left with a huge hole when that employee leaves and your business will suffer; if the employee fails to perform, you've just given that employee the chance to do a great deal of damage.

Instead, your responsibility is to delegate, but delegate using clear instructions and good systems. (I talk about creating systems in 'Building a Business with a Life of its Own', earlier in this chapter.) You never want an employee to become indispensable because, at that point, you have built a business that may not be dependent on you, but that sure as anything is dependent on someone else.

Chapter 12

Developing a Strong Marketing Plan

In This Chapter

▶ Thinking about the structure of your marketing plan

▶ Looking at who your customers are, and the kind of customer you want for the future

▶ Using your competitor analysis and crafting a positioning statement

▶ Finetuning sales goals and objectives

▶ Being creative about ways to support your sales goals

▶ Incorporating a feedback loop to keep yourself honest

*B*y its very nature, marketing is a creative process, usually driven more by impulse and instinct than by facts and figures. For this reason, I find that creating a structured marketing plan is every bit as important as creating a detailed financial plan.

In this chapter, I talk about the elements that make up a marketing plan, and look at the important groundwork in regards to defining your target market and understanding who your customers really are. What is it that you're really selling and who do you want to sell this to? How do you set realistic sales targets and put strategies in place to make sure these targets are met? This chapter helps you work through these aspects.

With any marketing plan, you also need an element of review. Reviewing and measuring the results of your efforts provides the perfect counterweight for the sometimes intuitive nature of marketing, and enables you to be objective about what's working and what's not.

Laying Down the Elements of Your Plan

If you browse through a dozen business books, you're likely to find a dozen different formats for marketing plans. Most of these formats have their merits, but here are the elements of a format I find work just fine:

- ✔ **Introduction:** Start with an engaging introduction that explains who you are, what you're selling, what kind of brand you're trying to build and your unique selling proposition. (I talk about these topics in the following section.)

- ✔ **Target market:** Who are you selling to? Is your typical customer young or old, from the city, or from the country? Later in this chapter, the 'Defining Your Target Market' section explains how to research this information.

- ✔ **Competitor analysis:** In this part of your marketing plan, you describe who your competitors are, and how you compare. Chapter 3 focuses on competitor analysis, but in this chapter (skip ahead to 'Summarising Your Competitor Analysis') I talk about condensing this information for the purposes of your business plan.

- ✔ **Sales targets:** How much are you going to sell, who are you going to sell to, and what is your pricing policy? See 'Setting Sales Targets' for details.

- ✔ **Sales strategies:** What strategies do you intend to put in place to support your sales targets? Later in this chapter, 'Creating Strategies to Support Your Targets' outlines possible tactics.

- ✔ **Customer service:** A marketing plan isn't complete without an overview of how you plan to provide the best possible customer service. See 'Planning for Customer Service', later in this chapter, to find out more.

- ✔ **Review process:** The last section of this chapter, 'Keeping Yourself Honest', explains how to monitor your sales results, tweaking targets and strategies if necessary.

Writing an eloquent introduction

In Chapter 2, I suggest that you start your business plan with a strategic advantage statement that explains how your product or service benefits your customers and what differentiates your business from its competitors. As I explain in Chapter 2, this strategic advantage could be many things, including having lower costs, a brilliant new idea, specialist skills, or a right to use certain intellectual property.

I reckon it works well if you start your marketing plan by reiterating this information — even if you choose to use different phrasing — so that you can reinforce what it is that you're trying to sell. Each business is different, but your strategic advantage usually forms the basis of the core messages that you need to convey to customers.

However, when you're selling this advantage to customers, and trying to encapsulate it in a few words, this advantage becomes your *USP* — your Unique Selling Point.

 If you're struggling to express your unique selling point in a few, punchy words, I suggest you go online and search for businesses similar to your own. For example, maybe you offer a piano-tuning service. Search for similar businesses all around the world and check out their marketing slogans: 'We're in tune with you', 'Music to your ears', 'Stay sweet with the high notes'. I'm not suggesting you pinch someone else's selling point, but you can use it for inspiration.

In Table 12-1, I list some different kinds of businesses, along with their strategic advantages and the USPs they could use to reach customers.

Table 12-1	Small Business Unique Selling Points (USPs)	
Type of Business	**Strategic Advantage**	**USP**
App development	Strong industry connections in tourism	'Specialising in mobile solutions for tourism professionals'
Carpenter	Specialist training in CAD software as well as a partner trained in interior design	'Free design and quote service'
Car spare parts	Strategic alliance with local courier service	'Delivery all suburbs'
Musician	Phenomenal ability to memorise songs and lyrics	'Repertoire of over 900 songs from the seventies'
Naturopath	Qualifications in both counselling and naturopathy	'A holistic service for body and mind'
Remainder books online	Connection with local publishers meaning very low cost of purchase, thereby subsidising freight	'Free freight'
Secretarial service	Strong working relationship with low-cost offshore virtual assistant service	'Same day service — guaranteed'
Your business . . . (fill in the blanks)	*Your strategic advantage . . .* (fill in the blanks)	*Your USP . . .* (fill in the blanks)

The beauty of developing your own USP is that you can hone in on the thing that makes you different from your competitors, which is an infinitely better approach than trying to be all things to all people. Have a think about what you want your USP to be (or what it already is) and how you can best exploit this in your overall marketing.

Building a brand that people want

I imagine that you have a pretty clear image of yourself and how you want the outside world to perceive you. You may see yourself as anything from a pearls and twin-set kind of gal to a double-income-no-kids executive, or from a freestyle hippy to a very straightforward farming bloke.

Your business needs to have an image in just the same way that you do. With a certain amount of forethought and awareness, you can build up this image. Businesses tend to have two types of image:

- ✔ The image of the business (sometimes also called *corporate branding*)
- ✔ The image of the things you sell (sometimes called *product branding*)

Think of your business as having its own identity, personality and image. This image is made up of lots of things, but includes the name and logo of your business, the quality of your products or services, and your displays and shop fittings. The appearance of your staff, the way in which you advertise, your colour schemes and the atmosphere that pervades your business premises all have a direct influence on the kind of image you present.

A pie shop opened in our village a few years ago in a location where many other businesses and restaurants had struggled. I don't know the owners, but I reckon that they may well have worked in a corporate environment before opening the pie shop. Smart signage, a huge product range, expensive shop fittings, staff uniforms, loyalty cards and slick advertising marked this venture as different from its predecessors, right from the start. Gone is the somewhat greasy meat pie served lukewarm from a bain-marie. Not surprisingly, this business has flourished.

Franchises are typically very good at delivering a clear image and a strong brand. If you know of a franchise group that operates in the same kind of business as yourself, have a close look at what they do, and see what you can take on board.

Branding and your website

If you're still defining and building your brand, pause for a minute to consider how people will look for your product or services. If people are likely to look for you online, you want a company name (and brand) that includes words that say something about what you offer.

Imagine you have a holiday house on the south coast called 'Beach Daze'. Sure, you could register www.beachdaze.com.au as the domain name. However, how often do people search on the term *beach daze*? Never. (Well, surely close to never.) You're much better having a domain name such as www.southcoastbeachhouse.com.au, or www.southcoastholidays.com.au.

Another example may help. Imagine your name is Rick Dark and you're a dentist in Auckland. Do you think www.rickdark.co.nz would be a good domain name? No. Instead, look for domain names such as www.auckland-dentist.co.nz, or www.dentist.co.nz. Then set up Facebook pages and other social networking pages using these same words.

Researching domain name availability is straightforward: Simply go to the website of a company that offers domain name registrations to see if the name you want is available.

When you're designing business cards, brochures, logos or signage, don't do things on the cheap. Even if you have access to software that can do the job, keep in mind that it takes years of experience to develop an eye for design. Your brand is at stake every time you update your website, send an email with your logo at the bottom, or create new advertising materials.

Defining Your Target Market

Traditionally, the second part of a marketing plan (the Introduction being the first part — refer to the section 'Writing an eloquent introduction', earlier in this chapter) is about defining your target market. For established businesses, defining your target market is largely about analysing who your current customers are; for businesses just getting started, defining your target market is about describing who you hope your customers are going to be.

Sometimes you may find that your customers end up being a different kind of customer than what you originally anticipated. You may be fine with this, or you may decide that you want to change your mix of customers. In this situation, you need to implement specific sales targets and strategies to effect this change.

Analysing your customers

So how do you describe your typical customer? (Either the kind of customer you already have, or the kind of customer you hope to have.) Try to use the following categories when painting this picture:

- **Demographics:** Is your typical customer male or female? How old are your customers and how much do they earn?

- **Geographic:** Where are your customers located? How many people live in this area? What's the climate?

- **Psychographic:** What kind of lifestyle does your typical customer aspire to? What motivates your customers?

- **Behavioural:** How often does a typical customer purchase from you? Are customers loyal to your business?

Figure 12-1 shows an example customer analysis for an online bookstore specialising in vehicle repair manuals. (Note that females make up a miniscule 5 per cent of sales and that the owner is content to leave this segment as is — ah, such is life.)

Go to www.dummies.com/go/creatingbusinessplan to access the Customer Analysis template, which you can use as your starting point for customer analysis.

You'll probably find that you don't have one typical kind of customer, but that your customers fall into several different types. If so, try to estimate how much of your product or service each group buys, or will buy in the future. Consider what proportion of your target market has used a product similar to yours before, and analyse how much repeat business you get (or are likely to get).

Consider how sensitive your target market is to external events such as interest rate rises, changes in government policy, overseas tourists or environmental changes. I talk more about these outside influences in Chapter 13.

Figure 12-1: Analysing your customers can be a fun process once you get started.

Market Segment	Analysis	Percentage split	How my Business Benefits This Market Segment	Do I want to Increase/Decrease Focus on This Segment? (or leave as is)	Strategy
Age bracket	0-19	5%	not much, we have very few kids books	increase	could look at kids books
	20-29	25%	should be our core market, but lack of ebooks doesn't help	increase	need to get ebook guides happening
	30-39	45%	prompt delivery of quality repair guides	leave as is	
	40-49	20%	ditto	leave as is	
	50+	5%	ditto	increase if possible	maybe consider big print books or different distribution techniques
Gender	Male	95%	supply of vehicle repair guides	leave as is	
	Female	5%		leave as is	
Income bracket	<$20,000	5%	repair guides help people repair their own vehicles	leave as is	
	<$40,000	43%	ditto	leave as is	
	<$60,000	37%	ditto	leave as is	
	>$60,000	15%	ditto	increase	more high-end books and maybe racing car coffee table guides
Customer comes from	Local area	35%	our local store in the city	leave as is	
	Interstate	55%	postal service with overnight delivery	increase	more online advertising
	International	10%	international service limited due to freight costs	leave as is	
Customer purchase frequency	At least monthly	15%	Lots of new releases	increase	mail monthly catalogue to all subscribers
	At least once a year	45%	Easy to find online	leave as is	
	One-off	40%	Lots of very specific titles	leave as is	

Thinking creatively about channels

In the next part of your marketing plan, devote some space to *channel analysis*. Sounds technical, but channel analysis is simply a description of each channel that you plan to sell through. Here are a few examples of channel analysis:

- Nina has a retail store in the suburbs. However, she also sells some clothes online. Her shop is one channel; eBay is another.

- A manufacturer making gourmet jams sells through three different channels: Direct to stores, in bulk to distributors, and direct to consumers at farmers' markets.

- Anita makes jewellery. She sells some at the markets herself, some to a local gift store and some through a party plan. Each of these outlets is a channel.

- An importer sells furniture via four different channels: Large department stores, independent stores, online portals such as eBay, and direct to customers from the warehouse shopfront.

Do you sell to more than one channel? (And if not, maybe you should!) Then devote some of your marketing plan to describing each channel. Analyse what proportion of your sales goes to each channel, and whether this channel is growing or declining.

Researching the market

If your business is very new or hasn't even started yet, I suggest you include some market research in your marketing plan. Market research sounds like such a technical term, but can be very simple in practice.

Here are some examples:

- My son was thinking of starting a business working with local publishers selling book remainders on eBay. He tested his model by selecting one publisher and a small number of titles. (I could tell you the outcome of his research, but it's not such a happy tale.)

- Years ago, I had an idea to start up an online training company in partnership with a couple of other educational providers, specialising in QuickBooks software. As part of my market research, I looked carefully at companies providing similar services in different parts of the world. I discovered how none of these businesses seemed to be doing well and concluded that the market wasn't yet ready for this system of online training delivery.

✔ One of my girlfriends started up a business selling gingham squares soaked in beeswax as an alternative to cling wrap. Part of her research process involved trialling different fabrics and sizes and giving samples to friends and family, asking for feedback about pricing and packaging.

Summarising Your Competitor Analysis

I focus on competitors in Chapter 3, and recommend analysing your competition early in your planning — because without a good understanding of your competitors and their pricing, you can't decide what you intend to charge. If you don't know what you intend to charge, you can't do any meaningful financial forecasts. Without financial forecasts, you don't know if your business model has any chance at all. And without having your essential idea confirmed, what on earth is the point of doing a marketing plan? (Phew!)

So, in Chapter 3, I explain how to perform a competitive analysis and devise a competitive strategy (scoot back to Chapter 3 for more info). In your marketing plan, you need to include this analysis and confirm whether your competitive strategy will be one of cost leadership, differentiation or niche marketing.

As well as including competitive analysis in your marketing plan, you also need to summarise the place that your business fills in your customers' minds when compared against your competition. The secret here is to use a word that ends in 'est' or has 'most' or 'best' in front of it. Here are some examples: Best, cheapest, quickest, highest quality, most popular, most efficient, widest range, best product knowledge, quietest, most secluded, best value.

You must do something better than your competitors, or be best at something. What is it?

Setting Sales Targets

To run your business well, you must first figure out the level of sales you require in order to break even (a topic I cover in Chapter 9), and also calculate what sales need to be in order for you to trade profitably. Next, you want to translate these financial benchmarks into how many units you need to sell of each item or each product range, or how much revenue you need to generate from services.

Slicing goals into bite-sized chunks

When you set sales targets for your business, avoid plucking random round figures out of the air; don't just plan to make sales of $20,000 every month, or sell 100 widgets in the next six months. Instead, break down your targets into bite-sized chunks, and apply a reality check to each one.

For example, a hairdresser could set targets as to the number of cuts and colours each week, a wholesaler might set targets for each geographic region (and sales rep), and an independent theatre could set targets for the number of tickets sold per day. (For more detail and templates to help you with this process, refer to Chapter 5.)

Expressing goals in other ways

True marketing is all about attitude, rather than just about selling stuff. For this reason, I sometimes like to set sales goals that aren't just expressed in dollars or units sold, but in other attributes as well. (This strategy makes sense when you think about it: Customers don't rate your service or product simply on price; they look at lots of other traits of your business as well.)

In Table 12-2, I list a few examples of sales goals that aren't measured in dollars. In the first column, I list long-term goals; in the second column, I list short-term goals; and in the third column, I list the strategies the business intends to employ in order to support these goals.

Table 12-2	Different Kinds of Sales Goals and How to Reach 'Em	
Long-Term Aim	*Sales Goal for the Quarter*	*Strategies to Support the Goal*
Develop business in eastern suburbs	One new customer a week in this locality	Advertise in local online trading website
Improve booking rates from email queries	Make 10 bookings for every 25 queries	Set up templates for email replies
Increase repeat business	Repeat business to be 25% of total sales	Set up yearly reminders on database for all existing customers
Increase quality of service	Aim to reduce complaints to one a month	Further training for field staff and review of procedures
Improve on quote accuracy	Aim to ensure actual costs and time are within 10% of original quote	Issue weekly variance reports for each sales rep and meet every fortnight to discuss variances

Getting SMART: Five essential ingredients for any goal

One of the acronyms consultants often employ when referring to goal setting is the SMART approach: A goal needs to be **S**pecific, **M**easurable, **A**chievable, **R**ealistic and **T**ime-specific.

I love the SMART approach and find it works really well. Here's the low-down on what each word means in practice:

- ✔ **Specific:** When talking about sales goals, are you being really precise about what you are hoping to achieve?

- ✔ **Measurable:** You need to able to measure every goal. (Dollars sold, units sold, new customers gained, email enquiries received, hits on the website and so on.)

- ✔ **Achievable:** Setting goals is pointless unless you can reasonably achieve them.

- ✔ **Realistic:** Even if a goal is potentially achievable, is it realistic? Do you definitely have enough time and enough funds to ensure the goal can be met?

- ✔ **Time specific:** Always specify the time frame for meeting this goal.

The sales goals outlined in Table 12-2 (earlier in this chapter) are pretty good in that they all seem to meet the SMART objectives (although, of course, it's hard for me to judge whether the goals in this example are definitely achievable and realistic).

Just for fun, here are some of the kinds of sales goals I really hate (they all sound cool at first glance, but scratch the surface and these goals are horrendously vague):

- ✔ 'I aim to increase online sales by 20 per cent.' (This goal fails the 'Time' test — by when will sales increase by this amount?)

- ✔ 'We plan to open a new store every six months for the next five years.' (Given that a new store costs about $80,000 to open, this goal almost certainly fails the 'Realistic' test.)

- ✔ 'My main goal is to improve customer satisfaction by 100 per cent.' (Unless you add a whole heap of detail, this goal fails the 'Measureable' test.)

> ✔ 'Our aim is to expand corporate sales and increase market share to 25 per cent.' (This goals fails the 'Specific' test in that it doesn't say how much corporate sales are going to expand by, and fails the 'Time' test in that it doesn't specify a time.)
>
> ✔ 'We will become a recognised brand.' (Yuck. I'm not even going to spell out all the tests this one fails.)

Creating Strategies to Support Your Targets

For every sales target you set, you want a marketing strategy that supports these targets. I like to organise strategies into four broad categories:

> ✔ Website and marketing materials
>
> ✔ Paid advertising (either online or in print)
>
> ✔ Public relations
>
> ✔ Networking (including social media)

In the next few pages of this chapter, I explore each one of these strategies in turn; however, before I do, I want to share a couple of suggestions regarding how you choose to go about selecting these strategies.

Making a list of your top ten

Gravitating towards marketing strategies that seem easy or appealing at the expense of strategies that are the most likely to succeed is tempting.

The instinct to stay in one's comfort zone can hold you back, big time. I regularly come across business owners who spend hundreds of hours mucking around with social media when what they really should be doing is knocking on doors and visiting people. Conversely, I also come across people spending too much money on printed catalogues or print advertising instead of making the transition to online strategies. Everyone has things they are good at and things they are bad at. However, your business doesn't want to know what you're good at; your business just wants what's good for it.

Steering clear of personal preferences and prioritising sales strategies objectively can be very tricky. With this in mind, here's my suggested plan of action:

1. **Read through the marketing strategies in this chapter (or any other business or marketing books for that matter).**

2. **Get together with your business partners or advisers and arrange a marketing meeting.**

   Of course, if the business is just you, take yourself out to a cafe or a quiet spot on a deserted headland. (Don't jump.)

3. **Brainstorm all the possible marketing ideas and write these down.**

   Remember the rules of brainstorming — even if someone comes up with an idea that's hopeless, or something that seems ridiculous pops into your head, you can't judge. Simply write down the idea and keep going.

4. **When the brainstorming process starts winding down, stop generating new ideas and instead highlight the 15 best ideas.**

   Ensure you have at least two ideas that relate to each of the four categories (websites/marketing materials, paid advertising, public relations and networking). If you don't, keep the ideas coming until you do.

5. **Next to the 15 best ideas, write approximate costs and the amount of time required. Score through any ideas that are plainly unaffordable.**

6. **Number these ideas from 1 to 15, with 1 being the idea you reckon will have most impact, and 15 the least.**

   Don't worry about how much these ideas cost or how long they may take at this point.

7. **Select the combination of ideas that you feel will give you most bang for your buck while falling within your total marketing budget. Then cross out any ideas that you know don't fit in your budget.**

   Make sure you continue to have a combination of ideas across the four categories. You don't have a marketing budget yet? Then skip back to Chapter 10.

8. **With the amount of time you have available in mind, number your remaining ideas, starting with the number 1.**

   So idea 'number 1' will be within your marketing budget, achievable in a reasonable amount of time, and guaranteed to generate sales. (If you still have more than 10 ideas on your list at this point, score through any ideas numbered 11 or higher.)

You now have a list of marketing ideas, all within your budget and hopefully achievable in the time you have available, numbered 1 to 10 in order of priority.

9. **Set a schedule for each of the ideas on this list, and list which sales target each idea supports.**

   For more detail about this process, refer to 'Setting Sales Targets' earlier in this chapter.

You may think that this process is a bit pedantic and, to be fair, it probably is. However, what this process safeguards you against is your own human nature. Your marketing priorities will be organised in a priority that hopefully fits the needs of your business, rather than what you're personally drawn to doing.

Several years ago, when websites were still relatively new, I went to see a design company about my website. Gerlinde (the female half of the husband-and-wife team who ran the business) was on the phone that afternoon, cold calling every single business in the area. When I enquired about what she was doing, she told me that she'd started at the letter 'A' in the business directory three days before and she was currently on the letter 'C'. I asked how successful this strategy was. 'Not one sale yet' her husband replied, 'but we think this strategy will work in the end'. Two weeks later, Gerlinde then proceeded to knock on the door of each of these businesses, doing a follow-up call in person. Personally, I couldn't think of anything worse than cold calling in this way, but I was filled with admiration for Gerlinde's persistence. This business is now the most successful website design and programming business in our region, and I have no doubt that a good measure of this success is due to Gerlinde's willingness to pursue marketing strategies that weren't necessarily easy or comfortable, but were likely to succeed in the long term.

Creating websites and marketing materials

The backbone of most marketing plans is your physical presence in the marketplace. Unless you are a retail store, this physical presence can be a website, an online store, brochures, business cards or even printed catalogues.

Probably the element that requires most planning for new businesses is the website. While a website is certainly more important for some businesses than for others, I can't think of a single business that doesn't benefit from some kind of online presence.

The technology behind websites changes as quickly as the weather, but in respect of planning, here are some general principles to bear in mind:

- **Be clear about how you will maintain and update your website.** You don't want your website to be static, nor do you want to pay a designer every time you decide to change the text on a webpage. Ensure that your website comes with some kind of *content management system*, software that enables you to log on to your site and make changes.

- **Go slow on e-commerce and shopping carts, unless they're the reason for your website in the first place:** For example, a musician friend of mine just created a new website with the aim of securing a few more gigs around town. He has a CD of his original songs for sale, but that product is the only product he sells. He decided the whole shopping-cart-ordeal wasn't worth the cost in order to maybe sell one CD every month or so.

- **If contracting out the website to a designer, check that the designer understands *search engine optimisation (SEO)*.** By SEO, I mean the art of getting sites to rank highly in search engines such as Google. Test the designer's expertise by selecting a handful of the designer's clients and checking out how the websites of these clients rank in Google.

- **Make sure your website is always backed up.** If your designer hosts as well as designs websites, clarify what backup facility exists for your site. What would happen if you or your designer accidentally wiped files from the server or if your site were defaced by a hacker?

- **Remember that eBay is often a viable alternative:** eBay provides a great way to test business ideas and customer reaction to your products. You may even find that eBay works so well that maintaining a separate website of your own (along with all the associated e-commerce hassle) becomes more trouble than it's worth. (Of course, the two aren't mutually exclusive: You can always have your own website *and* sell stuff on eBay — after all, the more ways customers can find you, the better.)

In regards to your marketing plan, your plan needs to include a clear strategy regarding your online presence, including social media. These strategies need to be closely linked to your sales targets. For example:

- Increase the dollar value of online sales by 20 per cent within six months by using sponsored advertising on Google (budget $200 per month).

- Increase traffic to website to 200 unique visitors per day by the end of March focusing on keywords and SEO techniques ($100 per month budget).

- Secure $1,500 additional sales per month within six months by opening eBay store.

A website is only part of your online arsenal, and needs to be supported by advertising, electronic communications and social media. Also, don't forget that traditional methods such as brochures, catalogues or point-of-sale material can still be surprisingly effective in spreading the word about your business.

Planning an advertising strategy

In your marketing plan, the name of the game is to list all your planned advertising expenditure (in other words, print advertising, sponsored online ads, trade shows, mail-outs and so on) and then against each one, include details that answer the following questions:

- ✔ Why have you decided to use this type of advertising?
- ✔ When are you going to do this advertising?
- ✔ How much is it going to cost?
- ✔ How are you going to evaluate whether this advertising was successful?

Table 12-3 shows a sample advertising strategy, covering these details.

Table 12-3	Planning Your Advertising Strategies			
	Why	*When*	*How Much*	*How to Evaluate*
Facebook campaign	Need to take advantage of new connections	Ongoing	Free	Number of friends, traffic back to website
Google ads	Increase online sales	Ongoing	$200 per month	Google sales conversion tracker
Industry magazine	Best way to reach industry professionals	Trial in April	$65 per ad	Use separate phone number and email address to identify interest generated
Business cards	Required for business networking events	Jan	$550	Tricky to measure, but can maybe evaluate long-term by documenting referral sources

Try to match your advertising strategies back to your sales targets. For example, if one of your targets is to increase local business by 20 per cent, you want to make sure that at least one of your advertising strategies helps support that goal.

Reaching out to the public

Don't underestimate the power of public relations (press releases, community sponsorships, long boozy lunches and so on), even though the effect on sales can be harder to measure than some other strategies.

Press releases are a common public relations activity. The idea of a press release is that you get a website, magazine, newspaper or radio station to publicise your business or product without you having to spend a cent. Look through any news-based website or local paper and you can find oodles of examples of press releases. An article about how the local butcher sponsored the school cricket team, an article about a band that's performing at the local pub, or a photograph of a famous author holding her latest book are all likely to be the results of press releases.

If you're not sure how to write a press release for your business, you can hire someone to do it for you. If you want to have a bash at doing it yourself, mind these points:

- ✔ **Make personal contact:** The trick is to establish some sort of relationship with the person responsible for publishing press releases, ideally the editor.

- ✔ **Donate something to a good cause:** The media are usually willing to give free press if your business is contributing to a local event or charity.

- ✔ **Use keywords in your headline:** Remember that most papers publish press releases online as well as in print. Jetstar dominated the term 'cheap flights' on the web for a long time, simply because every press release they issued included the words 'cheap flights' in the headline.

- ✔ **Broadcast some newsworthy or useful information:** If you don't have anything newsworthy, create something that is! For example, if your business has been around for ten years, throw a birthday celebration and let the media know.

- ✔ **Don't make your press release too long:** Aim for 200 words or so, use simple expression, and provide an interesting image if possible.

- ✔ **Be short and sweet (just like me):** Keep your sentences short and make each paragraph only two or three sentences long.

✔ **Publish your press release online:** Type 'free press release' into Google (or your favourite search engine) and you see a stack of services offering to publish your press release online, usually free of charge. Why not? And for a finishing touch, include links back to your website in your press release to maximise the benefits.

Here are some other simple examples of good PR:

✔ Sending Christmas gifts to customers and key suppliers

✔ Providing customers with free information about your products and their benefits

✔ Remembering key customers' birthdays and sending a card

✔ Throwing a birthday party for your business and giving away free balloons to kids

✔ Sponsoring events at the local school

Working your networks

People often think of networking as being a marketing tool (which indeed it is), and they head off to business meetings or hook up on LinkedIn with a view to finding possible clients.

Be brave when customers lapse

Don't just think of marketing as being about ways to generate new customers. Marketing is just as much about keeping the ones you already have (and, in fact, you'll find it easier and cheaper to keep existing customers happy than to generate business from scratch).

Think of the clients or customers you had one year ago, two years ago, maybe three years ago, and compare this list to the list of current clients you have now. Who's dropped away? Who hasn't rung you in months? Don't wait any longer for them to contact you. Instead, you contact them.

By the way, I'm not just talking about the stereotypical sales rep kind of business when I talk of chasing lapsed customers. Keeping in touch with customers (and if they've gone elsewhere, finding out why), is crucial to the success of heaps of businesses — everything from tyre services to dentists, and consultants to acupuncturists. Social media tools such as Facebook offer an ideal medium to keep contact alive.

However, if you think this way, you're missing the point: Networking is about building relationships, sharing and listening to people — not about doing a hard sell. With true networking, the name of the game is not to approach the world around you with the attitude 'what can I get?' but with the attitude 'what can I give?' If you're generous with your ideas, knowledge and referrals, you soon reap the rewards. As the law of reciprocity states, what you give out is what you get back.

Engaging in social media

Facebook isn't just one of the hugest time-wasters on the planet, but can also provide a great way to make connections and stay in touch with customers.

From a business branding perspective, remember to keep your *business* Facebook page separate from your *personal* Facebook page. (The last thing you want is your clients reading posts from your jilted lover, or looking up photos of you aged five.) The people most likely to blur these boundaries are those working in creative industries such as musicians and artists, or people whose personal and business lives are very intertwined. (Wondering how you create a business Facebook page? Go to www.facebook.com, and on the Sign Up Page, look for the Create a Page for a Celebrity, Band or Business link.)

Alternatively (or as well as Facebook), consider having a tweet on Twitter. Although I personally find Twitter one of the more inane and boring activities in my life — and yes, I do have a Twitter account and I do tweet — in some industries, Twitter certainly does help to get your name out there.

Social media sites come up and go (remember the rise and fall of MySpace?) but at the time of writing, the two other sites that I recommend you consider are LinkedIn at www.linkedin.com (which is kind of like a massive Yellow Pages directory of professionals) and YouTube at www.youtube.com.

Are you feeling that you'll never get any real work done if you engage with all these social networking options? Don't worry — most social networking sites offer the facility to spread your message in multiple locations with a single click of the button. For example, when I add a new posting to my WordPress blog, I can choose to add updates automatically to my Facebook page, and LinkedIn and Twitter accounts at the same time.

Employing more traditional networking techniques

Of course, networking isn't just about tapping away on your laptop at all hours of the day and night. Traditional networking techniques — you know the ones where you actually get to meet real, breathing humans — are just as valid and, in some industries, probably even more effective.

Struggling to imagine a life outside your computer? Here are some ideas:

✔ **Become a social animal:** Every club or social activity in which you participate is a chance to network, whether this be a mothers' group, Rotary, the bowling club or netball. By developing a wider social network, you increase the chance of business referrals. By the way, I don't mean that you have to sell your business services to everyone in your social group. Rather, you let people know what you do for a living as part of everyday conversation, in the normal way that everyone does. (Sounds weird? Skip back to Chapter 3 and read about elevator speeches.)

✔ **Form alliances:** Look for businesses that complement your own. I know of a naturopath who sends all her clients to a particular health food store; in return, the health food store displays her business cards on the counter. Similarly, I know of a computer trainer who teams up with his local computer retail outlet so that, in tandem, they provide hardware, software, support and training.

Who can you form a strategic alliance with? Think of cinemas and restaurants, plumbers and electricians, nurseries and landscapers, newsagents and bookstores. Which businesses also service your customers, both before they arrive at your door and after they leave you?

✔ **Get involved in the community:** If you're sitting at home twiddling your thumbs, get out and volunteer for stuff in the community. Always carry a few business cards with you, and don't be shy to tell people about your business.

✔ **Join a local business group:** Those intimidating business networking meetings are just the stuff for building up business, and networking is the kind of marketing that doesn't cost much at all. Contact your local chamber of commerce or ask around business colleagues to find out where your local business networking meetings are happening.

✔ **Sponsor local events:** If your marketing budget can stretch far enough, be willing to sponsor community events (everything from the school walkathon to the local radio open day). This is a great way to build both loyalty and recognition for your business.

Planning For Customer Service

Ask successful businesspeople what they think their secret is, and chances are they say something about their customers. In fact, the majority of established businesses list customer service right at the top of attributes vital to their success.

Doing the right thing by your customers is the best possible form of advertising. The way you treat your customers influences their decision to come back to you; and because customers are getting more and more vocal about the value they place on being treated properly, listening reaps rewards. So, if something matters to customers, it has to matter to you, too.

Customer service *does* mean different things to different people. I've heard excellent service described as 'being at your best with every customer' or 'figuring out new ways to help people'. Regardless of the description, the principle remains the same for all businesses — excellent service means always doing the right things, in the way customers want it done. Applying this principle in practice depends entirely on your business.

As part of your marketing plan, I suggest you include a few paragraphs summarising your customer service plan. In particular, you may want to include:

- Customer service goals (for example, your target response time for enquiries or order turnaround time)
- How you plan to get feedback from customers
- How your customer service standards compare with the competition
- How you intend to guarantee the consistency and quality of your products and/or services

Similar to your sales targets, your customer service goals should ideally be SMART (specific, measurable, achievable, realistic and time-specific — refer to the section 'Getting SMART: Five essential ingredients for any goal', earlier in this chapter, for more).

To read more about planning for quality customer service, go to www.dummies.com/go/creatingbusinessplan to download the Building a Customer Service Plan article.

Keeping Yourself Honest

The last part of your marketing plan is where you get to explain what systems you plan to put in place so that you track the effectiveness of your marketing campaigns.

Comparing dollar targets against actuals

Early in this chapter I mention that a key attribute of any sales target is that it should be measurable (refer to the section 'Setting Sales Targets'). For any sales targets that you express in dollars, one of the quickest ways to measure performance is to enter these targets as budgets in your accounting software. This way you can compare actuals versus budgets every month in a single click of a button, similar to how I do in Figure 12-2.

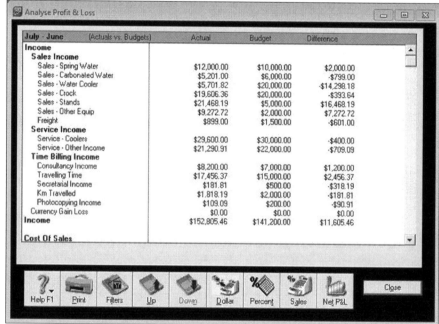

Figure 12-2: Try to compare actual sales results against budgets on a regular basis.

The downside about simply comparing actual results against budgeted targets is that you can only evaluate the overall success of your sales targets, and you don't get to see the detail that lies behind. For example, your total sales might be close to the combined total of your sales targets, but if you analyse the whole deal more closely, you could find that actual sales via your website exceeded targeted sales by 20 per cent, but actual sales made via the weekend markets fell short by about the same amount.

Tracking referral sources

You probably know the advertising maxim: 'You know that only one dollar of every hundred dollars you spend on advertising works. The thing you don't know is which dollar it is.' However, while this saying is chillingly true, you can still build up an idea of how effective your advertising strategies are with strategies such as the following:

- **Keep track of loyalty schemes:** If you offer discounts or loyalty schemes, record these discounts separately in your point-of-sale system (or cash register), or in a separate income category in your accounting software. This way you can keep track of how much you give out in discounts and, therefore, how well this type of advertising works.

- **Publish unique contact details:** If you want to test a new form of advertising, try publishing a unique phone number (a VOIP number is usually cheapest), email address or website landing page, so that you can readily identify all leads generated by the ad.

- **Record referral sources:** The easiest way to collect this data is when someone first makes contact — by asking how this potential customer heard about your business. Record the person's response in your database and/or accounting software. Later, when you generate sales reports, correlate how many sales were made as a result of each source.

Analysing online success

When analysing the effectiveness of online advertising, remember that the purpose of this form of advertising isn't just to create sales. Online advertising forms a part of your overall marketing strategy, one part of which is almost certainly to build customer awareness of your products and services. Don't get too hooked on measuring online advertising in dollars and cents — bear in mind that even if visitors didn't buy a product or make an enquiry today, they may return to your website at some point in the future.

With this in mind, here are some of the performance measures you can use for online advertising:

- **Analyse ranking on key search engines for keywords:** I don't really have scope here to talk in detail about keywords, but let's say that your business is holiday accommodation on the north coast. In this scenario 'holiday accommodation north coast' is almost certainly a keyword, and you can measure how you rank on this keyword by typing the phrase into Google (or any other search engine) and seeing where your website appears. For example, if you're the sixth entry on the second page, and each page has 10 entries, you rank 16th for this keyword.

Make a list of all possible keywords for your website and track your ranking for each of these keywords at least once a month. Monitor how your performance changes each month.

✔ **Analyse website traffic:** Subscribe to a website traffic analysis tool (Google Analytics is one of the best and it's also free) so that you can monitor how people find your website, what web pages they visit, and how long people stay after they get there. Correlate changes in traffic with any new marketing strategies you put in place, so that you can accurately measure the effect of these strategies.

✔ **Set up conversion tracking on paid online advertising:** Try to define what you want visitors to do as a result of browsing your website or Facebook page. Maybe you want them to make an enquiry, subscribe to your newsletter, buy a product from your online store, view session times, make an appointment or sign up to a forum board. In web-nerd lingo, each of these outcomes is called a *conversion*. Depending what web stats program you're using, you can add little bits of *HTML code* (the mark-up language used to publish web pages) that track every conversion made, and whether this conversion originated from paid online advertising or not.

Measuring overall conversion rates

Marketing folk talk a lot about *conversion rates*, an expression that sounds terribly religious, but actually refers to the gentle art of converting queries into sales.

For example, if you sell kitchens and you do ten quotes in one week and two of these quotes are accepted, the conversion rate is 20 per cent. Or, if you're a computer consultant and you receive enquiries over the phone, and an average of six out of every ten enquiries yields a booking, you have a conversion rate of 60 per cent. Similarly, if you're selling your wares online, and one in every hundred people who visit your site buys something, the conversion rate is 1 per cent. (Online conversion rates are typically very low, averaging between 1 per cent and 5 per cent for commercial sites.)

From time to time, measuring how effective your conversion rates are is good practice because, if you can improve them, you've got a handle on one of the most cost-effective and successful methods of increasing sales.

Part of your business planning process is to set up reporting systems for all aspects of your business, not just financial performance. Tracking referral sources, analysing online success and measuring conversion rates (the topics I cover in the last few pages of this chapter) are all very important non-financial ways to measure business success.

Chapter 13

Staying One Step Ahead

In This Chapter

▶ Reflecting on your industry and where it's heading

▶ Doing an honest no-holds-barred assessment of your abilities

▶ Spotting possible opportunities and threats

▶ Matching your strengths to opportunities, and guarding weaknesses from threats

▶ Building a winning action plan

*I*n this chapter, I talk about preparing your business for change. I reflect on all kinds of change — everything from new competitors to the latest influx of government regulation, and from the impact of a booming economy to the demands of new technology.

I have a feeling that this is the chapter in the book where you're most likely to find it hard to sustain interest, especially if you're just getting started in business. After all, if you're planning something relatively small (maybe beautician services, bookkeeping, jam-making or landscape gardening), it may feel irrelevant to be thinking about the rise and fall of the economy or the impact of changing technology.

However, almost every industry around the world is currently experiencing change, and the pace of this change is only increasing. Look at the way the retail industry has transformed in the face of online competition, or how smartphones, tablets and laptops have transformed the entertainment industry.

Even a simple business such as bookkeeping can be affected by new government regulations, in the same way as a landscape gardener could be impacted by climate change. Anticipating change so you don't miss out on new opportunities is a sure-fire ingredient for business success, in the same way as safeguarding yourself against threats or industry decline is essential for survival.

Taking an Eagle-Eye View

To be strategic in business, you need an understanding of how the industry in which you're operating is faring, and what outside factors may affect this industry in the near future.

Imagine you were the owner of a video and DVD rental business 15 years or so ago when this industry was thriving. Maybe your business was very profitable (you had great taste in movies, your shop was in a central location and you had no competitors). Despite all these advantages, chances are you would have ceased trading by now. Why? Because the movie-rental industry has transformed. Video streaming, online rentals and other internet-based entertainment means that the old-fashioned DVD rental store is fast going the same way as the dodo.

Looking at what's happening in your industry

Industry analysis may sound like a terribly technical term, but if you've been working in this industry a while, you probably know most of what's going on at an intuitive level. What I provide here is a bit of a framework so that you don't forget anything. Also, some of the questions I ask may prompt you to think a little deeper about the industry that you're in.

Here are the main areas I suggest you concentrate on:

- **Competitors:** Have any of your competitors gone out of business in the last 12 months? How many? Conversely, have any new competitors come on the scene? How many? (Chapter 3 also provides some insights into analysing future competitors, and provides a Future Competitor worksheet.)

- **Customer growth:** Is this industry experiencing growth in the number of customers?

- **Environment:** What environmental drivers affect your industry? (Consider climate change, ecological movements, environmental legislation, pollution, and so on.)

- **Exchange rates:** How do exchange rate variations affect your industry? Is your business model dependent on a certain level of exchange rate?

✔ **Globalisation:** How could the globalisation of products and services affect this industry? Could services be outsourced overseas?

✔ **Government legislation:** Could any government regulations, tax concessions, grant schemes or impending legislation affect your industry?

✔ **Pricing:** What are the trends regarding pricing? Are prices generally going up, or is the pressure downwards?

✔ **Technology:** What impact could technological change have on your industry? (Consider potential product obsolescence, changes in equipment, new customer demands, new skills and so on.)

✔ **Overall trends:** What would you say is the general health of the industry in which you operate? Can you source any statistics (either from government or from industry bodies) regarding industry trends?

I don't know about you, but I tend to go a bit numb when I look at a whole list such as the preceding one without being able to see where my business fits in the scheme of things. So in Figure 13-1, I bring this theory to life by doing an example industry analysis for three completely different kinds of businesses. Identify the business that's closest to yours and see if these examples help bring meaning to these concepts. I leave the last column blank so that you can complete the industry analysis for your own business.

If you like, you can download the Industry Analysis worksheet shown in Figure 13-1 from www.dummies.com/go/creatingbusinessplan.

A couple of quick comments about the Industry Analysis worksheet:

✔ In Figure 13-1, I'm fairly brief because all I'm trying to do is give you the general idea. You will need a fair bit more detail than what I've provided, ideally a paragraph or two for each of the nine headings.

✔ If you have outside reference sources with interesting data (such as graphs or charts or whatever), feel free to include these as part of your industry analysis.

✔ If you're referring to specific research, always quote the source of this research.

	iPhone app developer	Retailer of women's fashion	Solar panel installations	Your Business
Competitor trends	Huge growth in number of competitors	Decline in regular retail competitors but massive growth from online competitors	Sustained growth in number of competitors, particularly from larger operators and power companies	
Customer growth	Exponential growth in potential number of customers as demand for iPhone apps grow	Demand for women's fashion tends to sync with state of economy – currently stable	Demand for solar panels increasing 20 to 30% annually for the last five years	
Environment	Some concerns regarding components in smartphones; however, flipside is that apps are often a substitute for paper-based products such as maps	Although there could be a niche opportunity for organic clothing, particularly cotton, this isn't relevant to this particular store's demographic. Rising fuel prices do affect freight charges from suppliers, however.	Solar panels offer an alternative to fossil fuels and help meet national carbon emission targets. Some concerns regarding disposal/recycling of solar batteries, particularly long-term	
Exchange rates	Many customers are based overseas so exchange rates affect competitiveness of pricing	Most clothes are imported and so exchange rates affect pricing. However, most competitors also importing and so price changes tend to be across the industry.	Solar panels are imported and constitute approximately 50% of the value of any installation.	
Globalisation	Globalisation of labour market means competing with app developers around the world, including developers with significantly lower labour costs	Globalisation is part of the reason for the increase in online competitors. This trend will probably only continue.	Solar panels are heavy and impractical to ship internationally as individual units. They will always need a local person to install them.	
Government	This market is relatively unregulated by government although government departments themselves are a potentially lucrative customer base and relatively unwilling to offshore development	Overseas regulations regarding workplace health and safety may increase the cost of goods in the long-term	Government subsidies and R&D tax concessions continue to offer a major boost to the industry	
Pricing	The rates that app developers are able to charge is likely to decline long-term due to forces of globalisation	The average price per item of clothing sold has declined by 10% in the last 2 years due to competitive pressures. This trend is probably unsustainable.	The cost of solar panels has declined by 22% due to improved technology but the cost of labour has increased by 15% in the last 3 years due to government wage legislation. The price customers are prepared to pay has stayed constant due to steady demand.	
Technology	The impact of technology governs this industry, with changes in software and hardware dominating industry opportunities	Changing technology doesn't impact retail operations or clothing design significantly (although the costs of producing costs overseas continue to decline), but the burgeoning of online stores is a major threat to bricks-and-mortar retail.	Any technological progress that makes solar panels more affordable or efficient will translate to significant growth. Conversely technological progress in other green energy industries could cause solar panel sales to decline.	
Overall trends	Overall trends for the industry are very positive, with the average smartphone/tablet user spending 2 hours 10 minutes every day on their device	According to IBISWorld analysis, the clothing retail industry is in decline, with an average decline of 0.9% per year over the last 5 years	Rising costs in non-renewable energy sources will result in lower demand overall for power, but demand for solar energy is likely to continue to grow at current rates	

Figure 13-1:
Conducting an industry analysis.

Ha, ha. You can't catch me!

One of the points you may want to consider as part of your industry analysis is *entry barriers*. Barriers to entry are very high set-up costs that make it hard for other competitors to enter the fray. (I mention entry barriers in Chapter 3 also.)

Obvious examples are new airlines, car manufacturers or supermarket chains. (Although I guess it's unlikely that anyone reading this book would really be planning to start a new airline.) At a more everyday level, entry barriers can be expensive tools or specialist equipment, many years of study, big infrastructure costs such as software systems or warehousing, complex distribution networks or expensive real estate.

If you plan to start a new business within an industry where significant entry barriers exist, you may find growth is impossible because you don't have enough capital to invest. If this is the case, you need to be open to the idea of changing your business model.

On the other hand, changes in technology have caused entry barriers in many industries to crumble, opening up a gamut of opportunities. For example, owners of small businesses who formerly couldn't compete because they didn't have enough capital to fit out an expensive retail outlet can now sell direct to the consumer using online channels; authors who couldn't secure distribution without going through a publisher can now self-publish their own ebooks; recording studios that used to require hundreds of thousands of dollars of investment have now been replaced by the home computer and some audio software.

If you are a small player, see if you can identify any new technologies that present opportunities in markets where, up until now, the big players have dominated the field. Not only are entry barriers crumbling at an ever-increasing pace, but large companies can also be very slow to change.

Responding to industry trends

The idea behind doing an industry analysis is to get a sense of what's happening overall in the industry. Of course, an industry that's in decline is going to be a whole load tougher (if not impossible) to succeed in than an industry that's growing very fast.

I mention the decline of video and DVD rental stores earlier in this chapter, and when doing so, I was thinking of the video store that used to be in my village. The business was a solid one, and the store (as one of the only places open after 6pm) was always social and lively. In hindsight, I can look back and think, the owners should have changed to more DVDs and fewer videos earlier; they could have downsized and halved the rent; they could have explored a niche market and developed an online presence. Pish tosh. For this particular business, there was no hope. The best thing the owners could have done (which for whatever reason they didn't) is close their business while they were still ahead.

If your industry is in severe decline, your best bet is probably to try to sell your business now, close your business if it's already unprofitable or, if you're still at the planning stage, walk away from the idea of starting a new business. Closing a business can be particularly scary, because you may have significant funds invested that you'll never recoup. However, if you're already trading at a loss, selling your business in the context of a declining industry may be impossible. The longer you trade unprofitably, the more you stand to lose financially.

Aside from an industry in decline, what about other scenarios — such as enormous industry growth? Generally, industry growth is a great thing for anyone involved, and if you're in the right place at the right time, you can make handsome profits. The flipside is that any industry experiencing rapid change carries higher risks because the direction of change and new technology can be hard to predict.

Part of the secret to mitigating this risk lies in matching the internal strengths of your business against the potential opportunities of the industry. And guess what? That's what the next section of this chapter is all about . . .

Rating Your Capabilities

I'm sure you don't have to pause for very long to think of someone who always seems to choose the more difficult paths in life. Maybe you have a friend who's dyslexic but has chosen to be a linguist as a career, or you know someone in a wheelchair who travels the world.

Chasing one's dreams and persisting in the face of adversity is undoubtedly character building and often deeply rewarding. However, in the world of business, you will find that it usually pays to be more strategic about where you channel your energies. What you want to do is identify the possible opportunities and see if you can match these opportunities against your natural skills and abilities.

Putting yourself through the griller

I have a morbid fascination for those personality quizzes you see in magazines in doctors' waiting rooms — the ones where you get to answer inane multiple-choice questions and then read a chilling verdict at the end.

With these guilty pleasures in mind, Figure 13-2 provides you with your very own quiz, with the added benefit of not having to get stuck in a waiting room in order to enjoy it. (In the example shown in Figure 13-2, I've also included sample responses.)

If you like, you can also print out the Business Performance quiz shown in Figure 13-2 by going to www.dummies.com/go/ creatingbusinessplan.

When you answer the questions in Figure 13-2, respond from the perspective of your business, rather than from you as an individual. Think of the collective skills that you, your employees, any family members, business mentors or outside consultants bring to the party. Also, keep your competition in mind when you rate your business on things such as customer service or marketing. (For example, you may be aware of small areas where you can improve your customer service but if you know that you beat all of your competition hands down, you can probably award yourself a rating of 'awesome'.)

When rating how important each function is for your business (sales, finance, people and so on), I suggest you put a tick in the 'Yes' column for all aspects of financial management. Even if your business chugs along just fine and you're a shoebox-receipts kind of person, poor financial management is almost always a limiter to business success and growth.

Prioritising where you need to do better

If I'm a psychologist running a counselling business, chances are that cold calling or direct marketing skills aren't going to be that big a deal. (Although a bizarre image of someone door-knocking enquiring as to each resident's mental health does spring to mind.) On the other hand, if I'm selling a new product that few people have ever heard of, being able to sell anything to anyone is going to be an essential skill.

In Figure 13-2, can you see how I've highlighted some of the ticks in the strengths and weaknesses columns? What I've done is highlight all business functions where the capability rating is 'not great' or 'terrible' but the function itself is rated as being important.

The combination of something being both important to your business but a weakness in your capabilities is an unhappy one. Can you identify any business functions in which you're really weak, but which are crucial for your business?

	STRENGTH			WEAKNESS		Is This Important to Your Business?		
	Awesome	Pretty good	Average	Not great	Terrible	Yes	Sometimes	Not Really
Sales and marketing. How does your business rate in regards to . . .								
Cold calling, direct sales, or telesales?	✓							
Negotiating skills?		✓					✓	
Skills in social media?	✓					✓	✓	
The ability to organise and run strong advertising campaigns?		✓						✓
The ability to write a good press release?		✓						✓
Finance. How does your business rate in regards to . . .								
Keeping a good set of up-to-date books?						✓		
Invoicing customers and making sure you get paid on time?					✓	✓		
Financial reporting, particularly regular Profit & Loss reports?					✓	✓		
Cashflow management and tax planning?				✓		✓		
Availability of capital and ability to pay bills on time?				✓				
Management ability. How does your business rate in regards to . . .								
Depth (number of years) of experience?				✓		✓		
People-management skills?		✓					✓	
Range of experience in different business situations?				✓			✓	
People. How does your business rate in regards to . . .								
The balance and synergy of skills in the team?		✓				✓	✓	
The vibe and morale in the workplace?		✓				✓	✓	
Physical resources. How does your business rate in regards to?								
Physical location?					✓	✓		✓
Up-to-date tools and equipment?	✓					✓		
Customer service. How does your business rate in regards to?								
Ability to fulfil orders or respond to enquiries quickly?		✓				✓		
Ability to communicate well with customers?	✓					✓		
Responsiveness to customer requests?	✓					✓		
Computer systems. How does your business rate in regards to?								
Good reporting systems and sales management?		✓					✓	
Ability to manage websites, custom software or any other IT requirements?			✓			✓		
Product or service. How does your business rate in regards to?								
Range of products on offer?			✓			✓		
Technical expertise and ability?				✓		✓		

Figure 13-2:
Rating your business on key areas of performance.

Identifying Opportunities and Threats

Industry trends aren't the only things that can greatly affect your business but over which you have little control. What about changes in the economy, or the arrival of new competitors on the scene? For you to stay one step ahead, the name of the game is to try to anticipate the impact these outside factors may have on your business.

For each of the following categories, ask yourself what opportunities and what threats lie in store. Remember that any change can be an opportunity or a threat (or even both) depending on where you stand in the scheme of things. Organise these opportunities and threats in two columns, similar to Table 13-1. (Although bear in mind that Table 13-1 is a somewhat simplified example — your list will almost certainly have a bit more detail.)

Consider the following:

- **New competition:** How likely is it that new competitors could affect your business? Do you have special skills or a strategic advantage that safeguards you from competition? (I talk more about strategic advantage in Chapter 2.) Or is the thing that makes your business so successful easy to copy? What if the competitor has more capital, a better location or superior marketing abilities?

- **Emerging technologies:** How is technological change going to affect your business? Could new technology end up putting you out of business (think of the video store example at the beginning of this chapter)? Or are you skilled in the direction that new technology is heading, and could this be an opportunity?

- **Changes in demographics:** Demographic change is a long-term thing, but so (hopefully) is your business. If your business serves a local population (as opposed to having national distribution or being online), it pays to watch the trends in population patterns. (Running a children's toy store in a suburb with a rapidly growing retiree population and a declining birth rate may not be the most brilliant strategy ever.)

- **Changes in government regulations:** If your business is dependent in some way on government regulations (maybe you're a taxi driver, you work in health, or your business relies on government grants in some form or other), you're particularly vulnerable to changes in the political landscape. Ask yourself what impact changing regulations could have on your business, and how you could respond.

✔ **Changes in the economy:** Is your business very dependent on the ebb and flow of the economy? Some businesses (for example, a business selling staple food products) are relatively stable regardless of what's happening in the economy; other businesses (such as those selling high-end luxury goods) tend to move in tandem with booms and busts.

✔ **Changes in your domestic affairs:** You won't find personal stuff listed in other business-planning books, but if you're a small business, I know (from experience!) the impact that changes in your home life can have. A divorce can split business assets in two and turn a viable business into a struggling one, or the need for your family to move to another town for your spouse's job can dramatically affect your business. So if you think that a change of this nature is possible, don't be shy to include this in your plan.

Table 13-1	Summarising Opportunities and Threats
Opportunities	*Threats*
Analysis for iPhone app development company	
Huge growth in demand	Growth in number of competitors
Opening up of labour market means possibility to hire overseas programmers at lower rates	Offshore labour market means new competition often at very low prices
Some clients willing to sign up for profit-share arrangements in lieu of lower charges	Changes in programming languages make it hard to keep up, especially with small employee base and high cost of training
Lots of government contracts available as government bodies seek to create new apps for community info	Strong trend towards android phones, and expectation from clients for apps to be available for androids as well as smartphones
Analysis for solar panel installation company	
Huge growth in demand	Some serious new competitors with major muscle
If proposed government changes go ahead, major subsidies for consumers	Exclusive distribution licence ends in two years
Schools and government bodies obliged by their own policy to stick with local suppliers	Rapid growth requires high borrowings and puts pressure on cashflow
	If new government, all subsidies could finish

It's cool to be green

One overriding long-term global trend that's unlikely to change any time soon is the growth of environmental awareness, and the resultant demand for ecological products and services. Couple this with the growing acceptance of climate change as a reality, and you end up with a perfect example of something that is both a business opportunity and a business threat.

For those in the 'green' industry (ecological products, alternative energy, environmental consulting and so on) this long-term trend presents an opportunity. For those in industries with high energy demands, particularly those dependent on fossil fuels, this trend is a threat.

When you're thinking about opportunities and threats for your business, you may also want to refer to the industry analysis process earlier in this chapter ('Taking an Eagle-Eye View'). However, keep in mind that opportunities and threats in this context have a different scope than just one particular industry. For example, a global recession or a change in government isn't industry-specific. Or at the other end of the scale, the arrival of a new competitor may be a reflection of a growing population in one geographic region rather than an indication of general industry trends.

Keep your mind open to the fact that some things don't fit neatly into boxes as an opportunity or as a threat. Be willing to get creative. Although your analysis of threats and opportunities usually reflects your current position, stay open to new possibilities.

Doing a SWOT Analysis

If you've read any other business books or worked in larger organisations, you've probably already heard of a SWOT analysis (**S**trengths, **W**eaknesses, **O**pportunities and **T**hreats). As a model, the SWOT analysis sticks around while other business concepts come and go, simply because this way of looking at things is both easy to understand and surprisingly powerful.

Putting theory into practice

The idea of a SWOT analysis is simple:

- ✔ Aim to build on your strengths but minimise your weaknesses
- ✔ Endeavour to seize opportunities and counteract threats

Are you ready to try your own SWOT analysis? Then here goes:

1. **Make a list of the strengths and weaknesses of your business.**

   I explain how to do this earlier in this chapter in 'Putting yourself through the griller'.

2. **Make a list of possible opportunities and threats.**

   Refer to 'Identifying Opportunities and Threats' to find out how.

3. **Draw a grid similar to Figure 13-3.**

   You can use a whiteboard, butcher's paper or the nifty SWOT Analysis template that can be found at www.dummies.com/go/creatingbusinessplan.

4. **Divide your strengths into two categories: Strengths that can help you take advantage of opportunities, and strengths that can help you deal with threats.**

5. **Write down these strengths in the first row of your SWOT grid, along with the related opportunities or threats.**

   Strengths that help realise opportunities go in the top-left. Strengths that could help counteract threats go in the top-right.

6. **In the same manner, divide your weaknesses into two categories: weaknesses that may hinder you taking advantage of opportunities, and weaknesses that may make threats even more of a threat.**

7. **Write down these weaknesses, as well as the threats, in the second row of your SWOT grid.**

   Weaknesses that hinder opportunities go in the bottom-left; weaknesses that exacerbate threats go in the bottom-right.

Business SWOT Analysis		
	OPPORTUNITIES	**THREATS**
STRENGTHS	*Write strengths that assist with opportunities here, along with a description of the opportunity*	*Write strengths that help counteract threats here, along with a description of the threat*
WEAKNESSES	*Write weaknesses that may hinder you from exploiting opportunities here, along with a description of the opportunity*	*Write weaknesses that may compound threats here, along with a description of the threat*

Figure 13-3: The principles of a SWOT analysis.

Translating your SWOT analysis into action

After you've completed your SWOT analysis (refer to preceding section), what next? Put simply, this grid encapsulates four different business strategies:

- ✔ Aim to exploit any areas where your business is strong and is a good fit for an opportunity.

- ✔ Keep a watchful eye on any areas where your business is strong, but a threat may be looming.

- ✔ Try to improve on any areas where your business is weak but opportunities exist. (Maybe getting extra training, hiring employees with different skills, or employing consultants.)

- ✔ Take pre-emptive action and attempt to get rid of any areas in which your business is weak but a threat is looming.

Figure 13-4 shows a SWOT grid in action, matching the strengths and weaknesses of the iPhone app company in Figure 13-2 with the opportunities and threats identified in Table 13-1.

- ✔ **Top-left corner (where a strength meets an opportunity):** Strong marketing skills (as per Figure 13-2) balance perfectly with strong growth in customer demand, just as the use of domestic employees (rather than offshore employees) make a good fit for growth in government contracts. The business should aim to exploit these strengths.

- ✔ **Top-right corner (where a strength meets a threat):** Strong marketing skills also serve to mitigate the threat of rapidly increasing competition. The business needs to keep a watchful eye on both marketing strategy and new competitors.

- ✔ **Bottom-left corner (where a weakness meets an opportunity):** A significant weakness (identified against technical expertise in Figure 13-2) is that the business only develops apps for the iPhone platform, and not for androids. The business should aim to improve this area of their business, particularly as the emerging android market is a clear opportunity.

- ✔ **Bottom-right corner (where a weakness meets a threat):** The weaknesses in financial management may create problems as downwards pressure in pricing is likely, given growth of overseas developers. This weakness and threat create an unhappy synergy, indicating an area in which the business needs to take action.

Example Business SWOT Analysis for iPhone App Company		
	OPPORTUNITIES	**THREATS**
STRENGTHS	Strong sales and marketing skills, which are perfect for capitalising on huge growth in demand. Use of local (rather than overseas) labour mean we're well placed to secure work from government organisations	Strong marketing skills will assist in meeting the challenges of many new competitors
WEAKNESSES	Programming skill in only one platform may limit potential, particularly if android phones continue to take market share from iPhones	Weaknesses in financial management may leave us exposed as cheap overseas labour puts downward pressure on pricing

Figure 13-4: Plotting business strategy using a SWOT analysis.

Creating a Plan for Change

In some ways, creating a business plan can be very 'bitty'. You have missions and visions and financials and marketing plans, then industry analysis and more. Each one feels like a separate topic in its own right and may even require that you use a different mindset or different skills as you address each one. However, as you delve deeper and deeper into the process, you hopefully find that everything starts connecting.

Right at the beginning of this book, in Chapters 2 and 3, I talk about identifying your strategic advantage and analysing how your business compares to the competition. In many ways, the industry analysis and SWOT analysis in this chapter follow a similar process, but provide another layer of clarity regarding what areas in your business to exploit, as well as the weaknesses to guard against.

In your business plan, try to include the following:

✔ The issues or problems you face

✔ The opportunities that lie ahead

✔ A plan of action that outlines how you intend to mitigate your problems and exploit these opportunities

When drawing up a plan of action, try to express this plan in clear goals that are very specific and which have a timeframe. For example, 'A weakness in our business is our limited experience in creating android apps. We will attempt to hire a new employee with these skills within the next three months.' Or another example: 'A clear weakness in my business is the lack of financial skills and also the general lack of attention to my finances. I plan to focus on financial management with an aim to being able to produce and review my own Profit & Loss every month. If this proves too difficult, I will employ a casual bookkeeper.'

Are you a person who sees the glass half-full or half-empty? Sure, threats may be on the horizon, but do opportunities lie within these threats? As Winston Churchill said, 'A pessimist sees the difficulty in every opportunity; an optimist sees the opportunity in every difficulty'.

Chapter 14

Managing Risk

In This Chapter

▶ Staying vigilant about money, debts and cashflow

▶ Safeguarding your brand, image and life's work

▶ Limiting the amount of money you could lose if things go wrong

▶ Keeping squeaky clean in the eyes of the law

▶ Summarising your plan of action

*A*lthough people often think of running your own business as a risky activity, I don't. I've worked with many hundreds of businesses over the last 20 years and, although I can think of many businesses that have had to change radically or even had to close, I cannot think of one person who has lost their home or lifetime's savings as a consequence of business failure.

The time when you risk the most is usually when you first get started with a business, because you're still figuring out your business model, whether customers are going to want your products or services, and how you're going to be different from everyone else. However, after this critical first stage, the risk subsides.

With a bit of planning, you can minimise the risk that running a business entails. For example, you can register trademarks or patents to protect your intellectual property, take out insurance to protect yourself against litigation, set up company structures to limit your liability and implement strong reporting procedures to keep your finances as risk-free as possible.

In this chapter, I explain how to do all of these things, and more. Think of this part of the business-plan process as if you were putting up a bit of extra netting around the chicken coop so the foxes can't get in — something that's relatively quick to do, and which can save a whole load of pain and suffering.

Mitigating Financial Risk

When I talk about *financial risk*, I'm talking about the risk of a business being forced to close either because it's trading unprofitably or because it can't pay its debts when they fall due. (Interestingly enough, as I explain in Chapter 10, a business can be profitable yet still unable to pay its debts, particularly if it grows too fast.)

Any business carries financial risk, and some types of businesses are certainly more risky than others. On a positive note, if you can cultivate your financial management skills, plan conservatively *and* grow your business at a sustainable rate, you can usually stay in control. That's what the following sections are all about.

Maintaining profitability

The single most important thing you can do to protect yourself against financial risk is to maintain an accurate, up-to-date, well-organised set of accounts, ideally using accounting software.

I don't have the scope within this book to pick apart accounting software options, and indeed the software that works best for you will depend on where you are in the world, what kind of business you have, the size of your business and also what your accountant prefers to work with. However, I can say this: Unless you have a micro-business with no more than 10 or so transactions per month, don't even bother trying to do your books in Excel or by hand, but instead subscribe to some good accounting software.

With accounting software in place, your ongoing mission, week in and week out, is to keep a vigilant eye on sales, cost of sales and expenses:

- ✔ **Sales:** If you set targets for sales (refer to Chapters 5, 8 and 10), you probably also have an expense budget that's based on these sales targets. If you don't meet your sales targets, you're going to have to take quick action either to generate those extra sales or to pull back on your expenses (or both).

- ✔ **Cost of sales:** If your business has costs associated with sales (maybe you're a manufacturer, retailer, wholesaler or you use subcontract labour for your services), the relationship between cost of sales and sales can make or break your business. As I explain in Chapter 6, a difference of only 5 per cent in your gross profit margin can have a big impact. As financial manager, you need to be acutely aware of your target gross margins and be prepared to take action if these margins go off course.

✔ **Expenses:** I'm hoping you already have a budget for expenses. (If not, please feel free to check out Chapter 8.) Budgets exist for a reason, and your job is to make sure that expenses stay on track.

Although maintaining an overview of financial performance is vital, you don't necessarily have to be adept at bookkeeping or a whiz at interpreting reports. I sometimes think of a client of mine who has a great business selling soil-conditioning products. My client is a genius at sales (he could sell anything to anyone) and wonderful with people, but when it comes to financial reports and budgets, things get a little shadier. However, Russell is very talented at creating a good pool of skilled people around him, and he doesn't hesitate to seek assistance in the trickier areas of finance. The result? His business flies along, performing well in all areas.

If you struggle to understand Profit & Loss reports, or if you find it hard to set budgets and make projections for the year ahead, consider getting some extra training or paying for professional assistance.

Guarding against bad debts

Bad debts are when customers don't pay you what they owe. Maybe a customer has ceased trading, gone broke, is unhappy with your services or has left town in a puff of smoke. Whatever the reason, the reality is that you're not going to be paid.

In 2011, when I was working in publishing in Australia, a company called REDgroup Retail went bust. REDgroup was the parent company for the Australian and New Zealand divisions of Borders, and also owned two national bookstore chains: Angus & Robertson in Australia and Whitcoulls in New Zealand. For many publishers around Australia, sales to Borders and Angus & Robertson made up 30 per cent or more of total sales. These publishers not only lost 30 per cent of their turnover overnight, but many were left with hundreds of thousands of dollars of bad debts.

Bad debts can happen in any industry, but happily, you can do a few things to protect yourself:

✔ **Do credit checks:** If a customer applies for credit, ask the customer to complete a credit application form that includes at least two credit references. Follow up these credit references and see what other suppliers say.

✔ **Set credit limits:** Put strict credit limits on every customer's account and make sure your accounting software automatically alerts you (or anybody else who raises invoices) when a new sale could potentially take a customer over the limit.

✔ **Chase for dollars as soon as they're due:** The squeaky wheel gets the grease. If you offer a customer 30-day trading terms, chase for the overdue money as soon as 35 or 40 days tick over.

✔ **If possible, make chasing for money the sole responsibility for someone:** People hate getting on the phone chasing for money, and so if you ask an employee to be responsible for debt collection and this employee has lots of other responsibilities, human nature is such that debt collection will always slip to the bottom of the list. For this reason, if your business is big enough to afford it, consider making debt collection the sole task of a specific employee.

✔ **Consider credit insurance:** Credit insurance (also called bad debt insurance) means that if a customer goes belly up, you still get paid 80 to 90 per cent of the amount outstanding. Downside is, of course, that this kind of insurance can be really expensive.

✔ **Always consider your level of exposure:** If any one customer owes you enough that if that customer doesn't pay, you could go under, you're probably too exposed. Similarly, if any customer owes you more than 30 to 40 per cent of the total amount that you're owed, you are probably too exposed.

✔ **Develop a sniffer-dog instinct for businesses on the nose:** If a customer is repeatedly slow to pay, especially if that customer makes promises for payment and then doesn't deliver, be super careful about extending credit in the future.

If in doubt about extending credit, don't!

Managing cashflow

I talk lots about cashflow management in Chapter 10, where I explain how to create a Cashflow Projection for the next 12 months. However, just in case you don't want to do this whole process, I'll make one short (and not so sweet) point: Profit doesn't equal cash in the bank, in just the same way as cash in the bank certainly doesn't equal profit.

As I mention in Chapter 10, your business can quickly run short of cash if you need to pay tax, you purchase new equipment or have major start-up costs, make large loan repayments, or if you increase the value of credit you offer to customers or the value of inventory you hold.

Managing cashflow takes strong financial skills, particularly if a business has been unprofitable in the past or is tight on capital. A good financial manager is a master of timing. He or she will know when to delay payments, when to get short-term finance, how to order stock for last-minute delivery and how to predict a cash crunch before it happens.

At the time of writing, my stepdaughter is planning to start a new venture in the gourmet food industry. This weekend we spent all of Saturday going through the figures, looking at prices, building Profit & Loss Projections, setting sales targets and so on. (Aja makes a perfect test bunny for this book, reviewing each chapter as it unfolds.) On Sunday we arrived at the Cashflow Projection report and we made a prediction for how much cash would be in the bank at the end of the year. Despite the fact I'd just been completely immersed in writing the cashflow chapter, even I was shocked at how different the cash situation was compared to the profit. (The conclusion? White wine is indeed good medicine for almost any circumstance.)

If you have weak financial skills, a key strategy to counteract this weakness and reduce your financial risk is to get assistance with cashflow reporting and projections.

Staying on top of stock levels

A business that's saddled with stock that isn't selling is a business that's strapped for cash. Wholesalers and distributors are particularly vulnerable to this problem.

Managing stock levels sounds easier than it actually is. Most wholesalers have to order well in advance, often importing goods from overseas, and good prices — something that's so important for wholesalers — are usually contingent on ordering bulk quantities.

Here are some tips for keeping stock levels as low as possible:

- ✔ **Invest in inventory software:** Software that tells you the quantity and cost price for each item is a must.

- ✔ **Don't hang onto stuff:** If you only have 150 units of something on hand, you may think that's not so much. However, if you only sell 10 units or so a year, you have a whopping 15 years' worth of stock! Get rid of any stock that has been around for more than 12 months, and be grateful if you can get cost price for it. Certainly don't hang onto stock waiting to make a profit, because this strategy only costs you money.

- ✔ **Be wary of customers who promise like lions but order like mice:** I've seen chain stores in particular indicate 'order expectations' to small wholesalers that are completely inflated compared to what happens in reality. Meanwhile the wholesaler commits to importing hundreds of thousands of dollars of stock, most of which ends up lying dusty in a warehouse.

Rein in that personal spending

Creative impulse and generosity often go hand-in-hand with an entrepreneurial spirit. Predictably enough, this spontaneity often translates to overspending as soon as a business starts to turn a dollar. All that needs to happen next is a couple of big tax bills and, within a few months, a business that was going really well may start to struggle financially.

If you have been poor as a church mouse for months or even years as your business gets established, the good news is that you know how to survive on slim pickings. So if cash does start to roll through the door, hold onto your wallet for just a wee while longer until you know for sure you can go on exotic holidays, buy diamond rings or splash out on a sports car. (Sigh!)

Protecting Your Intellectual Property

Intellectual property (otherwise known as IP) sounds like such a grand term, doesn't it? Makes me think of professors, brilliant writers, inventors and scientists.

Intellectual property doesn't need to be anything particularly intellectual, however. In fact, the moment you start your business you start establishing your own intellectual property, no matter whether you're a carpenter or a chef, an astrologer or a zoologist.

Your intellectual property can be as simple as your company name, website name and logo, or as complex as your designs, method of manufacture or recipes, or as subtle as your procedures and your list of customers. Looking after your IP is an important part of the business-planning process.

Safeguarding your name, brand and designs

Creating intellectual property doesn't mean you own the rights to it. With the exception of copyright and circuit layout rights (which are automatic), in order to own the rights to intellectual property, you have to first register this property. If you don't, you may put your business at risk.

Fortunately, you can actively protect the intellectual property of your business in several ways:

- ✔ A *trademark* is a word, name, symbol or device that indicates the source of a product and distinguishes this product from others. Usually, you register a trademark under a specific *class* (usually using an international system of classification known as the *Nice Classification System*). For example, Lonely Planet is a trademarked term, and is registered under four classes: Software and publications, luggage and backpacks, travel agency services and restaurant services.

  Registering a business name doesn't mean you have ownership of that name. Even if you have registered as a company (which in most parts of the world affords a slightly higher level of protection than registering a trading name as a sole trader or partnership), the only sure way to protect your business name is to register a trademark.

- ✔ A *patent* offers protection for new and brilliant inventions, and can protect the rights for any device, substance, method or process. When you register a patent, you acquire exclusive rights to commercially exploit this invention for the life of the patent.

- ✔ A *registered design* gives you the exclusive rights to commercially use or sell a specific design, so long as this design is new and distinctive. This design refers to the shape, configuration, pattern or ornamentation that gives a product a unique appearance.

Other types of intellectual property include trade secrets (such as the secret recipe for KFC's chicken), copyright for original written material, and plant breeder rights for new plant varieties.

The process for registering trademarks and patents depends on where you are in the world and the different regulations that apply in each country. In most jurisdictions, you can now register trademarks and patents yourself without requiring expensive legal assistance and, accordingly, the cost can be surprisingly affordable.

When choosing a company name and registering a corresponding domain name (that is, a website address), try to grab the most common 'core' domains while you're at it. For example, if your business is in Australia and you decide to purchase 'www.petcrazy.com' as a domain name, try to purchase 'www.petcrazy.co', 'www.petcrazy.com.au' and 'www.petcrazy.net' as well.

Making sure you're not on someone else's patch

The flipside of protecting your own name and assets is ensuring you don't tread on the toes of someone else's.

In 2012, an eco-clothing label called 'I Am Not A Virgin' received a 'cease and desist' notice from the Virgin Group, stating that the company's name infringed on the Virgin brand and that the company had 30 days to cease trading or change its name. A tale of woe (because, of course, the Virgin Group had their way) but with a twist of humour as the Virgin lawyers dared to suggest that the company change their name to 'I Am Not Chaste' instead. (To hear more and maybe have a bit of a giggle, type 'I Am Not A Virgin' followed by the words 'Richard Branson' — Branson is the founder of Virgin Group — into YouTube.)

The moral? Before you invest too much in your company name and brand, conduct a thorough search of registered company names, trademarks and domain names.

Restricting employees with a view to when they move on

Any confidential business information that provides your business with a competitive edge can be considered a *trade secret*. Typically, this kind of information includes things such as customer lists, supplier pricing structures and manufacturing processes. This information can even include 'negative knowledge': services or products that you've tried but that didn't work out.

The most likely people to divulge your trade secrets (whether intentionally or inadvertently) are your employees or ex-employees. Here are a few ways to guard against this risk:

- ✔ **Get your employees to sign a confidentiality agreement:** When employees commence employment with you, get them to sign a confidentiality (or nondisclosure) agreement as part of their employment agreement.

- ✔ **Label stuff that's confidential accordingly:** If an email is confidential, include the word 'Confidential' in the subject line. If a report is confidential, type 'Confidential' at the top. If everything in a particular folder on your computer is confidential, password-protect this folder.

✔ **Let employees know why confidentiality is important:** Explain to employees (or include this information in your employee procedures) why keeping information confidential is important to the company and how it could hurt your company if secrecy were to be breached.

✔ **Consider a future non-competition provision:** This kind of provision prohibits ex-employees from setting up in direct competition when they leave your employment. (Seek legal advice if you're considering a clause of this nature, because this kind of provision can be tricky to enforce.)

Limiting Your Liability

As I mention right at the beginning of this chapter, for every risk in a business, you can usually find a way to counteract that risk. Two of the simplest methods involve choosing your business structure carefully and taking out a sensible level of insurance.

Choosing a business structure

What type of legal structure is going to be best for your business? The three main structures to choose between are sole trader, partnership or private company. (Other less common structures include co-operatives, limited partnerships and trusts.)

A *sole trader* structure means that it's just you who controls and owns the business, and that you're entitled to receive all of the profits. A *partnership* is when two or more people go into business and share profits in agreed proportions. With both of these structures, the business and the owners are one and the same thing in the eyes of the law.

In contrast, a *company structure* is a separate legal entity in its own right. The office-holders who run the company are called *directors*; the investors who own the company are called *shareholders*; the people who work for the company are the *employees*. What this means is that if you set up a simple company (even just with $2 of capital) and you're the only person earning a living from the company, you're simultaneously the sole director, the sole shareholder and the sole employee.

Each of these business structures has pros and cons, but a company structure has one key advantage when compared to other structures: *The liability of the directors is limited to a maximum of the net assets of the company.* Sounds very technical, but imagine a company has been trading at a loss and now has $30,000 in assets and $100,000 owing to creditors. If this company were to go bust, the director (or directors) wouldn't be personally liable to pay the creditors, despite the fact that the company doesn't have enough funds to pay all of its creditors. Similarly, if this company were sued by a customer and the company were found to be at fault, the directors wouldn't be personally liable.

Sounds good? I need to qualify this explanation of limited liability on three counts:

- ✔ If your company seeks to take out a loan, many lenders require a personal guarantee from directors, overriding the limited liability offered by a company structure.

- ✔ If your company is sued and you as a director are found to have been negligent (maybe you didn't follow health and safety regulations, or you knowingly used faulty components), you may be personally liable.

- ✔ If your company keeps trading while knowingly insolvent (in other words, you know you won't be able to pay your suppliers, but you purchase goods anyway), you may be personally liable.

Despite these three qualifiers, a company structure really does provide you with an extra layer of protection and helps protect your personal assets. If you don't already have a company structure, you should probably discuss this idea with your accountant.

Signing up for insurance

On the business-mentoring course that I'm involved with, a requirement of the course is that every person starting a new business takes out some form of insurance.

This policy may sound a little bureaucratic, but it works very well in practice because it forces the students to think really hard about what insurance they require.

Beware the risk of a lease that ends

If your business is very dependent on its location, don't forget to formulate a 'Plan B' for the eventuality that your lease may not be renewed when it comes to an end.

I know of a couple of businesses that have had either a great location in a central shopping strip or have had a quirky location that's perfect for their needs (such as a converted theatre or the old post office) and, when the lease has ended, the landlord hasn't renewed. For these businesses, relocating and reinventing the business has been a real struggle. (Particularly in one scenario when the landlord started up exactly the same kind of business in the location they had forced the tenant to vacate.)

You can't completely guard against this kind of situation, but you can always try to lessen the risk by negotiating for longer lease terms and keeping on really good terms with your landlord.

Business insurance falls into three broad categories:

- ✔ **Assets and revenue insurance:** Typical policies include insurance for building and contents, burglary, deterioration of stock, electronic equipment failure, employee dishonesty, goods in transit, interruption of business, machine breakdown and many different kinds of motor vehicle insurance. You almost certainly don't need all these policies, but you'll definitely require motor vehicle insurance of some kind, and probably contents insurance as well.

- ✔ **Liability insurance:** As soon as you interact with the public in any way, you need public liability insurance. You may also require professional indemnity and product liability insurance.

- ✔ **People insurance:** In almost all situations, you're obliged by law to have insurance that covers your employees in the event of an accident in the workplace. You may also want to take out income-protection insurance to cover yourself in the event of long-term sickness or disability.

The moment you tell the average insurance broker you're looking for business insurance, dollar signs replace the part of the eye where you normally find the pupil. While insurance is a must for any business, it's also an added expense. So go through any policy suggestions in detail and, if it makes sense to do so, minimise costs by not taking out policies you don't really need, or by increasing your excess or lowering your level of coverage.

Staying on the Right Side of the Law

Is this chapter at risk of being a bit doom and gloom? I hope not. If you do the right thing and comply with the various government rules and regulations, no harm should come to you . . .

Keeping your products safe

Licenses and permits are one thing, but the moment you manufacture products you step into a whole new realm of complications. I just had a look at the regulations that would apply if I were to make some homemade biscuits to sell at a stall in the village and I discovered that I would need to get local council approval, comply with the Food Standards Code, register with the Average Quality System and complete a full risk assessment. I don't actually want to bake biscuits so I didn't dig any deeper, but I suspect this list of regulations is only the tip of the iceberg.

Essentially, if you're manufacturing anything, a whole heap of regulations is certain to apply. Go to your local business advisory centre or ask your industry association for more information, so that you can be sure you meet all regulatory requirements.

From a slightly different perspective, these regulations usually exist for a good reason. Sure, you don't want to risk getting whacked with huge penalties, but you also don't want to run any risk of your products actually hurting someone else. Ultimately, causing injury to someone else would be a much harder thing to live with than having to pay a fine of some kind. (My son Finbar who is looking over my shoulder as I write this has just declared, 'Your biscuits aren't *that* bad, Mum'.)

Complying with employment legislation

It's a great feeling when your business grows big enough to be able to afford your first employee. However, you may find the number of laws surrounding employment a bit daunting at first. Suddenly, you need to understand about tax, pension schemes or superannuation, insurance, workplace safety and much more.

I'm not going to go into the different rules and regulations that apply (and besides, the regulations vary so much depending on where you are in the world). You can find heaps of information about hiring employees online, particularly from government websites, and this information provides a great starting point. However, after you think you've found out everything, get some follow-up advice from your accountant, business adviser or lawyer.

My daughter started her first full-time job last week and was catapulted straight into payroll administration with scant in-house supervision. The business had just won a contract and was hiring several new employees. Isla spent days trawling through paperwork, looking up information on websites, negotiating deals and setting up pays. By the end of the week, she felt quite confident that she had covered everything. Then she rang me for a chat and asked one brief question, which soon led to another, and then another. She was horrified by just how much she had missed or not been aware of in regards to employee entitlements, conditions and pay rates.

When it comes to employing people, what will get you in trouble is the stuff that you don't know even exists. For example, if you don't even know that payroll tax exists, how can you calculate it? If you don't know that laws exist regarding unfair dismissal of employees, how will you know to follow the correct procedures when firing someone? In terms of your business plan, it pays to identify whether your knowledge is weak in this area. If it is, try to mitigate any risks involved by seeking expert help or improving your own knowledge.

Ensuring a safe workplace

Workplace safety isn't just about preventing people from getting their legs chopped off in sawmills or being run over by tractors, but covers all types of workplace environments, including such things as how long employees should sit at a computer without a break, how hot the urn in the kitchen should be or how to organise work schedules to reduce stress.

In regards to you minimising risk for your employees (and, therefore, for your business), try to integrate safety practices into your business, and supplement these practices with some kind of written workplace policy. The idea is that as time goes on, safety becomes a habit, with both you and your employees working together to keep your workplace safe, on an ongoing basis.

If all this sounds a little heavy on theory but light on practicality, here are some everyday ways you can work towards making your workplace as safe as possible:

✔ Set limits on lifting weights. From a workplace safety perspective, claiming 'it was my employee's choice to lift the heavy sack' is no protection against prosecution.

✔ Display clear operating instructions next to any machinery — even the food processor in a kitchen or that urn in the back office.

✔ Always have a first-aid kit that's adequate for the sort of injuries and situations you're most likely to encounter on the premises. Try to make sure at least one employee has a First Aid qualification.

✔ Provide a smoke-free workplace.

✔ Ensure you have measures in place to prevent common injuries such as slips, trips and falls, manual handling, and ergonomic and repetitive strain injuries (these last two items apply particularly to staff working on computers all day).

✔ Ask employees to actively watch for risks and dangers in their workplace. Place health and safety on the agenda of every staff meeting and document these discussions as proof that you work actively on your health and safety procedures.

✔ Provide all new employees with a health and safety overview as part of their induction.

Understanding planning regulations

Planning regulations vary enormously locally, regionally and nationally. However, here are just a few things to be aware of:

✔ **Fumes, noise and waste:** Describes my teenage son's rock band perfectly. I'm sure he doesn't comply with environmental regulations. Maybe some authority could fine him for me.

✔ **Home offices:** Most one-person businesses can be operated from home without a problem, but as soon as you start employing staff or requiring customer parking, you need to find out what regulations apply in your area.

✔ **Licences:** If you're familiar with the industry, you probably already know what you need. But you almost certainly can't start a business wiring new homes just by following the step-by-step guide from WikiHow.

✔ **Retail approval:** Opening up a shop in any retail precint usually requires some kind of local council development approval, even if you have a legitimate lease in place. You also have to consider things such as opening hours and parking.

If you feel bamboozled by the number of regulations that apply to your business, your industry association is often a great source of practical advice.

Deciding What Goes in the Plan

In an aim to avoid this chapter feeling as if it's one drawn-out cautionary tale, I've tried to suggest some kind of preventative action for every risk you think you'll face. However, you may be wondering how you translate these suggestions into something practical to include in your business plan.

For the purposes of your plan, I suggest you create a table similar to the one in Table 14-1, which shows a risk analysis for one of my client's businesses (actually, I've merged a couple of businesses here to protect confidentiality). Table 14-1 identifies the risks you think you face, and what you plan to do to guard against these.

If you like, you can also download a Risk Action Plan template with the headings from Table 14-1 from www.dummies.com/go/creatingbusinessplan.

Table 14-1		An Example Risk Action Plan	
Type of Risk	**Details of Risk**	**Planned Action**	**Time Frame**
Financial risk	Poor profitability	Hire a consultant to look at our reporting systems so we can get regular P&L reports	Next month
		Monitor sales targets more closely	Hold a monthly sales meeting and compare budgets to actuals
		Try to improve gross profit margins (consider outsourcing production)	Six-month project
	Risk of bad debts	Set up credit policy	This month
		Employ someone to chase debts	Now
		Reduce credit limits for problem customers	ASAP
	Poor cashflow	Get additional help with Cashflow Projection reports	Speak to accountant next week
	High stock levels	Commission new aged stock report	Next month
		Consider not buying into new ranges unless sales more certain	Long-term
Risk of intellectual property getting copied	A competitor imitating our brand	Register trademark for business name and business logo	Next month

(continued)

Table 14-1 *(continued)*

Type of Risk	Details of Risk	Planned Action	Time Frame
Risk of intellectual property getting copied *(continued)*	Domain name confusion (if you type 'co' not 'com' at the end of the domain name, you get a different business)	Approach domain-name holder and make an offer to purchase domain name	February (when funds likely to be available)
	Employees starting up in competition when they leave	Draft formal confidentiality agreements with non-competition clauses and request employees to sign	Before Christmas
Risk of litigation	Risk of faulty product	Company structure provides reasonable protection, and high production standards are in place. Product and public liability insurance policies are also in place. No action required at present, other than constant monitoring that procedures are followed	Ongoing monitoring
	Risk of employee accident in the workplace	Workplace safety procedures are in place, but could probably be updated and employees could be involved more.	Call a staff meeting next week to work on this project
Risk of fines	No risks identified in regards to planning regulations	No action required at present	Ongoing monitoring
	Risk of contravening employment law	Employment agreements in place in regards to pay and conditions, and all approved by accountant. No action required at present	Ongoing monitoring
Risk of trade secrets being stolen/copied	Employees could divulge confidential information (on purpose or inadvertently)	Update employment agreements and company policies to include requirements regarding confidential information	ASAP

Chapter 15

Pulling Together Your Written Plan

. . . .

In This Chapter

▶ Stripping back to the skeleton of your plan — a quick anatomy lesson

▶ Creating a one-page concise summary of who you are and where you're at

▶ Assembling key financial documents

▶ Bringing together the other key elements of your plan

▶ Keeping yourself on track — a schedule for each turn on the road

. . . .

*I*f you've been working on your plan over the course of the last few days or even weeks, you may be feeling like your brain is turning to mush. You may have ended up with a random pile of notes, a folder of partially written Word documents, and a ragtag assembly of financial projections and reports.

Don't worry. In this chapter, I look at how the pieces of the business-plan jigsaw fit together. This stage is undoubtedly the most exciting part of the whole planning process. You get to take a step back, see how everything interconnects and experience that warm glow of self-belief as you think, Yes, I can succeed, and this plan explains just how.

In this chapter, I also share heaps of tips for keeping things real. Business plans too quickly slip into buzzwords and woolly promises. I reflect on the relative merits of mission statements and emphasise the importance of financials, sales targets and clear marketing plans. I also explain how to translate your big-picture goals into bite-sized chunks that you can plan to achieve next month, next week or right this very moment.

Reviewing the Overall Structure

You can organise your business plan in any way you like, but a format that works well (and which reflects how I've organised the chapters in this book and in the sample plan in the Appendix) is as follows:

- ✔ **Cover page and table of contents.** Your final business plan will probably end up being between 15 and 20 pages long, so a table of contents helps you and others find what's what.

- ✔ **Business overview, company description (including your strategic advantage), and a summary of key goals.** See 'Introducing Yourself and Your Business' next in this chapter to find out more.

- ✔ **Financial reports, including Profit & Loss Projections (essential) and Profit & Loss historical reports (essential unless you're a brand new business).** Other optional reports include break-even analysis, Cashflow Projections, ratio analysis, Balance Sheet reports and budgets. See 'Plunging into the Financials', later in this chapter, for more details.

- ✔ **A people plan and a summary of operations.** In this part of your plan, you summarise the skills of yourself and others involved in your business. Depending on your business, you may also include a summary of operations. See 'Selling yourself and your team' and 'Providing a quick summary of operations' later in this chapter.

- ✔ **Your marketing plan.** Chapter 12 provides a complete summary of how to construct a marketing plan.

- ✔ **A summary of industry and economic trends, opportunities or threats, and your risk-management plan.** I cover these topics in Chapters 13 and 14, as well as a summary of how to present these topics later in this chapter. (See 'Explaining how you're going to manage change and risk'.)

- ✔ **A summary of goals and an action plan, along with any appendices or extra information.** See 'Setting Milestones for Every Step of the Way', later in this chapter, for more info.

Please don't feel obliged to stick to my suggested structure. In particular, you may find that the industry analysis section sits better in the first part of your plan, immediately following your business and strategic overview. Also, if you've chosen to use business-planning software (a topic I cover in Chapter 1), you'll almost certainly end up with a structure that's slightly different. I reckon the sequence of information is irrelevant, so long as you end up covering the topics I list in the checklist in Table 15-1.

Table 15-1	Your Business Plan Checklist	
Planning Item	*Essential or Optional?*	*Completed?*
OVERALL SUMMARY		
Non-disclosure agreement	Include if your plan contains confidential information	
An inspirational description of your company and what it does	Essential	
A mission statement	Optional, but an expected part of a standard business plan	
A values statement	Only include if you truly intend to commit to these values	
A clear statement of how your business is different and a summary of strategic advantage	Essential	
A summary of the major goal or goals for your business for the next 12 to 24 months	Essential	
FINANCIALS		
Detailed sales budgets for the next 12 months, along with a summary of how you arrived at these budgets	Essential	
If you've been trading for more than a year, a Profit & Loss for the last 12 months	Essential	
If you've been trading for more than a year, a Balance Sheet generated for the last day of your Profit & Loss reporting period	Essential	
A Profit & Loss Projection for at least 12 months ahead	Essential	
A Cashflow Projection	Essential if you're predicting growth and you carry stock or offer credit to customers	
A budget for the next 12 months (your Profit & Loss Projection may be able to double as a budget)	Essential	
Moving annual turnover analysis	Useful for seasonal businesses	
Detailed product costings	Essential for manufacturers	

(continued)

Table 15-1 *(continued)*

Planning Item	Essential or Optional?	Completed?
MARKETING		
An analysis of who your customers currently are, and (if different) who you want them to be in the future	Essential	
A detailed competitor analysis	Essential	
A summary of the sales strategies you have in place, or intend to have in place, to support your sales targets	Essential	
A customer service plan	Essential	
PEOPLE		
A description of the skills and experience of both yourself and the others in your team	Essential	
STRATEGIC		
A summary of operations (distribution methods, premises, manufacturing processes and so on)	Often not relevant for service businesses	
An analysis of the industry in which you belong, the trends in this industry, and how you intend to be responsive to change	Essential	
A summary (and action plan) of strengths, weaknesses, opportunities and threats	Essential	
A risk-management plan	Essential	
ACTION		
A summary of goals and objectives	Essential	
An action plan summarising the timeframe for achieving these goals and objectives	Essential	

Go to www.dummies.com/go/creatingbusinessplan to download a copy of the Business Plan Checklist in Table 15-1. I've included a column where you can tick off each item as you complete it.

Introducing Yourself and Your Business

Most business plans start with a one-page summary that includes a mission statement, a brief company description and a summary of overall strategy (including a description of what makes this business different from other similar businesses). Many plans also include a values statement.

Although this one-page summary forms the first page of your plan, I suggest you delay writing this summary until you've worked on the other elements of your plan, including defining your strategic advantage, financial projections, marketing plan and so on. This page requires a strong, well-defined overview and if this is your first ever business plan, this clarity usually isn't something that you gain straightaway, but instead is something that emerges as your understanding of business deepens.

Developing a mission statement

Now for something a little radical: I'm not sure I really believe in mission statements. (Wondering what I'm talking about? A *mission statement* is a simple sentence or couple of sentences describing what your business is about.) Unless such a statement is superbly crafted with great insight, I reckon mission statements are about as useful as an umbrella in a bushfire.

I'm in good company with this opinion. In an interview with *Entrepreneur* magazine, Richard Branson (founder of Virgin Group) had this to say about mission statements: 'Most mission statements are full of truisms and are anything but inspirational. A company's employees don't really need to be told that "The mission of XYZ Widgets is to make the best widgets in the world while providing excellent service." They must think, "As opposed to what? Making the worst widgets and offering the lousiest service?" Such statements show that management lacks imagination, and perhaps in some cases, direction.'

Despite this general cynicism, if you intend to share your plan with others, a mission statement will be expected. So what's involved?

✔ **Keep your statement short and sweet.** Don't be tempted to write too much — if your mission statement is more than two sentences long, or it can't fit into the standard Twitter 140-character template, ditch it and begin again.

✔ **Make your statement inspirational.** 'My mission is to earn lots of money and retire by the time I'm 40' just isn't going to cut it, especially in the eyes of employees or customers. Try to create a mission with the potential to inspire and motivate others.

✔ **Reserve jargon for public servants.** For a humorous read on this topic, I recommend *Death Sentence: The Decay of Public Language* by Don Watson and published by Random House.

✔ **Look for inspiration online:** No-one but you can come up with an authentic mission statement, but if you run short on ideas, try checking out the missions of other businesses similar to your own. Go to a search engine like Google and type the words **mission statement** plus a word to cover whatever line of business you're in (for example, type: **mission statement plumbing company**).

✔ **Don't just cobble a few words together:** A good mission statement is no substitute for a bad business plan. Your customers aren't idiots, and generally have a sniffer-dog instinct for drivel.

What do you think of the mission statements from these well-known companies?

✔ Apple designs Macs, the best personal computers in the world, along with OS X, iLife, iWork and professional software. Apple leads the digital music revolution with its iPods and iTunes online store. Apple has reinvented the mobile phone with its revolutionary iPhone and App Store, and is defining the future of mobile media and computing devices with iPad.

✔ Pixar's objective is to combine proprietary technological and world-class creative talent to develop computer-animated feature films with memorable characters and heartwarming stories that appeal to audiences of all ages.

✔ At Bunnings, we are committed to delivering the lowest prices, widest range and best service to our customers every time they come in to our stores.

✔ Google's mission is to organize the world's information and make it universally accessible and useful.

✔ Dell's mission is to be the most successful computer company in the world at delivering the best customer experience in markets we serve.

For me, I like the mission statements from Pixar, Bunnings and Google but I feel that the statement provided by Apple (which seems to be little more than a product listing) lacks inspiration. Similarly, Dell's mission statement also lacks oomph, and the appalling syntax makes me want to send them a grammar manual.

Some companies talk about creating *vision statements* as well as mission statements. In this context, a vision statement encapsulates long-term goals and aspirations, along with the ideals that a business is striving for, whereas a mission statement is more about stating what you do, why you do it and whom you do it for. I find that the boundaries between these two kinds of statements get blurred, and for most situations, believe that a simple mission statement does just fine.

By the way, after you create your mission statement, don't forget to update your website or any other key marketing materials with what you state in your mission statement.

Crafting a company description

Imagine that someone who has never met you or traded with you before is reading your plan. How would you describe your business so that this person gets a good sense of who you are and what you do? With this scenario in mind, start writing, aiming for three of four paragraphs in total and keeping the following in mind:

- ✔ **Your strategic advantage and what differentiates you from your competitors:** This point is the single most important thing to include on the first page of your plan. For more on this topic, refer to Chapter 2.

- ✔ **How long your business has been running:** If your business has been running for some considerable time, say so. Be proud of your accomplishment.

- ✔ **The turnover of your business and the number of employees.**

- ✔ **The kind of services your business provides:** Be specific. If you're a physiotherapist, say what your area of speciality is and who your customers are. If you're a consultant hydro-geologist, explain what it is you do and what this activity involves.

- ✔ **The kind of industry your business belongs to:** Talk about your particular industry, what the trends are and what factors are peculiar to it.

- ✔ **Your main goal or goals:** If your goal is to reach sales of 10,000 units within two years, say so. If your goal is to expand your product range to double its size, say that.

- ✔ **The scope of opportunity:** Flesh out the full extent of any possible opportunities, particularly if your plan is going to be read by a possible investor.

You can find an example of a company description (also sometimes referred to as an executive summary) in the Appendix.

Talking about your values

Many business-planning experts suggest you include a values statement at the beginning of your plan, as part of the first page summary. While this idea sounds good in theory, I find it doesn't work so well in practice.

I knew a couple who started up a home-delivery service of organic fruit and vegetables. One of the values in their business plan was 'A 100 per cent commitment to organic produce'. However, as the business grew, they soon realised that what their customers valued was fresh produce and the convenience of regular home delivery. They discovered that if given the option, many customers were just as happy with locally grown (non-organic) produce, especially if it was cheaper. Commercial reality soon saw this couple change their offering, even though this conflicted with the values that they had supposedly committed to. In real life, they needed to make a living and weren't too fussed whether produce was organic or not, so long as it was fresh.

Of course, values are important — ethical behaviour is the bedrock of any society. However, don't put something in your values statement just because it sounds impressive to customers. If a value isn't something to which you're deeply committed, leave it out.

I reckon that a values statement is an optional part of your business plan, and you should only incorporate this statement if it genuinely adds meaning to the way you run your business.

Shhh, it's a secret

I'm a glutton for crime fiction and TV murder mysteries, and get a morbid thrill when a character who I've come to love and trust turns out to have been the baddie all along. Who can you trust? Nobody, it seems.

If you're planning to share your business plan with people outside of your company, I suggest you carry a little bit of that suspicion into your interactions with others. Almost any business plan contains confidential information that competitors would find helpful.

One neat way to ensure confidentiality is to ask outsiders to sign a *non-disclosure agreement* (a legally binding agreement that commits that person not to disclose any confidential information). You can find a sample Non-Disclosure Agreement template at www.dummies.com/go/creatingbusinessplan. Feel free to download this agreement and adapt it to your own requirements.

Plunging into the Financials

In working on the financial part of your plan, you may well have ended up with a wide selection of documents — everything from product costings to price comparisons, from historical sales reports to budgets for the years ahead. Which reports should you include in your final plan, and in what sequence should you present these?

Presenting your key reports

Here's a summary of the key financial reports you should consider including in your plan:

- ✔ If your business is new, include a summary of start-up expenses and how you plan to finance these.

- ✔ Always include a Profit & Loss Projection for at least the next 12 months. If your business is growing quickly, extend this projection and include figures for the next 24 to 36 months as well. (For subsequent years, you can summarise projections to include one column per quarter, rather than one column per month.)

- ✔ If your business has been trading a while, include a historical Profit & Loss for the last 12 months. Hopefully you use accounting software and so you can generate this report easily. If you don't, you may need to supply the Profit & Loss report from your most recent tax return. If the figures for the past 12 months are unusual for any reason, include some notes as to why.

  Consider including a column on your Profit & Loss that expresses each line as a percentage of sales. For example, if your sales are $100,000 and your wages $8,000, the percentage of sales column would say 8 per cent. This information helps benchmark your financials against other similar businesses. (For more about benchmarking, refer to Chapter 7.)

- ✔ Similarly, if your business has been trading a while, include a Balance Sheet right up to the end of the period that your Profit & Loss spans. (So if your Profit & Loss report goes from April to March, generate a Balance Sheet for 31 March.) Again, if you use accounting software, you can generate a Balance Sheet with a click of a button.

- ✔ If your business teeters on the edge of profitability or fails to generate enough profit for you to live comfortably, break-even analysis can be very helpful. In Chapter 9, I explain how you can calculate break-even analysis in several different ways.

 ✔ A Cashflow Projection report can be technical and time-consuming to create. However, you only really need this report if you're predicting growth for your business *and* you offer credit to customers or carry a significant amount of inventory.

 ✔ A Balance Sheet Projection predicts the value of assets, liabilities and equity at the end of the period that your Profit & Loss Projection spans. (So if your Profit & Loss Projection goes from April 2014 to March 2015, your Balance Sheet Projection forecasts account balances for 31 March 2015.) Unless you use business planning software, creating your own Balance Sheet Projections is normally out of reach for most ordinary mortals, and a Cashflow Projection is (mostly) a valid substitute. I talk more about this topic in Chapter 10.

 ✔ Depending on your business, you may want to provide more detail for some expense items in your Profit & Loss Projection, so that you can set down clear budgets for the year ahead. For example, you may want to grab the total figure for Advertising Expense and split this into a detailed budget for different marketing activities.

When you create financial projections, you have to make many assumptions along the way. Maybe you've assumed that you're going to hire a new employee in three months' time, that you're going to shift premises, or that a new sales contract is going to come through. Even if the plan is for your eyes only, include these assumptions in your narrative. (The sample plan in the Appendix shows what format this narrative may take.)

You may even want to include multiple scenarios in this part of your plan: What if sales were 10 per cent higher or expenses 20 per cent lower? (Chapter 8 explains how to create multiple scenarios easily and quickly.)

Pleading for finance

If one of the purposes of your plan is to apply for a loan or hustle for investor funds, you want to include a coherent plea for finance in your plan. This plea should include how much finance you require and when, how long you want to borrow this money for, the interest you expect to pay, and your proposed repayment schedule. (Chapter 4 explains about how to calculate loan repayments and interest.)

Be ultra-careful to ensure your financial projections reflect the need for finance and the proposed repayment plan. Your Cashflow Projection is ideal for corroborating the need for additional finance, because this report predicts your cash balance at the end of each month and quickly highlights predicted cash shortfalls.

Don't forget to include the anticipated loan interest as an expense in your Profit & Loss Projection, and also include the full value of proposed loan repayments in your Cashflow Projection. Alternatively, if your plan doesn't include a Cashflow Projection, show the full value of the loan repayment in the Profit & Loss Projection.

Lenders and investors tend to look for different things in a business plan. Lenders typically look for strong profitability and assets such as the family home to use as a guarantee. Lenders also focus on the accuracy of your financial reports, as well as details regarding your personal assets and credit rating. In contrast, investors are on the hunt for the opportunity that lies within a clever business idea, and for the chance to get above average returns. For this reason, investors are often less concerned about the accuracy of financial reports, and are focused on examining competitor analysis and sales trends.

Adding extra information

I try to keep the financial stuff pretty simple for most plans but, depending on your business, you may want to add some additional information beyond the reports I suggest in the preceding sections. Three things that I often look at when reviewing a business are moving annual turnover, the accounts receivable ratio and the stock turnover ratio.

Moving annual turnover analysis

If you have a seasonal business, with big spikes in trade at certain times of year, analysing overall sales trends can be very tricky. However, moving annual turnover (MAT) analysis provides a clever solution that enables you to map trends more accurately.

The idea is that at the end of every month, you add up the sales for the last 12 months, including the month just completed. So at the end of February 2015 you add up sales for the period March 2014 to February 2015, and at the end of March 2015 you add up sales for the period April 2014 to March 2015. Continue this for 12 months and the end result is a graph that shows you the true trends of what's happening in your business.

I show how this report works in Figure 15-1. The first graph shows the sales figures for a retail store for the last 24 months. As you can see, the figures go up and down but don't seem to head anywhere in particular. The second graph shows MAT for the past 12 months, based on the same figures. Can you see how the general trend is one of steady growth?

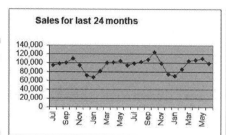

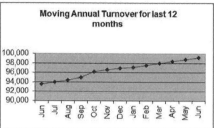

Figure 15-1:
Analysing
moving
annual
turnover.

Accounts receivable ratio

Your *accounts receivable ratio* is a ratio that calculates how many days, on average, it takes between invoicing a customer and getting paid. If you keep an eye on this ratio and how it changes from month to month or from year to year, you can get a real insight into the effectiveness of your invoice collection procedures.

To calculate this ratio, simply divide your total sales for the past 12 months by the current value of accounts receivable. For example, if total sales for the last 12 months for your business were $300,000 and you're currently owed $65,000, your accounts receivable ratio is:

$$\$300,000/\$65,000 = 3.75$$

If you get really excited by this calculation, go one step further and divide the number of days in a year by this ratio:

$$365/3.75 = 97$$

This ratio means that it takes an average of 97 days for your customers to pay up, which incidentally would be a poor average in most industries.

I worked as a consultant for a medical insurance company a few years ago. Almost all the clients were government departments or insurance companies, with convoluted payment approval procedures. On average, it took 90 days to get paid. I calculated that if we could get this average down to 30 days, the company would save $45,000 a year in interest. I used this argument to justify the employment of a dedicated debt-collection officer for 3 days per week, and also commissioned several custom reports that assisted clients with the information they needed to get invoices approved quickly. I monitored the debt collection ratio every month, observing how our changes in procedures were slowly making an impact. (We did succeed in a payment average of 35 days in the end, something everyone was really pleased about.)

Stock turnover ratio

If you carry stock for resale as part of your business, your turnover ratio is a handy analysis tool.

Turnover ratio = total sales divided by cost value of stock on hand

For example, if annual sales for your business are $600,000 and the current cost value of your stock on hand is $80,000, your turnover ratio is:

$600,000/$80,000 = 7.5

Now divide the number of days in a year by this ratio:

365/7.5 = 48.6

In other words, this means that it takes an average of 48 days for a stock item to sell. Whether this average is good or bad depends on the kind of business you're running (an average of 48 days for selling something would be poor for a store selling food, but excellent for a store selling furniture).

If you have a high turnover ratio, you have less money tied up in stock, new products to attract customers and higher sales for the same amount of space. If you have a low turnover ratio, chances are you're investing in some poor stock choices or buying far more than you need at one time.

Completing the Rest of Your Plan

The last ten or so pages of your plan include your people plan, a summary of operations, your marketing plan, SWOT analysis and risk-management plan. When collating this information, keep returning in your mind to your overall goals and business strategy. How well do the pieces fit together?

Look for consistency. If your marketing plan budgets for a significant growth in sales, is this growth reflected in your people plan (in other words, do you intend to recruit more staff)? If your SWOT analysis shows a weakness in working with social media, does the Facebook strategy that forms the keystone of your marketing plan make sense?

Selling yourself and your team

One of the things I try to convey to people just getting started in business is that you must think of your business as being separate from yourself. In order to grow, you need to involve others so that you can leverage your business idea and expertise. This need to conceive of your business as a separate entity in its own right is why the people part of your plan is so important. (I explore this topic in some depth in Chapter 11.)

For the purposes of your plan, all you need to do is write a concise description about the key people involved in the business and who is responsible for doing what. If you're only just getting started — maybe you don't have any employees yet — include details of people in your network who are assisting you, such as your accountant, business mentor, or family and friends. Write a short description of each person's role, including relevant work experience and qualifications, and don't hesitate to emphasise the unique skills that each person contributes. (I don't normally suggest you include résumés or CVs in a business plan, but if you feel such a document would be relevant, stick it in your plan's appendices.)

If you've identified any particular weaknesses within your company — maybe you're not strong on financials or you don't have anybody in your business who's confident with social media — consider addressing this weakness in your people plan and explain how you intend to manage this.

Providing a quick summary of operations

I don't really dwell much on operations elsewhere in this book, but if you're a manufacturer or wholesaler, I suggest you include a brief summary of operations management at this point in your plan. This summary typically describes the process of manufacture, where and how your product is manufactured, and what mechanisms you have in place for order fulfilment and delivery.

What you include in this part of a plan is very specific to each business. Maybe you're tossing up whether to manufacture in-house or to outsource production; maybe you have issues with the premises where you manufacture goods; maybe supply and demand are difficult to manage and you have long lead times when ordering materials. Order fulfilment can also be tricky: Do you plan to distribute goods yourself? How will you manage freight? Are the costs of order fulfilment so high that you need to get a certain level of orders before you can break even?

The name of the game with most manufacturing and wholesale businesses is profit margins, where a change of 1 or 2 per cent can spell the difference between success and failure. The operations side of things (warehouse rent, warehouse staff, freight, order processing and so on) is often where a significant chunk of profit gets chewed up, especially for growing businesses where staff requirements change frequently.

Introducing the killer marketing plan

In Chapter 12, I run through the key elements of a marketing plan: The introduction, a target market analysis, a competitor analysis, a summary of sales targets, a summary of sales strategies and a customer service plan. This structure works well regardless of whether a marketing plan is a stand-alone document or forms part of an overall business plan. Probably my only comment related to the marketing section of a business plan is that it typically provides a bit more information as to how you arrived at your monthly sales budgets, such as splitting up sales by agent, customer channel, product or location.

The main thing when working on the marketing section of a business plan is to ensure that the figures in your marketing plan correlate dollar for dollar with the figures in your financials. So if your predicted sales for the next 12 months in your marketing plan are $252,000, ensure your Profit & Loss Projection says exactly the same thing. Similarly, if the total for Advertising Expense in your Profit & Loss Projection is $5,000 for the year, ensure this correlates with your marketing strategies and marketing budget.

Explaining how you plan to manage change and risk

In Chapters 13 and 14, I talk about managing change and trying to minimise risk. These topics are broad in nature, so how do you decide what information to include in your plan? Consider including the following:

- ✔ **An analysis of your industry:** As I explain in Chapter 13, try to include at least one to two paragraphs on each of the following topics (unless a particular topic is irrelevant to your industry): the potential impact on your business of any changes in competitor activity, environmental factors, exchange rates, outsourcing patterns from overseas, government legislation or technology. The analysis should also include a general overview of overall trends in pricing and the growth or decline of the industry as a whole.

   With this analysis, if you have sourced expert reports regarding industry trends, summarise the gist of these reports in one or two sentences in the main body of your plan, but consider including the full report at the end of your plan as an appendix.

- ✔ **Your SWOT analysis:** I explain how to do a SWOT analysis in Chapter 13. It's up to you whether you only include the final 'SWOT grid' or you choose to include the workings that lie behind this grid, including the detailed analysis of your strengths and weaknesses. I generally feel that the more information you include in this part of your plan, the better.

- ✔ **A risk-management plan:** Chapter 14 explains how to look out for risk and take action to minimise risk in your business, and provides a suggested framework for a risk action plan at the end of the chapter. Make sure you include this action plan as part of your business plan. Also as part of this action plan, ensure that you adequately cover the topics of protecting intellectual property and insurance. (Any lender or outside investor is going to want reassurance that you have these areas covered.)

Setting Milestones for Every Step of the Way

As you progress through your plan, you inevitably end up with a whole heap of goals, including financial goals, sales goals, customer conversion goals, personal goals and product goals. Some of these goals may reflect that you still have extra distance to go with the planning process, or some may reflect the necessity to keep reviewing your plan every six months or so.

In the last part of your plan, I suggest you bring all of these goals together into a single schedule and create the planning calendar from hell.

Translating your plan into clear goals

Start by reading through every line of your business plan and thinking about what action you need to take. For example, maybe in your SWOT analysis you identified a weakness in that you haven't yet trademarked your logo and business name. Translate this weakness into a plan of action — decide when you want to initiate trademark application procedures, and set a timeframe.

 When creating an action plan, you may want to try to differentiate between *goals* and *objectives*. Goals are the overarching aim of the game; objectives are the means by which you get there. Table 15-2 gives you an idea of how to make this distinction.

If you don't want to bother with the semantics of separating goals and objectives, that's fine too. The main thing is to remember that the best goals are always SMART: **S**pecific, **M**easurable, **A**chievable, **R**ealistic and **T**ime-specific. (I explain this terminology in Chapter 12, but the words give you some idea of what's required.)

Table 15-2	Creating an Action Plan	
Goal	*Objective*	*Time Frame*
Stay aware of changes in competitors	Review competitor analysis	Six-monthly
	Visit at least five competitor shops and report back	March
Stay within 5% of budgets for the next 12 months	Enter monthly budgets into accounting software	Annual
	Compare actuals against budgets in Profit & Loss	Monthly
Get on top of bookkeeping and produce accurate financial reports	Hire a bookkeeper ASAP and ensure accounts are reconciled weekly	Weekly check
Manage cashflow hiccups and pay all creditors on time for the next 12 months	Arrange for short-term loan finance over summer period	Apply in Nov

(continued)

Table 15-2 (continued)

Goal	Objective	Time Frame
Increase gross profit margin by 5% within 6 months	Research ways to reduce product costs, particularly packaging	Ongoing
	Look at changing freight companies to reduce shipping	Ongoing
Meet or exceed sales targets for the next 12 months	Sign up one new customer every week	Weekly
	Aim to find one new distributor to serve western seaboard	By October
	Update email templates	Now
	Sign up for Google Adwords (budget equals $40 per week)	Do now, review monthly
	Report actuals against marketing budget every month	Monthly
Increase proportion of online sales to 10% of overall sales	Start a blog, aim for one post every fortnight	Fortnightly
	Sign up for online marketing course at local business centre	September
Protect intellectual property and brand	Get help to create formal employee agreements and include a non-disclosure agreement as part of same	October
	Commence trademark application	September
	Register .com and .co domain names	April
Stay abreast of industry trends	Attend monthly industry association meetings	Monthly
	Review industry statistics	Six-monthly
Secure business against potential litigation	Draw up a product recall policy	Feb
	Review all insurance policies	Annual

Creating a calendar

After you clarify your various planning goals, along with the time frame and frequency for each goal, I suggest you transfer these goals onto a business-planning calendar for the next 12 months. Figure 15-2 shows an example of a calendar that corresponds to Table 15-2 from the previous section of this chapter. (I only show one month here, but I suggest you include a full 12-month calendar in your plan.)

Depending on the size of your business, you may find creating several business planning calendars according to who is responsible for what makes more sense than creating only one overall calendar. However, as the owner, you still want to keep an overall eye on everyone else's planning calendar, not just your own, so that you can be sure nothing falls by the wayside. Alternatively, you can use different colours to indicate different people's responsibilities, as I do in Figure 15-2 (with one colour for the general manager's responsibilities, another for the marketing manager's and another for the bookkeeper's).

When looking at Figure 15-2, you may wonder why I put something as routine as keeping accounts up to date in a planning calendar. Fair question. I do so only because in this scenario, one of the goals for the business is to hire a bookkeeper to try to get their finances under control. Once the bookkeeper is on top of things and routines are established — with the clear expectation that accounts are updated weekly — this item could probably drop off the planning calendar. The same could arguably apply with weekly goals to sign up one new customer per week or even the fortnightly blog posting. However, until activities become a routine part of a person's job, the planning calendar acts as a great prompt to ensure these new ideas or systems actually happen.

OCTOBER Planning calendar

MONDAY	TUESDAY	WEDNESDAY	THURSDAY	FRIDAY	SATURDAY	SUNDAY
		1	2 MONTHLY Compare sales targets against budgets	3 WEEKLY: Ensure accounts up to date and reconciled.	4 FORTNIGHTLY: Write blog posting for website.	5
6 WEEKLY: Sign up one new customer this week	7 MONTHLY Finalise accounts for previous month	8 MONTHLY Compare budgets against actuals for P&L	9	10 WEEKLY: Ensure accounts up to date and reconciled.	11	12
13 WEEKLY: Sign up one new customer this week	14 ONGOING: Follow up packaging quotes and test new cartons	15 Submit loan application for anticipated Jan cash shortfall	16	17 WEEKLY: Ensure accounts up to date and reconciled.	18 FORTNIGHTLY: Write blog posting for website.	19
20 WEEKLY: Sign up one new customer this week	21 BI-MONTHLY: 7.30pm Industry Association Meeting	22	23 Contact solicitor regarding employee agreements	24 WEEKLY: Ensure accounts up to date and reconciled	25 WEEKEND COURSE at local business centre (social media marketing)	26
27 WEEKLY: Sign up one new customer this week	28	29 Follow up trademark paperwork	30 MONTHLY Review Google Adwords report	31 WEEKLY: Ensure accounts up to date and reconciled.		
		NOTES:				

Figure 15-2: Creating a planning calendar.

Part V
The Part of Tens

Enjoy an additional (and free!) online Part of Tens chapter about creating business plans. Visit www.dummies.com/extras/creatingbusinessplan.

In this part . . .

- Discover ten Excel tips to make creating your business plan quicker and easier.

- Learn how to format your plan to look polished, presentable and professional.

- Find out the ten questions you must ask yourself before you finish your plan.

Chapter 16

Ten Tips for Using Excel in Your Business Plan

. . . .

In This Chapter
▶ Adding stuff up in the blink of an eye
▶ Discovering tricks to speed your work
▶ Tweaking formats so your worksheets look smart
▶ Connecting one worksheet to another
▶ Splashing out with charts and graphs

. . . .

*I*n this chapter, I focus on the stuff you need to know about Excel when creating a business plan. I realise this is a business planning book, not an Excel manual, but I believe that being able to create budgets and financial projections using Excel (or any other spreadsheet software) is a pretty important skill for anyone involved in business, and one that gets overlooked by most business books.

This skill is important simply because of the many hours you'll save. Instead of adding up columns of figures using a calculator and recalculating totals each time a figure changes, Excel adds up everything for you, automatically updating totals along the way.

If you find that an instruction in this chapter doesn't make sense (for example, maybe I mention the View menu but you can't see a menu by that name), don't stress. The exact instructions can vary a little depending on what spreadsheet software you're using, particularly if you're using an open-source spreadsheet such as OpenOffice or Google Docs rather than Excel. Simply click the Help button and search on whatever it is that I'm trying to explain (such as AutoSum, freezing panes, or copying and pasting), and you should find instructions to help you out.

If you haven't worked with Excel before, don't feel anxious. If you can use a calculator, you can use Excel.

For more assistance on any of the topics covered in this chapter, you can watch a fee 'how-to' video. Visit `www.dummies.com/go/creatingbusinessplan`.

Get Things to Add Up Automatically

At its simplest, Excel is a grid of rows and columns. Each square in the grid is called a *cell*. To see how this concept works, have a look at the worksheet in Figure 16-1. Can you see the column labels along the top (A, B, C and so on) and the row labels down the left side (1, 2, 3 and so on)? Now look at the text in the top-left that says 'Sales Region A'. This text sits in Column A and Row 2. The cell reference for this text is cell **A2**.

With this technical understanding of cell references in place, you're ready to create your first formula. I'm going to demonstrate how to add up figures automatically, probably one of the most important things that Excel can help with when it comes to your business plan. Here's how:

1. **Click in the cell where you want the total to appear.**

   You normally click in the cell at the bottom of a column of figures or to the right of a row of figures. For example, in Figure 16-1, I click in cell B6.

2. **Go to the Formulas menu and click the AutoSum button.**

   Can you see the AutoSum button in the top-left? Simply click here and Excel inserts a formula that totals all the figures in the column above (or all the figures in the row to the left).

   Don't worry if you can't find the AutoSum button (this button does move around from version to version). You can always type a formula instead. The formula for adding up figures is =**SUM** followed by the cells you want to add. For example, in Figure 16-1, the formula is =**SUM(B2:B5)**.

3. **Press the Enter key (return on a Mac).**

   The total appears automatically (which should be $54,100 in this example).

Can you see how the formula appears in the formula bar just above the column labels? If the formula bar doesn't appear when you're working in Excel, I suggest you change your view settings. Depending what version of Excel you're using, try some permutation of the following: Go to the View tab and tick the Formula Bar option; go to the View tab, click the Show button, and then tick the Formula Bar option; select Formula Bar from the View menu.

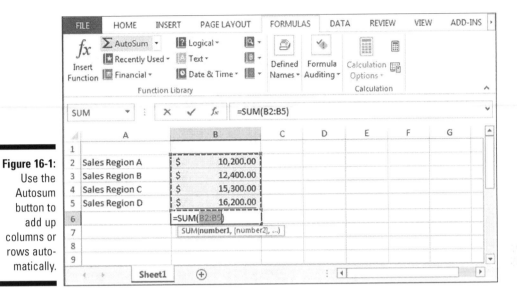

Figure 16-1:
Use the
Autosum
button to
add up
columns or
rows auto-
matically.

Learn to Drag and Copy

The *fill handle* is a small black dot or square that appears in the bottom-
right of an active cell. You can use the fill handle in a few different ways,
including copying a cell's contents to adjacent cells or to create a series.

First of all, imagine I want to copy a formula from one cell to the next. For
example, in Figure 16-2, I already have a SUM formula for January's sales.
Although I could click on the bottom of each column for February through
to April and insert a formula for each one, a much quicker approach is to
copy the formula I already have.

Here's how to copy the formula across this row for three more months:

1. **Click in the cell that has the formula you want to copy.**

2. **Rest your mouse on the black square in the bottom-right corner.**

   A black crosshair symbol appears, a little like a plus sign.

3. **Click with the mouse and holding the mouse button down, drag the black crosshair symbol to the right across three columns (as far as Column E in Figure 16-2).**

4. **Let go of the mouse.**

Your formula should now appear across that row, totalling each month.

	A	B		C		D	E	F
1		Jan		Feb		Mar	Apr	
2	Sales Region A	$	10,200.00	$	11,300.00	$ 9,100.00	$15,000.00	
3	Sales Region B	$	12,400.00	$	12,100.00	$ 8,200.00	$ 7,000.00	
4	Sales Region C	$	15,300.00	$	16,200.00	$ 7,600.00	$17,000.00	
5	Sales Region D	$	16,200.00	$	17,050.00	$19,000.00	$16,020.00	
6		$	54,100.00					
7								
8								

Figure 16-2: Click and drag the little back square in the bottom-right of an active cell and see what happens.

You can use the fill-handle principle to extend a series of numbers or labels. In the context of a business plan, I often use this technique to automatically complete the months of the year along the top of a worksheet. To do this, I type the names of the first two months (for example, 'Jan' and 'Feb'), click on the second month and grab the fill handle, then drag my mouse to the right. Quick as a teenage fridge-raid, the name of each month of the year appears.

Format Cells so They Make Sense

If you want the financials in your business plan to look good, spend a little time on formatting. Here are some tips:

✔ **Show the dollar signs.** To include the dollar sign next to your numbers, highlight the cells you want to format and click the $ sign on the Formatting toolbar. (If you can't see this icon, go to the Home tab, select Format from the Cells group and select Currency as the Number style.)

✔ **Don't clutter up financial projections with cents and decimals.** To hide the cents from view, select Format from the Cells group followed by the number 0 in the Decimal Places field. Alternatively, highlight the cells and click the Decrease Decimal arrow (the arrow that points to the right) from the Number group of commands on the Home tab.

- ✔ **Format percentages correctly.** To express a figure as a percentage, go to the Home tab, and click the % option from the Number group of commands.

- ✔ **Get headings to fit.** If you have a long heading that doesn't quite fit in a column, first increase the height of the column. To do this, drag down the dividing line that separates the row labels (for example, drag down the dividing line that appears between numbers 1 and 2 on the left side of your worksheet). Then go to the Home tab and click Wrap Text from the Alignment group of commands.

- ✔ **Merge cells when required.** To add a heading that spans multiple columns, highlight the cells in this row, go to the Home tab, and select Merge Cells from the Alignment group of commands.

One more thing. Don't be tempted to use more than one font in a financial projection. For example, don't use Times New Roman for the headings and Arial for the numbers. Just stick to one font across all your financial reports. People want to concentrate on the figures, not be distracted by fancy design.

Freeze Rows and Columns

When working on financial projections, you often end up with a whole heap of columns and rows. All too quickly, your column and row headers slip out of sight, and you can't see what month you're working on or what expense you're meant to be budgeting for.

The solution is to 'freeze' the rows or columns you want to keep in view.

To freeze the very top row, so that when you scroll down you can always see this row, go to the View tab and select Freeze Top Row from the Freeze Panes menu. (If Freeze Panes is greyed out, select Normal rather than Page Layout as your View settings.) Similarly, to freeze the first column, so that when you scroll to the right you can always see this column, select Freeze First Columns.

To freeze a row that's near the top of your spreadsheet but isn't actually at the top — maybe the names of the months aren't in the top row, but in the second or third row down — click in a cell that's just below the row you want to freeze and select Freeze Panes. (This will also freeze the columns to the left of wherever you had clicked.) You can see how my worksheet looks after I've frozen both panes in Figure 16-3. To remove this split, click Unfreeze Panes from the Freeze Panes menu.

Figure 16-3:
Freezing
panes
enables
you to
always keep
column
and row
headings in
sight.

Apply Conditional Highlights

Conditional highlighting is one of the neatest features in Excel. With financial projections, I like to apply conditional highlighting so that all the negative results show up in pink.

In Figure 16-4, I take the Cashflow Projection from Chapter 10, but this time I apply conditional formatting. Can you see how all the negative amounts come up in pink (or grey, if you're reading this as a printed book rather than an ebook)? You can get this to happen automatically by doing the following:

1. **Select the cells to which you want to apply formatting.**

   In most situations, I just highlight the whole worksheet.

2. **On the Home tab, in the Styles group, click the arrow next to Conditional Formatting, and then click Highlight Cells Rules.**

3. **Select Less Than as the rule, enter 0 as the amount, then click OK.**

   Admire your handiwork as all negative amounts turn pink.

	A	B	C	D	E	F	G	H	I	J	K	L	M
1		Jun	Jul	Aug	Sep	Oct	Nov	Dec	Jan	Feb	Mar	Apr	May
54													
55	**Net Profit**		- 6,882	- 5,602	- 2,187	- 4,287	- 72	41,423	- 13,757	- 5,487	- 3,637	- 4,007	6,893
56													
57	**CASH INFLOWS**												
58	Cash Collected From Sales		25,000	31,070	35,440	41,150	36,450	47,260	174,890	13,400	31,350	50,850	56,770
59	Loan Finance		120,000										
60	Total Cash Inflows		**145,000**	**31,070**	**35,440**	**41,150**	**36,450**	**47,260**	**174,890**	**13,400**	**31,350**	**50,850**	**56,770**
61													
62	**CASH OUTFLOWS**												
63	Purchase of New Equipment		12,000		25,000				12,000				5,000
64	Purchases of Stock		24,000	26,000	23,000	29,000	110,000	24,000	15,000	34,000	37,000	43,000	50,000
65	Expenses		18,857	19,007	17,407	17,957	17,207	16,907	17,957	17,507	21,907	24,157	17,207
66	Company Tax					2,000			2,000			2,000	
67	Loan Repayments		2,500	2,500	2,500	2,500	2,500	2,500	2,500	2,500	2,500	2,500	2,500
68			**57,357**	**47,507**	**67,907**	**51,457**	**129,707**	**43,407**	**49,457**	**54,007**	**61,407**	**71,657**	**74,707**
69													
70	Opening Cash		1,000	88,643	72,207	39,740	29,433	- 63,823	- 59,970	65,463	24,857	- 5,200	- 26,007
71	Cash Inflow less Cash Outflow		87,643	- 16,437	- 32,467	- 10,307	- 93,257	3,853	125,433	- 40,607	- 30,057	- 20,807	- 17,937
72	Closing Cash		**88,643**	**72,207**	**39,740**	**29,433**	**- 63,823**	**- 59,970**	**65,463**	**24,857**	**- 5,200**	**- 26,007**	**- 43,943**
73													
74													

Figure 16-4: You can use conditional formatting to automatically highlight negative results.

Hide Stuff You Don't Need

Often when you're working on financial reports, you want to create a summary of results. For example, if you're working on a Profit & Loss Projection, maybe you want to summarise this report so you view totals for total sales, gross profit, total expenses and net profit only.

The solution is easy. Simply highlight the rows you want to hide from view, and then from the Home tab, go to the Cells group of commands and select Hide & Unhide from the Format menu. Click Hide Rows and the rows obligingly disappear from sight.

To reveal rows that you've hidden, return to the Format menu but this time select Unhide Rows.

Link One Worksheet to Another

In Chapter 8, I explain how you can create several worksheets within a single Excel file, and that you can link information from one sheet to another. For example, you can have a Profit & Loss Projection on one sheet and a Cashflow Projection on another, and when you change a figure in your Profit & Loss, this change automatically flows through to the Cashflow.

The same principle applies across different Excel files. For example, imagine that you're running a business where the sales manager maintains a detailed worksheet with sales budgets for each sales agent and territory, and that you need the grand total of these sales budgets to use in your Profit & Loss Projection. You can link your Profit & Loss Projection worksheet to your sales manager's budget worksheet so that when sales budgets are updated, your Profit & Loss is automatically updated too. Working in this way saves time and reduces the chance for error.

When you copy or link data from one spreadsheet to another, be super clear about whether you're copying and pasting formulas, values or links:

- If you simply click Paste in the destination spreadsheet, Excel copies any formulas that you created. You often find that these formulas won't make any sense when copied to a new spreadsheet.

- If you click Paste Special and then select Values, Excel copies the text or dollar values only. This works just fine at first glance, but remember that if you work in this way, the destination spreadsheet won't update if you later change a figure in the source spreadsheet. To use my earlier example, if your sales manager updates their sales budget, your financial projection won't update if you only paste values.

- If you click Paste Special and then select Paste Link, Excel copies a link to the source spreadsheet. The values appear in your destination spreadsheet as a mirror of the values in your source spreadsheet. The beauty of pasting a link in this way is that if you change a value in your source spreadsheet, the destination spreadsheet updates also.

Chapter 8 explains the fine details of linking worksheets, but the main thing to remember is that if you link data from one spreadsheet file to another (as opposed to simply linking worksheets within a single file), you need to be consistent about how you name your files and where these files are stored. If you rename or move a file from which you've created a link, your destination worksheet won't be able to find the data it needs and won't be able to update data automatically.

Remember that you can watch a video of all the Excel tips explained in this chapter at www.dummies.com/go/creatingbusinessplan.

Don't Type Values into Formulas

Try to avoid entering dollar values into formulas for cells — instead, type the value into its own cell on a worksheet.

An example is probably the best way of explaining what I mean. Imagine you know that cost of sales is 30 per cent of sales. To calculate cost of sales in your Profit & Loss Projection, you could create a formula for each month that multiplies the sales forecast by 30 per cent. Sounds okay, but if you later find out that cost of sales is actually 29 per cent, you would have to edit every formula. Instead, you're better to insert a new row at the top of your worksheet, type **Cost of Sales** in the first cell and then **30%** in the adjacent cell. Right-click, select Define Name, and give this cell a unique name. (For more about naming cells, refer to Chapter 8.) Next, create formulas for each month that relate back to this cell. Later, if you need to tweak the percentage, all you have to do is change a single cell, and you don't need to edit the formula for every month.

Similarly, imagine that the sales price of a product you sell is $20 per unit and that your sales forecast includes a row forecasting monthly sales quantities. In order to calculate total sales for the month, you could create a formula for each month that multiplies the quantity by $20. However, what's better is to type **Average Price** in the top-left corner followed by **$20** in the adjacent cell. Name this cell **Average Price** and then create formulas for each month that multiply the forecast for quantity sold by Average Price.

Spell Out Your Logic

One downside of working with spreadsheets is that you can get lulled into a false sense of security as to the reliability of your figures. However, making a mistake is actually very easy, especially if you use long, complicated formulas.

For this reason I always to try to show one calculation at a time in my financial projections, and keep my formulas as simple as possible. For example, in the extract from my Cashflow Projection in Figure 16-5, I don't really need to include row 71, which calculates Cash Inflow less Cash Outflow, as I already show both these amounts just above. However, I spell out my calculations row by row, doing one step at a time. I not only find it easier to spot mistakes this way, but also find that if I don't return to a spreadsheet for several months, I can more easily remember how everything works.

57	**CASH INFLOWS**	
58	Cash Collected From Sales	25,000
59	Loan Finance	120,000
60	Total Cash Inflows	**145,000**
61		
62	**CASH OUTFLOWS**	
63	Purchase of New Equipment	12,000
64	Purchases of Stock	24,000
65	Expenses	18,857
66	Company Tax	
67	Loan Repayments	2,500
68		**57,357**
69		
70	Opening Cash	1,000
71	Cash Inflow less Cash Outflow	87,643
72	Closing Cash	**88,643**

Figure 16-5:
Try to show the logic of your calculations, step by step.

Create Graphs and Charts

A business plan without any graphics is like winter without hot chocolate. Happily, Excel makes it really easy to grab your financial projections and create charts.

The easiest way to see how to create a chart is to give it a go. Here's how:

1. **Create a new worksheet in Excel.**

2. **Enter the names of a few months along the top row, starting in column B, and in the first column create three headings:** Total Sales, Gross Profit and Net Profit.

3. **Fill in some figures for each month.**

   If you just want to see how charts work, fill in any old figures. Alternatively, populate these rows with figures for your own business.

4. **Highlight the first two rows, then go to the Insert tab and from the Charts group, select any graph that takes your fancy.**

   For sales figures, I tend to like bar charts, similar to what I create in the left graph in Figure 16-6.

5. **Now highlight all your data (the column and row headings, as well as the figures), then go to the Insert tab and create a line chart.**

   Line charts work best if you have a few rows of data that you want to show on a single chart.

6. **Use your intuition to tweak colours and formats to get a chart you're really happy with.**

   I could write a whole chapter about formatting charts, but in lieu of this instruction, just follow your nose and experiment.

Want to know how to copy your graph or chart into Word? The next chapter, Chapter 17, explains just how.

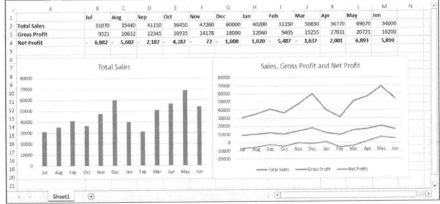

Figure 16-6:
Creating charts and graphs isn't just easy, but fun too.

Chapter 17

Ten Ideas for a Well-Presented Plan

In This Chapter

▶ Impressing others with a professional-looking plan

▶ Tweaking financial projections to fit neatly on a page

▶ Flipping information from Excel into Word

▶ Choosing fonts wisely, adding graphics and saving your plan as a PDF

▶ Keeping your language correct and concise

*T*his chapter is about getting your plan to look good and read well, something that's particularly important if you plan to share your plan with prospective partners or investors.

Some of the tips I share are pretty obvious, others are less so. Have a quick flick through to select your pick of what's hot, and what's not.

Do a Cover Sheet

Any business plan needs a decent cover sheet. I provide a sample cover sheet in the Appendix for your reference, but every cover sheet varies. If in doubt, here's what to include:

✔ Your company name and physical address

✔ Your email address and website

✔ Social media pages, such as your business Facebook page or Twitter account

✔ The date

✔ Your name and phone number

If possible, try to liven up your cover sheet with a picture or graphic, such as your business logo, an image of your product or a photo of your location. If you can't find anything relevant, go to a stock images website such as www.istock.com and search in the Illustrations section for images relating to your industry.

Create a Table of Contents

A table of contents is simply a list of the main headings in your business plan, along with a page number for each one.

Although you can create a table of contents by typing a list of headings and page numbers, the quickest approach is to insert a dynamic table of contents that automatically updates as your plan changes. Here's how:

1. **In Word, scroll through your business plan and apply a style to every heading.**

   On the Home tab, can you see the buttons saying Heading 1, Heading 2, Heading 3 and so on? Simply highlight each heading in your plan, and then click Heading 1 if this is a main heading, or Heading 2 if this is a subheading. If you don't like the fonts that Word applies to these headings, right-click the heading button and select Modify.

2. **Go to the page of your plan where you want the table of contents to appear.**

3. **Click the References tab and select Insert Table of Contents from the Table of Contents options.**

   A table of contents appears, complete with page numbers. (If you end up with something that looks like { TOC \o "1-3" \h \z }, simply press the Ctrl key followed by F9 to change your view settings.)

You can now format your table of contents to your heart's delight. If you end up changing something in your plan, click anywhere on the table of contents and then press F9 on your keyboard to update the headings and page numbers.

Get Your Financials to Fit

Have you tried to print any of your financial projections yet? Unless you're experienced with this kind of thing, chances are you've ended up with a report that stretches across several sheets of A4 paper. Maybe you've even resorted to using sticky tape to join the pages together, as if the business plan process were some kind of protracted craft workshop.

Printing a set of financials onto a single page is easy when you know how. Click Print→Scaling→Fit on One Page (or, on a Mac, ask to Fit to 1 page wide by 1 page tall). Change the Page Orientation to Landscape and you're done.

Printing financial projections in the preceding manner is only one solution. Often, what you really want to do is include these financials as part of your business plan. In other words, what you want to do is incorporate the figures you've generated using Excel into the narrative of your business plan Word document.

Sounds tricky, but where there's a will there's a way:

1. **In your Word document, insert a section break where you want the financial report to appear.**

   In most versions of Word, you do this by going to the Page Layout tab, and selecting Next Page from the Breaks menu (which appears in the Page Setup group of commands).

   Inserting section breaks is what allows you to change page orientation within a single document, so that some pages are orientated as portrait and others as landscape.

2. **Still on the Page Layout tab, select Landscape as the Orientation.**

   Generally, financial projections span a 12-month period and figures end up ridiculously small if you try to fit them across an A4 portrait page.

   For this reason, what you need to do is select landscape orientation for any pages that include several months of financial projections, even though the rest of your business plan is portrait orientation.

3. **In Excel, highlight the figures you want to copy into Word.**

   Don't highlight the whole worksheet but instead highlight only the cells you want to copy.

4. **Right-click with your mouse and select Copy.**

   Or on a Mac, control click.

5. **Return to Word, go to Home→Paste and select Paste Special from the Paste Options.**

6. **Select Microsoft Excel Worksheet Object as the Source, and click the Paste Link radio button on the left side.**

   Figure 17-1 shows what this window looks like. The neat thing about pasting a link is that your Word document automatically updates if you change anything in your financials.

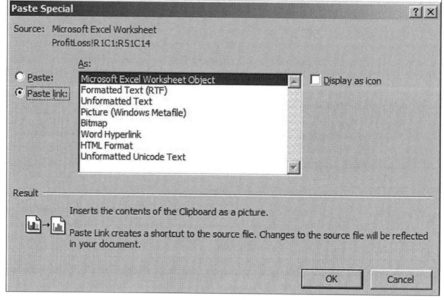

Figure 17-1:
Inserting
an Excel
worksheet
object into
Word.

7. **Click OK.**

   An image, or part of an image, appears on the page.

8. **If only part of an image appears, right-click the image, select Format Object→Layout→Square as the Wrapping Style.**

9. **Right-click and select Format Object again, but this time click the Size tab. Tweak the percentage settings for height and width (similar to what I do in Figure 17-2) so that the entire report fits onto a single page.**

10. **After you get your financial report to look good on the page, insert another section break so that you can return to portrait orientation.**

    Alternatively, if you have more than one financial projection to insert, insert a section break after the last one.

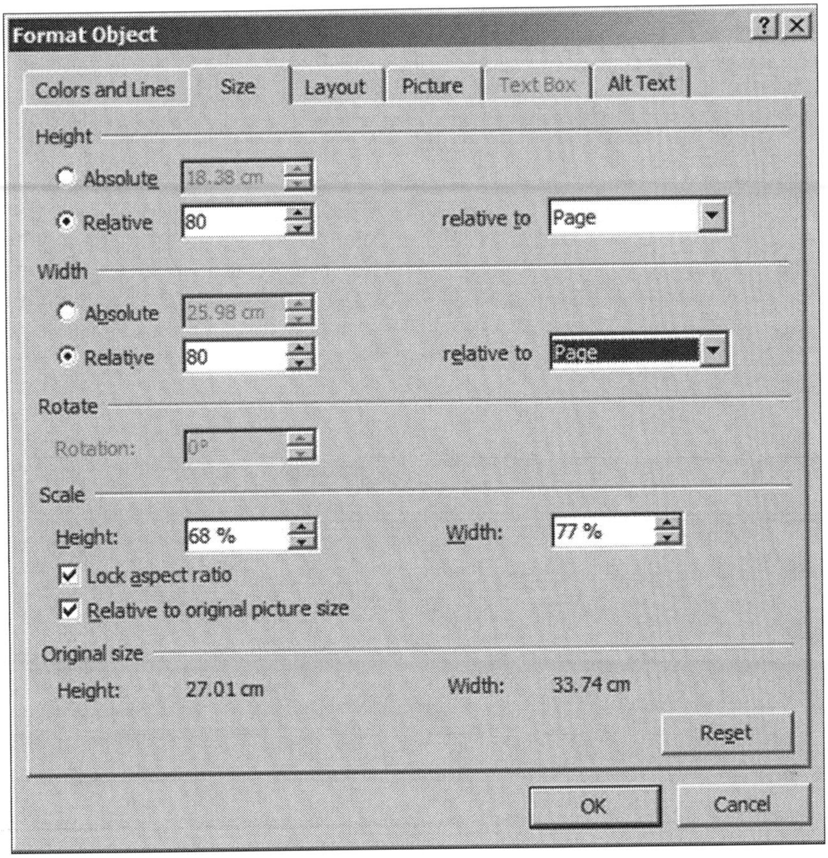

Figure 17-2:
Tweak the
size settings
so your
report fits
comfortably
on a single
page.

Copy Charts into Word

In Chapter 16, I explain how to highlight your Excel sales projections to create neat-looking charts and graphs. You can liven up your business plan by copying these graphs from Excel directly into Word.

1. **Create your graph in Excel.**

   Chapter 16 explains how to do this.

2. **Once you're happy, right-click on graph and click Copy.**

   Or on a Macintosh, press the Control button and then click Copy.

3. **Navigate to your business plan Word document, right-click once more and click Paste.**

   In the blink of an eye, the chart you just created in Excel becomes part of your business plan. The whole deal is so clever that you can't fail to marvel at your own brilliance.

When you copy a graph from Excel directly into Word, Word retains the link to the Excel file. So long as you don't change the name of the Excel file nor move the file into another folder, the graph in Word will update if you change any data in Excel. For example, if you change a sales figure for one month in Excel, not only will you update all your Excel totals, but the chart in your business plan updates too.

Use a Single Font, Keep Text in Black

This heading says it all really. If you mix and match fonts within a single document, you end up looking like someone dressed in a flowery shirt with striped pants. Creative, but maybe not that professional.

Ideally, keep to the same font for your column and row headings in Excel as well, and stick to black for all text.

By the way, feel free to vary the font size — headings certainly need to be a larger font size than the body of your text — just don't vary the font itself.

Include a Picture or Two

Try to brighten up your plan with some graphical element, such as your logo in the footer of each page, an image or images of your product, or graphs of your sales projections (refer to Copy Charts into Word, earlier in this chapter, for more info about graphs).

Also, don't be a cheapskate — after all, you're probably not going to print many copies of your plan — and show any images in full colour, not just black and white.

Save Your Plan as a PDF

If you want to email your plan to someone, the best approach is to save the whole document as a *PDF*. (A PDF is simply a special file format that captures everything within a document as an electronic image for anyone to view.) A PDF looks more professional than a Word document, and the file size often ends up a little smaller too.

To save a Word document as a PDF, in Word go to File→Save As. Enter a filename and then in the Save As Type menu, select PDF as the file type. You can then choose whether to create a Standard PDF (which retains the full quality of all images) or a Minimum Size PDF (which reduces image quality). I usually stick to a Standard PDF format.

Click Save when you're done. Word will think for a few seconds before your PDF opens automatically, ready for review.

Consider Interactive Elements

Your plan doesn't have to be a static printed document. If you save your plan as a PDF, consider including links to dynamic content such as websites or even video.

My husband runs a recording studio business, and you can find information about his studio in many places online. When he created his business plan, his cover page included links to his Facebook page and his website. His SWOT analysis included a link to a YouTube video promoting the location of the studio, and his company profile included links to some of the better-known artists who have worked at the studio.

Run a Spell Check

I worked as an editor of a magazine once, and from time to time I'd come across an article submitted by a freelancer that obviously hadn't been spell-checked. So you may think I'm stating the obvious by suggesting you spell-check your document, but if professional journalists can forget to do so, I reckon almost anyone can. If you're seeking to impress with your plan, you don't want to create unnecessary distraction with words that aren't spelt correctly.

Before running a spell check, review your language settings. (In Word, go to Review→Language→Set Proofing Language.) I find that Microsoft Word has a tendency to revert to US spelling at the drop of a hat, even if I've never specified the US as my region. Spelling rules can be surprisingly different from one English-speaking country to another, so it pays to get this setting right.

Check Language for Simplicity

In my opinion, a business plan is where plain, simple English should reign absolute. So after you get to the end of your plan, run a few simple language reviews:

- **Check for super long sentences.** A sentence that's longer than 30 words can probably be cut in two.

- **Review your plan for corporate buzzwords.** Consider substituting buzzwords with something more straightforward. For example, replace:

    'action item' with 'goal'

    'upskill' with 'train'

    'engagement' with 'customer involvement'

    'synergy' with 'great combination of skills'

    (Wondering what counts as a buzzword? Visit www.theofficelife.com and click the Ridiculous Jargon tab for a dose of inspiration regarding words that should probably be banished from public life.)

- **Keep paragraphs to a maximum of eight lines.** Any longer than this, slice the paragraph in two.

- **Make your language active.** Specify the person doing the act, don't talk about the act being done by someone. For example, don't say 'A Facebook campaign will be launched next spring' but instead say 'We plan to launch our Facebook campaign next spring'.

- **LOL?** Never use acronyms or abbreviations unless you know for sure that people reading your plan will understand them.

- **If you can substitute a noun with a verb, do so.** For example, instead of writing 'we have given consideration to general retail trends', write 'we have considered general retail trends'.

Word has some pretty good stylistic policing within its grammar checker. To switch this facility on, press F7 to open up the spell check, click Options→Writing Style→Settings. Select all the writing style checks, similar to Figure 17-3, and then recheck your document.

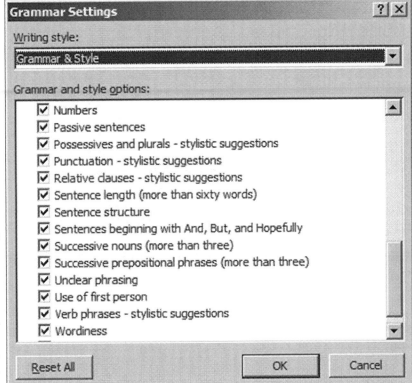

Figure 17-3:
Word
provides
not only a
spell and
grammar
check, but a
writing style
check also.

Chapter 18

Ten Questions to Ask before You're Done

In This Chapter

▶ Doctoring the spin in 30 seconds or less

▶ Facing up to your competition

▶ Making sure the numbers are right

▶ Imagining a future beyond this business

▶ Letting your dreams take flight while keeping your feet on the ground

Do you feel you've created a plan that's as good as can be for the time being? Great. Before you sign off, check your plan one last time, asking yourself the ten quick questions contained in this chapter.

Can You Summarise Your Business in 30 Seconds or Less?

When I was mentoring start-up businesses at a local business college, I would always begin the very first session by asking students to summarise their business in 30 seconds or less. Each student had to include both a description of their business as well as what made their business special. I was strict about the time limit, holding a stopwatch and calling out 'STOP' as soon as 30 seconds ticked around.

At that first session, I'd usually find that only one or two students could jump this hurdle. So I would persist, starting at least one session every week (the course ran for eight weeks) by going around the room and repeating the exercise. As everyone's business plans progressed, more and more students were able to articulate the essential purpose of their business, and why they felt their business had potential.

How do you rate at this exercise? Try this:

1. **Ready? Lay your hands on a recording device.**

   Your smartphone or the Sound Recorder application on your computer will do the job.

2. **Set? Find a timepiece.**

   Does anybody still have a watch? I know I don't. But I do have a great big red clock in my kitchen with the noisiest most infuriating tick in the world.

3. **Go! Click Record and talk aloud, describing your business and what's so special about it.**

   Don't talk for more than 30 seconds and if you stuff up your speech the first time, try again straightaway.

How did you go? When you listen to yourself, do you feel impressed by your succinct expression and winning communication style? Hopefully! But if not, take heart. First, head back to Chapter 2 to read about identifying strategic advantage for your business. Then continue to Chapter 3 where I explain how to craft the elevator speech from hell.

After working on your 30-second summary, read through the introductory section of your business plan one more time. If you can't articulate the essence of your business at the drop of a hat, chances are the introduction to your plan may be a little weak. Read through these pages and rework if necessary.

Does Your Plan Truly Evaluate Competitors?

One thing I've observed when looking at business plans, particularly plans for new businesses, is how many people gloss over competitor analysis. I find this a real worry, because understanding competitors is so essential to doing well in business.

I think I've figured out the psychology of this head-in-the-sand behaviour. When businesses are new, the 'dream' is still relatively intact. Spending too much time looking at competitors can make you feel like this dream is getting crushed, and in place of hope you may get a sense of anxiety about going head-to-head with the big guys in town.

Don't worry. Although competition is always a little scary, it can be inspirational too. By analysing your competitors in depth, you may find ideas that you want to imitate, ways you can adapt your pricing to increase profits, or new market niches that you hadn't been aware of.

So remember, if you haven't analysed competitors properly, your plan isn't complete. (If you're wondering what form a 'proper analysis' takes, skip back to Chapter 3.)

Have You Double-Checked Your Numbers?

I spend a fair chunk of this book discouraging you from adding up figures using a calculator and instead advocating the use of a spreadsheet. Now I'm going to eat my hat. Before you finalise your plan, grab a copy of every financial report you've created using a spreadsheet and add up at least one column using a calculator.

Have I gone bananas? Not really. Spreadsheets provide an excellent way to create financial projections, but they can be prone to error. For example, if you insert a sum at the bottom of a column of figures and then later you insert an additional row just above this sum, the formula may not always update automatically. You may end up with a total at the bottom of a long column of figures that misses the last number, thereby misleading you and everyone else.

 As well as the automatic summing in Excel, check other logic too while you're at it. For example, if your sales projections involve multiplying units sold by a particular unit price, manually check at least one or two months of sales projections to ensure the totals are correct.

Do Your Numbers Match Your Goals?

In Chapter 15, I talk about setting goals and objectives for every element in your plan, along with a time frame for each one. As one final check, evaluate how much each one of these objectives is going to cost (in both time and money), and then return to your Profit & Loss Projection to see if the numbers match up.

For example, if one of your goals is to launch a Google Adwords campaign next March, does your budget for Advertising Expense increase in March accordingly? Or if one of your goals is to open a new retail outlet in November, does your Profit & Loss Projection show a corresponding increase in Rental Expense and Wages Expense from that month onwards?

In addition, if any goals involve a time commitment from you, pause to consider whether this time involves any additional costs. For example, maybe one of your goals is to call on at least three new stores per week from February onwards. If the person calling on those stores is you, do you have enough time? If your intention is to do this task but maybe flick-pass something else you currently do to an employee, have you budgeted enough in Wages Expense?

Does Your Plan Play to Your Strengths?

Does the people part of the plan — the bit that lists who does what — play to your natural strengths?

One of the skills of growing a business is for you to focus on the things you're good at and then delegate the rest. (If your business is a service business, I don't necessarily mean that you focus on providing the service itself, which you're probably naturally good at and what inspired your business in the first place. Rather, I'm talking about focusing on the parts of business management that come most naturally to you.)

List the functions of your business: Administration, Finance, Marketing and People Management, plus Production if you're a manufacturer. Which of these functions appeal to you, and which of these functions correspond to your natural abilities? Think about what others recognise in you as your skills.

Even if you don't have any employees yet, try to delegate or get assistance with the business functions that aren't your areas of strength. Consider hiring a virtual assistant, employing an office junior, delegating the books to a subcontractor, or getting help from a marketing consultant.

One of the reasons many entrepreneurs fail in business is that they try to do everything themselves. Avoid this trap, if you can.

Have You Cast Your Net as Wide as Possible?

I love this part of the review process. Here's what you're going to need:

- ✔ **A kid-free zone.** Things are looking up.

- ✔ **At least two hours free time.** Hard to find, easy to lose.

- ✔ **No TV, internet or mobile phone.** Can't bring yourself to switch off? Drive to a place with no signal.

- ✔ **A couple of sheets of A3 paper and a few coloured pens.** I'm sounding really old school but believe me, this method works.

Now with your feet up and your mind free from distractions, let yourself dream. How big could your business be? What avenues have you yet to explore? Whom could you partner with? Do you have any crazy ideas that just won't go away?

Give these ideas some oxygen, and see where the journey takes you. Then return to your business plan and see whether these fresh insights can help you to boost the visionary element of your plan.

Have You Made Any Assumptions You Can't Justify?

Almost any business plan includes some assumptions. Maybe you've assumed that sales will grow at a certain rate, that you're going to adopt a new line of products, that your lease will be renewed or that you're going to upgrade your equipment. Or, if you're planning for a new business, maybe you've made assumptions about the size of the market, what price points customers are going to find acceptable, or the rate of repeat business.

For every assumption that you make in your plan, try first to spell out the assumption and second provide the rationale. Here are some examples:

- ✔ A plan assumes certain product costs, and provides detailed costing sheets in the appendix to justify these.

- ✔ A plan shows sales growth of 5 per cent per year, and explains this by graphing last year's sales and showing this as a trend.

✔ A plan shows sales growth of 20 per cent, but includes wages for a new sales agent in the budget.

✔ A plan shows a move away from bricks-and-mortar retail towards online sales, and justifies this by including an industry report that indicates this trend.

Industry-specific analysis is like gold for a business plan. If you can get hold of a good industry report, especially one analysing long-term trends, refer to this report in your plan and possibly include this report in the appendix.

Similarly, try to demonstrate a sophisticated, in-depth understanding of who your customers are, including who buys from you and why, and in what quantities.

What Do Others Think?

Once you reckon you've done as much as you can on your business plan, start sharing your plan with others. Show the financial section of your plan to your accountant, share your plan with family or friends, or, if you have employees, ask them to look through the plan and provide feedback.

Next, seek professional feedback from a business adviser or mentor. If you can't afford a consultant, that's fine. Many government business advisory centres offer free business advice, and the good thing about a written plan is that you have something concrete to offer as a starting point. (An adviser is going to find it much easier if they have something to work with, as opposed to if you rock up and say, 'Hey, I need help figuring out how to sell my stuff'.)

And remember, your business plan isn't a literary work. Not just because your plan doesn't include mystery murders, engaging dialogue and risqué sex scenes — more's the pity — but also because, unlike a novel, your business plan is never finished. Be open to feedback and comments, and be prepared to let your plan continually evolve.

Do You Have a Plan for Getting Out?

When I first drafted this chapter, my proposed heading for this section was 'Do You Have an Exit Plan?'. Sounded perfectly reasonable, until I stumbled across a website that listed the phrase 'exit plan' as one of the top 'corporate buzzwords the world would be better without'. Having reflected upon this, I tend to agree.

Never mind. The question you need to ask yourself is do you have a plan for selling your business? You may be bemused by this question, especially if you haven't actually started your business yet and you're still at the planning stage. However, if you're able to conceive of a future for your business that's independent of you and that you can sell to someone else, you've made the leap in thinking from being a businessperson to being an entrepreneur.

Is Your Plan Inspirational?

I'm not naturally a risk taker, which is probably one of the reasons I find business planning a comforting activity. Much of the business plan process focuses on being *sensible*: Checking financials, looking at margins, evaluating risk and so on.

Yet often it's the wackiest business ideas that work. Who would have thought that Crocs, those ugly spa shoes made from brightly coloured resin, could become an international fashion item? Or that the Pet Rock would be a fad that swept the world? (The Pet Rock was nothing more than a plain grey pebble packaged in a small box accompanied by a tongue-in-cheek Pet Rock training manual. With a statistic that does nothing to credit human intelligence, entrepreneur Gary Dahl sold over 5 million units in less than six months.)

Balance figures with fun, caution with creativity and budgets with belief. Let daring and hope be the spark that energises your business plan, and endeavour to infect yourself, your plan and others with an overriding sense of optimism.

Appendix

Sample Business Plan

*I*n this appendix, I provide a sample business plan for you to refer to. Please bear in mind that any resemblance to an existing business is entirely coincidental. (I did search for the business name 'Just for Kids Parties' and couldn't find any business by this name, so I'm optimistic that I'm not treading on anybody's toes.)

I follow the structure described in Chapters 1 and 15, with the result that I include detailed financials early in the plan, and move onto industry analysis and strategy second. As I mention in Chapter 1, if part of the purpose of this plan were to apply to a lender for finance, an emphasis on financials works well. However, if this plan were written for the eyes of a prospective investor, it may be better to shift the industry analysis and strategic direction sections so that they appear before the financials and the marketing plan.

Due to page constraints, I don't provide quite as much detail in this plan as I would like. For example, I include cross-references to additional information such as historical Profit & Loss reports, scenario analysis and a month-by-month action plan, but I don't actually include this information in the sample plan.

As I was working on this plan, I was reminded how every business plan ends up being quite different. In writing this book, part of the challenge has been to provide a universal explanation for a process that varies enormously from business to business. After all, a plan for a brand new business providing a simple home-based service is going to be very different from a plan for a manufacturing business with a substantial turnover and 40 employees.

The important thing isn't the format of the final document that you end up with. Instead, what's important is the process of planning itself and the inspiration that comes from the journey of setting goals and creating a vision for your future. And on this final note, I wish you the very best of luck.

BUSINESS PLAN

JUST FOR KIDS PARTIES

sarah@justforkidsparties.net
www.justforkidsparties.net
Tel: 02 8446 2354

just for kids parties
http://twitter.com/justforkidsparties

June 2014

Table of Contents

Executive Summary 3
    What's special about us 3
    Our mission...4
    Our values...4
    Our ultimate goal 5
Financials...5
    Gross Profit Projection...5
    Profit & Loss Projection...6
    Sales trends...8
    Cashflow Projection..8
Our Team...9
Marketing Plan..10
    Our branding 10
    Target market analysis 11
    Competitor analysis...11
    Summary of marketing strategies...12
Strategic Direction..13
    Industry analysis...13
        Demographic change..14
        Potential competitors...14
        Government legislation..14
        Sustainability and health concerns.................................14
        Technology and offshoring..15
    What we do best (and worst) 15
    Opportunities and threats 15
    Summary of strategic priorities..17
    Managing risk 18
Summary of Goals 19

Executive Summary

Just for Kids Parties is a relatively new but rapidly growing business based in Georgetown. In addition to ourselves (the owners), we have one full-time employee and a team of 12 casual entertainers. The turnover of our business for the financial year just past was $385,000.

Our focus is on kids' parties and corporate events such as shop openings and product launches. We service the area within a 100-kilometre radius of central Georgetown but seek to expand to Newcastle and Dunregan within the next 12 months.

Industry trends for the children's party business are positive, with parents and grandparents spending more money than ever on children. Demographic trends are positive due to the spike in the birth rate in 2007 (when the government introduced baby bonus legislation). These children are now in their first years of school and are the prime age group for parents to hire entertainers.

Our goal is to expand our turnover to reach $500,000 within the next 12 months. We are currently pursuing the possibilities of aligning ourselves with a party hire business (which rents out inflatable castles and slides) as a way of further differentiating our business.

Our ultimate goal is to create systems that enable a highly consistent service for customers, focusing on training and recruiting staff, delivery of games, systems for face-painting and availability of add-on products and services. We would hope to create a national franchise using our systems.

What's special about us

We believe that we have a unique set of skills. Not many business couples can say they met working as clowns in a circus. Both of us have over ten years' experience as performance artists and, unlike most of our competitors, we don't just do face-painting and party games, but juggling, magic tricks, hula-hoop workshops and more.

We have a unique network with other entertainers and are confident that the people we employ as children's entertainers have the best skills of any entertainers around. We have established a strategic alliance with a circus skills workshop company, whereby the best students of each semester are given an opportunity to work with us. This helps secure enrolments for the workshop company and assists with the recruitment of quality entertainers, which is probably the most challenging aspect for this industry.

Our credentials and diversity also give us a competitive edge for the more lucrative corporate work, and Sarah's experience working with corporate sponsorship has provided us with many openings.

Our mission

Our mission is to spark a sense of fun and wonder in every child we entertain.

Our values

We believe every child should have an equal chance to celebrate important occasions, and that our parties should help inspire children to be creative, have fun and share with others. Our values are represented in the following ways:

- When recruiting entertainers, we give preference to those who speak a second language.

- We do not offer 'pamper parties'. (We believe that pamper parties reinforce unrealistic notions of body image and beauty for girls.)

- We aim to foster the spirit of creativity, offering a wide range of craft parties, as well as juggling workshops and hula-hoop workshops.

- Parties are expensive and out of reach for many families. We aim to increase accessibility to our parties by offering a range of prices and packages including a low-cost, 90-minute party (available weekdays only).

(4 of 20)

📌 We aim to build the spirit of cooperation and sharing in the way we structure our games, with prizes for all participants and the inclusion of games where older children help the younger ones.

Our ultimate goal

We aim to build a strong and profitable business model using innovative systems for recruiting and training entertainers, as well as clear systems for providing the very best children's parties. Our aim is to franchise our business model within three years.

Financials

Just for Kids Parties has been in operation since 2011. The years 2011 and 2012 showed a small loss, 2013 showed a modest profit, and the 2014 financial year is set to make a slim profit after allowing for director salaries of $48,000 each. Historical Profit & Loss reports, as well as Balance Sheets, can be found in the appendix for this plan.

Gross Profit Projection

In calculating our Gross Profit Projection for the next 12 months, we separate the parties we still do ourselves as owners from the parties where we hire casual entertainers on a fee-per-party basis. Costs are based on average amounts paid to casual entertainers (actual amount paid varies on the travel time involved).

The following Gross Profit Projection shows a steady increase in gross profit over the next 12 months. The pace is quite demanding, however — you can see that we need at least 200 party bookings a month to make a relatively modest monthly gross profit of $20,000.

	Price	Cost	Jul-14	Aug-14	Sep-14	Oct-14	Nov-14	Dec-14	Jan-15	Feb-15	Mar-15	Apr-15	May-15	Jun-15	TOTAL
1 hour 30 Package	$195.00	$115.00													
2 hour Package	$220.00	$130.00													
Corporate Package	$275.00	$145.00													
Parties with owner's labour															
1 hour 30 Package			12	12	12	12	12	12	12	12	12	12	12	12	
2 hour Package			4	4	4	4	4	4	4	4	4	4	4	4	
Corporate Package			2	2	2	2	3	4	-	2	2	2	2	2	
Parties with subcontract labour															
1 hour 30 Package			80	85	90	90	120	180	60	70	90	95	100	105	
2 hour Package			75	80	85	80	100	160	45	60	75	80	90	95	
Corporate Package			2	3	4	4	5	8	4	6	6	7	7	8	
Income Generated															
1 hour 30 Package			$17,940	$18,915	$19,890	$19,890	$25,740	$37,440	$14,040	$15,990	$19,890	$20,865	$21,340	$22,815	$255,255
2 hour Package			$17,380	$18,480	$19,580	$18,480	$22,880	$36,080	$10,780	$14,080	$17,380	$18,480	$20,680	$21,780	$236,060
Corporate Package			$1,100	$1,375	$1,650	$1,650	$2,200	$3,300	$1,100	$2,200	$2,200	$2,475	$2,475	$2,750	$24,475
Total Sales			$36,420	$38,770	$41,120	$40,020	$50,820	$76,820	$25,920	$32,270	$39,470	$41,820	$44,995	$47,345	$515,790
Costs															
1 hour 30 Package			9,200	9,775	10,350	10,350	13,800	20,700	6,900	8,050	10,350	10,925	11,500	12,075	$133,975
2 hour Package			9,750	10,400	11,050	10,400	13,000	20,800	5,850	7,800	9,750	10,400	11,700	12,350	$133,250
Corporate Package			290	435	580	580	725	1,160	580	870	870	1,015	1,015	1,160	$9,280
Total Cost of Sales			19,240	20,610	21,980	21,330	27,525	42,660	13,330	16,720	20,970	22,340	24,215	25,585	$276,505
Gross Profit			$17,180	$18,160	$19,140	$18,690	$23,295	$34,160	$12,590	$15,550	$18,500	$19,480	$20,780	$21,760	$239,285

Profit & Loss Projection

Our Profit & Loss Projection (following) for the next 12 months shows a very small profit of $625 for the year. However, we have included $96,000 of wages for ourselves (as company directors) for this period.

When working with scenario analysis, we ran several different Profit & Loss Projection reports. On our most conservative model, we decreased sales by 10 per cent and increased expenses by 10 per cent. This scenario showed a substantial loss and highlights our vulnerability to fluctuations in sales or expenses.

To this end, we have set strict budgets for expenses and will review these expenses every 12 weeks. Note that we do have a buffer in that we can reduce the wages we draw out of the company, if required.

PROFIT & LOSS PROJECTION JULY 2014 TO JUNE 2015

	July	Aug	Sep	Oct	Nov	Dec	Jan	Feb	Mar	Apr	May	Jun	Total
Total Sales	36,420	38,770	41,120	40,020	50,820	76,820	25,920	32,270	39,470	41,820	44,995	47,345	515,790
Total Cost of Sales	19,240	20,610	21,980	23,330	27,525	42,660	13,330	16,720	20,970	22,340	24,215	25,585	276,505
Gross Profit	17,180	18,160	19,140	18,690	23,295	34,160	12,590	15,550	18,500	19,480	20,780	21,760	239,285
Accounting Fees	-	-	-	-	-	-	-	-	-	1,500	-	-	1,500
Advertising	750	750	750	750	750	750	750	750	750	750	750	750	9,000
Bank Charges	100	100	100	100	100	100	100	100	100	100	100	100	1,200
Computer Consumables	150	150	150	150	150	150	150	150	150	150	150	150	1,800
Consultant Expenses	300	300	300	300	300	300	300	300	300	300	300	300	3,600
Electricity	500	-	-	500	-	-	500	-	-	500	-	-	2,000
Insurance	-	-	-	-	-	-	-	-	-	3,000	-	-	3,000
Interest Expense	250	250	250	250	250	250	250	250	250	250	250	250	3,000
Internet Fees	150	-	-	150	-	-	150	-	-	150	-	-	600
License Fees	700	-	-	-	-	-	-	-	-	500	-	-	1,200
Merchant Fees	320	320	320	320	320	320	320	320	320	320	320	320	3,840
Motor Vehicle rego & insurance	-	-	-	-	-	-	-	-	1,500	-	-	-	1,500
Motor Vehicle Fuel	347	347	347	347	347	347	347	347	347	347	347	347	4,160
Motor Vehicle Repairs & Maint	167	167	167	167	167	167	167	167	167	167	167	167	2,000
Motor Vehicle Tolls	120	120	120	120	120	120	120	120	120	120	120	120	1,440
Office Supplies	150	150	150	150	150	150	150	150	150	150	150	150	1,800
Parking	80	80	80	80	80	80	80	80	80	80	80	80	960
Rates	400	-	-	400	-	-	400	-	-	400	-	-	1,600
Rental Expense	800	800	800	800	800	800	800	800	800	800	800	800	9,600
Repairs and Maintenance	500	500	500	500	500	500	500	500	500	500	500	500	6,000
Replacements	250	250	250	250	250	250	250	250	250	250	250	250	3,000
Security Expenses	120	120	120	120	120	120	120	120	120	120	120	120	1,440
Staff Amenities	300	300	300	300	300	300	300	300	300	300	300	300	3,600
Storage Expenses	150	150	150	150	150	150	150	150	150	150	150	150	1,800
Subscription and Dues	200	-	500	-	-	-	-	300	-	1,200	-	-	2,200
Telephone (inc mobile)	400	400	400	400	400	400	400	400	400	400	400	400	4,800
Travel Domestic	350	350	350	350	350	350	350	350	350	350	350	350	4,200
Wages and Salaries	3,683	3,683	3,683	3,683	3,683	3,683	3,683	3,683	3,683	3,683	3,683	3,683	44,200
Wages - Directors	8,000	8,000	8,000	8,000	8,000	8,000	8,000	8,000	8,000	8,000	8,000	8,000	96,000
Wages oncosts	1,168	1,168	1,168	1,168	1,168	1,168	1,168	1,168	1,168	1,168	1,168	1,168	14,020
Website expenses	300	300	300	300	300	300	300	300	300	300	300	300	3,600
Total Expenses	20,705	18,755	19,255	19,805	18,755	18,755	19,805	19,055	20,255	26,005	18,755	18,755	238,660
Net Profit	-3,525	-595	-115	-1,115	4,540	15,405	-7,215	-3,505	-1,755	-6,525	2,025	3,005	625

Sales trends

Our sales chart for the next 12 months, after allowing for seasonal variations (November and December are always peak months), shows an aggressive growth in sales, when compared to the same months last year, of 33 per cent. Although this is ambitious, this increase is in line with current trends and will be supported by increased advertising expenditure.

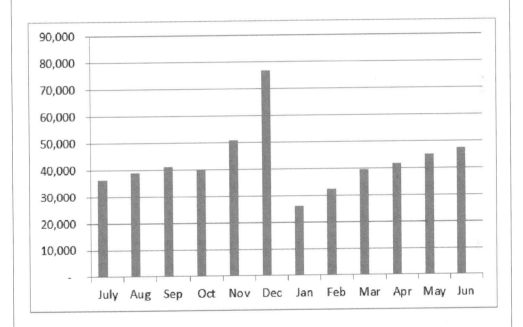

Cashflow Projection

Our Cashflow Projection (following) highlights the urgent need for finance. Although our company is profitable overall, we hope to invest in new computers and a custom online booking system during the coming financial year. Without finance, we would have a significant cash shortfall.

CASHFLOW PROJECTION JULY 2014 TO JUNE 2015

	Jun	Jul	Aug	Sep	Oct	Nov	Dec	Jan	Feb	Mar	Apr	May	Jun	Total
Total Sales		36,420	38,770	41,120	40,020	50,820	76,820	25,920	32,270	39,470	41,820	44,995	47,345	515,790
Cash Collected		37,136	38,300	40,650	40,240	48,660	71,620	36,100	31,000	38,030	41,350	44,360	46,875	
Debtors at Month End	8000	7,284	7,754	8,224	8,004	10,164	15,364	5,184	6,454	7,894	8,364	8,999	9,409	
Total Cost of Sales		19,240	20,610	21,980	21,330	27,525	42,660	13,330	16,720	20,970	22,340	24,215	25,585	276,505
Gross Profit		17,180	18,160	19,140	18,690	23,295	34,160	12,590	15,550	18,500	19,480	20,780	21,760	239,285
Total Expenses		20,705	18,755	19,255	19,805	18,755	13,755	19,805	19,055	20,255	26,005	18,755	18,755	238,660
Net Profit		3,525-	595	115-	1,115	4,540	15,405	7,215-	3,505-	1,755-	6,525-	2,025	3,005	625
CASH INFLOWS														
Cash Collected From Sales		37,136	38,300	40,650	40,240	48,660	71,620	36,100	31,000	38,030	41,350	44,360	46,875	514,321
Loan Finance		30,000												30,000
Total Cash Inflows		67,136	38,300	40,650	40,240	48,660	71,620	36,100	31,000	38,030	41,350	44,360	46,875	544,321
CASH OUTFLOWS														
Purchase of New Equipment & Software		3,000		2,500				8,500				5,000		19,000
Payments to Subcontractors		19,240	20,610	21,980	21,330	27,525	42,660	13,330	16,720	20,970	22,340	24,215	25,585	276,505
Expenses		20,705	18,755	19,255	19,805	18,755	18,755	19,805	19,055	20,255	26,005	18,755	18,755	238,660
Company Tax				2,000				2,000			2,000			6,000
Loan Repayments		300	300	300	300	300	300	300	300	300	300	300	300	3,600
		43,245	39,665	44,035	43,435	46,580	61,715	43,935	36,075	41,525	50,645	48,270	44,640	543,765
Opening Cash		1,000	24,891	23,526	20,141	16,946	19,026	28,931	21,096	16,021	12,526	3,231	679	
Cash Inflow less Cash Outflow		23,891	1,365-	3,385-	3,195-	2,080	9,905	7,835-	5,075-	3,495-	9,295-	3,910-	2,235	
Closing Cash		24,891	23,526	20,141	16,946	19,026	28,931	21,096	16,021	12,526	3,231-	679	1,556	

Our Team

The directors of Just for Kids Parties are Sarah Beadle and Tom Lloyd. Both Sarah and Tom have worked in theatre and circus since their teens, and are accomplished acrobats, clowns, musicians and all-round performers. Sarah is also a hula-hoop performer and fire-dancer; Tom is a natural artist and loves creative face-painting. Sarah also worked in circus management for two years, primarily focusing on corporate sponsorship programs.

In terms of the roles each director plays, Sarah is responsible for marketing and finance. Tom is responsible for staff management, staff training and day-to-day operations, including supervision of booking placements.

Just for Kids Parties has only one full-time employee, Sadhana Scott, who runs the office on a day-to-day basis. In addition, Just for Kids Parties employs 12 casual entertainers, all of whom work on a per-party fee basis.

Just for Kids Parties also employs a contract bookkeeper, a marketing consultant and a web design company that specialises in search engine optimisation.

Marketing Plan

Due to the highly fragmented nature of the party industry and the large number of small competing companies, it is very important that Just for Kids Parties differentiates itself from other companies.

We aim to differentiate ourselves in two main ways:

✔ We are a professional business (in a fun, party kind of way!) that is utterly committed to children's entertainment.

✔ We provide a customised service to our multicultural community with bilingual entertainers and culturally sensitive party formats.

We do not seek to compete on price alone. However, in contrast to competitors who generally offer the same price for each service, regardless of location, time of week or entertainment provided, we offer a hybrid pricing system, from 'no-frills' midweek packages to premium corporate packages.

Our branding

In our brand message, we seek to convey that we are not just serious about the party business, but want the children at our parties to have the most fun ever.

Our core message is that our parties 'Spark a Sense of Wonder'. We incorporate these words on all our advertising materials and communications.

Just for Kids Parties is unique in the range of packages offered and communities served. Our Unique Selling Proposition is this:

'Just for Kids Parties has the widest range of party packages available. Our wish is to give your child the best party ever.'

(10 of 20)

One of the challenges for our marketing campaign is to find ways to highlight our superior quality of service and choice of party packages in a market that is highly price sensitive. (On a head-to-head basis against key competitors, Just for Kids Parties does not offer the cheapest prices for most types of packages.)

Target market analysis

Our typical customer (with our customers being the parents, rather than the children in this case) is typically female (we find 8 out of 10 parties are organised by the mother), and aged between 30 and 50.

While we don't know the average earnings of a typical customer, what has been surprising for us is that our typical customer is not necessarily very well off. We think this is because we started out in our business being highly competitive on price, which attracted price-sensitive customers in lower-earning suburbs. The word-of-mouth referral network means that probably two-thirds of our parties still occur in what would be the lower-earning suburbs of the city. While this provides us with a solid base, it means that our customers are more price sensitive than we would like, and we aim to focus on growing our business into the eastern suburbs.

The cultural background of our customers is incredibly diverse, reflecting the population of the city. However, again due to referral and word-of-mouth, our business has a relatively high percentage of Spanish-speaking customers.

For most customers, motivations for hiring our services are to provide the best party possible for their children and to reduce stress. The average spend per party is $250.

Competitor analysis

Looking online, over 20 kids' party companies offer entertainment within a 50-kilometre radius. Most of these companies offer some combination of face-painting, party games, pamper parties and disco parties. The other indirect competitor is the indoor play centre at the local aquatic centre, which provides a popular and affordable party venue.

Super Hero Parties is probably our fiercest competitor, and is on average 20 per cent cheaper than us. However, it doesn't have the same variety of pricing or packages and only does face-painting and games at its parties (no magic tricks, hula hoops, clowns or craft parties).

Does this competitor . . .	Super Heros	Fairies for Kids	Fabulous Parties	Indoor Play Centre
Have cheaper pricing than me?	yes	varies	no	depends
Offer longer opening hours or availability?	no	yes	no	yes
Offer specific services that I don't?	no	no	no	yes
Have better distribution or service a wider region?	yes	no	no	no
Offer a larger variety of pricing packages?	no	no	no	no
Have more expertise and a higher level of skill?	no	no	no	no
Service all the niches that I service?	no	no	no	no
Have respect and trust in the community?	yes	yes	don't know	yes
Have an active social media presence?	yes	no	yes	no
Have a good online marketing strategy?	yes	no	yes	yes
Have more capital and power to expand?	don't know	probably not	yes	yes

Summary of marketing strategies

One challenge of our business is that even when we provide excellent service, a typical non-corporate customer only uses our services once. The challenge for us is to provide easy ways for a satisfied customer to refer us to others, and also provide a range of different party experiences so that this customer will be tempted to use our service again.

Our website remains our core marketing strategy, with social media, print advertising, networking and referral mechanisms all serving to complement this strategy and drive additional traffic to our website.

Our marketing goals for 2014 are summarised below. (Specific time frames for each objective are summarised in the Planning Calendar at the back of this plan.)

Goal	Objective
Develop culturally specific niche markets, expanding Spanish-speaking and Hindi-speaking parties by 40% within 12 months	Upgrade website to select from multiple languages, starting with Spanish and Hindi as additional languages.
	Advertise in speciality community papers
Increase traffic to website to 500 hits per day	Engage a specialist in search engine optimisation to improve website rankings
	Upgrade website content to include tips about party games, face-painting and so on
	Boost Google Adwords budget to increase enquiries
Boost social media presence	Build Facebook and Instagram pages
	Start a Twitter feed
Run test for focused local advertising campaign in five key suburbs (Ainslie, Gladstone, Hatton, Preston and Sully) and measure outcomes	Distribute flyers in local shopping centres, childcare centres and community noticeboards every 8 weeks
Increase brand awareness	Get both motor vehicles painted with company logo and USP
	Sponsor local soccer club sausage sizzle
	Ensure emails, website and all marketing materials have a consistent message
Develop word-of-mouth referrals	Place flyers with discount code in visible area at every party for other parents to take
	Advertise face-painting workshops for parents so that schools can raise additional funds at their events. (These workshops are great for referrals and networking, and are a source of revenue midweek when bookings are scant.)
Build affiliate programs	Implement affiliate advertising schemes with other party-related businesses (in particular party hire and catering businesses)
Increase corporate sales by 25% from last year	Telesales campaign focusing on major retail chains
Increase conversion rate to 60% for enquiries (currently 45%)	Set up templates for email responses
	Follow up enquiries via phone within 24 hours of each enquiry. (Modify web enquiry form to make phone number a compulsory field.)
Establish a reputation for excellent, consistent customer service	Invest in sophisticated online booking system
	Increase accuracy of bookings with system of automated text messages and confirmations
	Pursue feedback forms from every events. Collate reviews and testimonials

Strategic Direction

In times of economic change and increasing globalisation, the party entertainment business is more stable than most. Our overall strategic direction is to create a business that is highly professional and the market leader in our region.

Industry analysis

According to IBISWorld Market Research, the party planning industry is highly fragmented, with the majority of party and events planners controlling less than 1 per cent of the market. Because the industry provides a discretionary service, sales are mainly driven by corporate profit, per capita disposable income and the unemployment rate. Any recessions hit the industry hard, with many companies and families holding fewer, smaller events.

(13 of 20)

The majority of companies operate on a highly localised and niche basis. The diverse tastes of customers forces industry operators to adapt their party packages, and this in turn tends to limit expansion. In addition, low industry barriers to entry allow a large number of firms to operate in the industry.

Demographic change

Parents are working harder than ever before, with an increasing rate of both parents in full-time employment. Parents are increasingly keen to minimise stress and delegate the work of hosting parties to others.

Potential competitors

In this industry, new competitors emerge all the time. Customers tend to look for entertainers in one of two different ways: Either by personal referral or by looking online. New entrants to the market can grab a fair chunk of market share quite quickly simply by having a good-looking, high-ranking website.

Government legislation

Legislation requires that all entertainers who have direct physical contact with children must have a current Working with Children Check, and some states also have recommended health and hygiene procedures in regards to face-painting. Changes in government legislation are unlikely to affect the children's entertainment business, although the Working with Children Check will probably become more stringent over time.

Sustainability and health concerns

Global trends point towards increased health consciousness and environmental sensitivity. Overall, these trends are unlikely to affect the children's entertainment industry.

The possible exceptions here could be additional expense for premium face paints (some question exists over current supplies regarding possible heavy metals in the product), and additional expense for party prizes that meet eco-packaging requirements.

Technology and offshoring

The children's entertainment industry is delightfully robust when faced with changes in technology and offshoring. The human experience of entertainment, face-painting and magic is timeless and cannot be easily replaced by a smartphone app or a computer program.

What we do best (and worst)

The main strength of Just for Kids Parties is our skill and experience as entertainers, the wide range of packages we offer (again due to our broad skills), and our understanding of our market and our customers. Our main weaknesses are in online marketing (both in websites and social media) and financial management.

A summary of our strengths and weaknesses is as follows:

	STRENGTH			WEAKNESS		Is This important to Your Business?		
	Awesome	Pretty good	Average	Not great	Terrible	Yes	Sometimes	Not Really
Sales and marketing. How does your business rate in regards to . . .								
Cold calling, direct sales or telesales?	✓							✓
Negotiating skills?		✓					✓	
Skills in social media?				✓			✓	
The ability to organise and run strong advertising campaigns?		✓				✓		
The ability to write a good press release?		✓					✓	
Finance. How does your business rate in regards to . . .								
Keeping a good set of up-to-date books?							✓	
Invoicing customers and making sure you get paid on time?					✓	✓		
Financial reporting, particularly regular Profit & Loss reports?					✓		✓	
Cashflow management and tax planning?					✓	✓		
Availability of capital and ability to pay bills on time?				✓		✓		
Management ability. How does your business rate in regards to . . .								
Depth (number of years) of experience?				✓		✓		
People-management skills?		✓				✓		
Range of experience in different business situations?				✓		✓		
People. How does your business rate in regards to . . .								
The balance and synergy of skills in the team?	✓					✓		
The vibe and morale in the workplace?	✓						✓	
Physical resources. How does your business rate in regards to?								
Physical location?			✓				✓	
Up-to-date tools and equipment?			✓			✓		
Customer service. How does your business rate in regards to?								
Ability to fulfil orders or respond to enquiries quickly?			✓			✓		
Ability to communicate well with customers?	✓					✓		
Responsiveness to customer requests?	✓					✓		
Computer systems. How does your business rate in regards to?								
Good reporting systems and sales management?			✓					✓
Ability to manage websites, custom software or any other IT requirements?				✓		✓		
Product or service. How does your business rate in regards to?								
Range of products on offer?	✓					✓		
Technical expertise and ability?	✓					✓		

Opportunities and threats

We identified several key opportunities and threats in the kids' party business overall:

(15 of 20)

✔ **An opportunity to provide consistent standards:** One of the problems facing any kids' party business is providing a consistent experience for children and their families. A major challenge is that 90 per cent of parties occur on the weekend, and so it is almost impossible to offer employees full-time employment. This means relying on casual employees, many of whom are students, and this in turn results in a high turnover of staff. The skills involved in being a good entertainer are very specific and, therefore, finding good staff is very challenging, especially as the business grows. At Just for Kids Parties, we see this recruitment issue as a challenge, but also an opportunity, because we believe we have a unique network and strategy for locating quality staff, and our own expertise helps us to set up strong training systems.

✔ **An opportunity to exploit online marketing:** The other short-term opportunity is online marketing. Not all competitors have focused on web promotion and social media, but we know from our own sales analysis that almost 80 per cent of our customers find us online.

✔ **An opportunity to expand services to time-poor parents:** Parents are increasingly time-poor, and we think there is an opportunity to provide a 'one-stop shop' service for parents. We are keen to explore the idea of aligning ourselves with a party inflatables business, and possibly providing costume hire and party extras such as piñatas, prizes or party bags.

✔ **A threat of being vulnerable to fluctuations in the economy:** The biggest threat to us is the economy. We know that whenever consumer confidence falls (as it did in the months before our recent election), people become more concerned about price. We aren't the cheapest party company and, indeed, because of our professional standards, we cannot operate a viable business if we aim to compete only on price.

✔ **A threat of large competitors with marketing clout:** The other long-term threat is if one of the major competitors based in another city develops a strong franchise model or opens up in town.

✔ **A threat of small competitors competing on price:** An ongoing threat will always be single owner-operators without the same costs as our business who open up and compete hard on price.

Summary of strategic priorities

When analysing the strengths and weaknesses of Just for Kids Parties against the opportunities and threats, the following strategies emerge:

Business SWOT Analysis		
	OPPORTUNITIES	**THREATS**
STRENGTHS	*Our key strength is our expertise in entertainment. An opportunity exists in this highly fragmented industry for any business that can provide consistency.* *We aim to exploit our expertise by setting up unique training systems for all our entertainers to ensure quality entertainment every time.* *An opportunity also exists to differentiate ourselves as 'professional'. This is something parents will pay for. We aim to exploit this opportunity by emphasising our professional service (range of packages, range of staff, robust health and hygiene practice while face-painting, and so on).*	*Our main threat is the emergence of a competitor with a similar strategy, or a competitor who seeks to copy our main strength, which is our systems.* *We need to be vigilant to this threat, ensuring employees sign restriction of trade agreements and guarding the confidentiality of our training and recruitment systems.* *We also need to focus on building strong word-of-mouth referral networks, which will help counteract the entry into the market of a strong competitor.*
WEAKNESSES	*A major weakness for us is that neither owner is particularly savvy with social media or websites, and yet probably 80 per cent of our enquiries come through this channel.* *We need to improve our skills in this area so that we can take advantage of this opportunity.*	*One of the threats in this industry is price pressure and, therefore, reduced margins. (Parents are very price sensitive.) This threat forms an unhappy combination with our relatively poor financial management skills.* *We need to prioritise putting good financial systems in place and setting up quarterly review meetings with our financial advisor.*

(17 of 20)

Managing risk

A risk analysis identified the risks outlined in the following table. (Note: The schedule for taking action to deal with each of these risks is outlined in the Action Calendar at the back of this plan.)

Risk	Details of Risk	Planned Action
Financial risk	Low margins on many of our base party packages	Focus more on marketing of premium packages where margins are higher
		Recruit entertainers from a more diverse range of locations so less travel involved
		Look at ways to increase margins (such as add-on products, costume hire or piñatas)
	Poor cashflow	Get additional help with Cashflow Projection reports
Risk of IP getting copied	A competitor imitating our brand	Register trademark for business name and business logo
	Ex-employees starting up in competition	Draft formal confidentiality agreements with non-competition clauses
Risk of litigation	Risk of faulty equipment	Implement procedures for equipment checks on all disco equipment every 13 weeks; product and public liability insurance policies are also in place
	Risk of employee accident while onsite	Ensure insurance policy covers both employees and casual entertainers
	Risk of improper behaviour towards children by employee or casual entertainer	Ensure Working with Children Checks in place for all; follow up at least two separate referees before employing staff; ensure diligent follow up of all parent feedback
Risk of fines	No risks identified in regards to planning regulations	No action required at present
	Risk of contravening employment law	Ensure employment agreements in place in regards to pay and conditions, and all approved by accountant

Summary of Goals

Our main goal for the next 12 months is to pursue aggressive sales growth. We aim to achieve this by additional investment in marketing (particularly online) and through building cultural and geographical niche markets.

At the same time, we aim to consolidate the finances of our business to provide a solid base for the future. We also need to focus on the continual creation of systems for our business — recruitment systems, training systems, booking systems, party format systems and so on — so that we can move towards our ultimate goal of creating a franchise model.

The following yearly calendar planner summarises our key goals. A more detailed month-by-month action plan can be found at the back of this plan.

(19 of 20)

Date	July	August	September	October	November	December	January	February	March	April	May	June
Week 1	Enter budgets in accounting system	Review Google Adwords campaign stats	Organise advertising on vehicles	Review Google Adwords campaign stats	Review all staff agreements and Working with Children Checks	Review Google Adwords campaign stats		Review Google Adwords campaign stats		Review Google Adwords campaign stats	Review all staff agreements and Working with Children Checks	Review Google Adwords campaign stats
Week 2	Monthly Profit & Loss review meeting	Monthly Profit & Loss review meeting	Quarterly budget review / Monthly Profit & Loss review meeting	Monthly Profit & Loss review meeting	Monthly Profit & Loss review meeting	Quarterly budget review / Monthly Profit & Loss review meeting	Monthly Profit & Loss review meeting	Monthly Profit & Loss review meeting	Quarterly budget review / Monthly Profit & Loss review meeting	Monthly Profit & Loss review meeting	Monthly Profit & Loss review meeting	Quarterly budget review / Monthly Profit & Loss review meeting
Week 3	Review all insurance policies in light of products/public liability	Set up email templates for all enquiries	Set up Facebook and Instagram pages	Initiate local advertising campaign test suburbs	Look into registration of trademark/logo	Review competitive analysis	Review local advertising test campaign	Review pricing packages and structure		Review local advertising test campaign	Meet with accountant to discuss finance for growth	Review competitive analysis
Week 4	Sign up new SEO contractor for website / Explore affiliate party partners	Commission website upgrade to include additional languages	Initiate advertising campaign in local newspapers (language-specific) / Measure conversion rates for enquiries and report on same	Write up specs for online booking system	Follow up online booking system	Measure conversion rates for enquiries and report on same	Look at party add ons (party bags, pinatas and so on)		Measure conversion rates for enquiries and report on same	Commence formal business plan for next year	Review customer feedback mechanisms and customer satisfaction reports	
Ongoing	Corporate telesales campaign, work on system documentation	Corporate telesales work on system documentation	Corporate telesales, social media postings, work on system documentation	Corporate telesales, social media postings, work on system documentation	Corporate telesales social media postings, work on system documentation	Corporate telesales, social media postings, work on system documentation	Corporate telesales, social media postings, work on system documentation	Corporate telesales, social media postings, work on system documentation	Corporate telesales, social media postings, documentation	Corporate telesales, social media postings, work on system documentation	Corporate telesales, social media postings, work on system documentation	Corporate telesales, social media postings, work on system documentation

Index

• A •

accounting software
  exporting financials to, 125
  when to use, 260
accounts payable, 181, 187, 189, 192
accounts receivable
  managing, 73, 261–62
  ratio, 285–86
  showing in Cashflow Projection, 184–185
action plan
  checklist, 278
  creating, 256, 290–292
  example of, 347
  importance of, 17, 256
  risk-management, 290
  template for creating, 273
advertising
  budgets, 194
  customer service, 239
  marketing cycle, 22
  online, 241–242
  strategies, 230–235
  tracking referrals, 241, 242
  your brand, 223
advice
  business advisory centres, 11, 270, 324
  importance of, 324
  industry associations, 129, 164, 270, 272
  specialists, 11
American Express forum, 130
angel investors, 75
annual expenses, 125
appendix (sample plan), 327–347
Apple, 34, 79
assets
  management strategies for, 69, 73
  on Balance Sheet, 197
  owned personally, 63
  versus expenses, 61
assumptions, justifying, 284, 305, 323
audience, tailoring your plan to, 10–11, 23, 327
AutoSum command, 122, 298

• B •

bad debts, 261
Balance Sheet
  defined, 196
  historical, 17
  Projections, 196–198, 284
  versus Cashflow report, 197
  when to include, 276, 283
bank accounts. See cash management
barriers to entry, 43, 247, 341
behavioural characteristics, analysing, 225
benchmarking
  as a way of reducing risk, 164
  how to do it, 128–132
  Profit & Loss Projections, 283
  sales targets, 227
  services, 129
billable hours, calculating, 86, 88
bookkeeping equation, 197
borrowing. See finance, loans
brainstorming marketing strategies, 231
branding
  building, 212
  creating a message, 337
  your website, 223
break-even analysis
  calculating, 169–178
  changing, 174
  formula, 170

break-even analysis *(continued)*
  including personal expenses, 171
  template, 177
  when to include, 176, 283
budgeting and forecasting
  comparing against actuals, 16
  creating a formal budget, 193–196
  definition of, 127
  for expenses, 119–144, 196
  for marketing, 231
  for sales, 86, 89
  for start-up, 59–76
  goal setting, 194
  linking to financial projections, 304
  psychology of, 21, 142
  sales versus finance, 21
  techniques, 142
  versus actuals, 195, 240
  versus Profit & Loss Projections, 193
business advisory centres, 11, 270, 324
business angels, 75
business benchmarking. *See* benchmarking
business environment
  barriers to entry, 43, 247, 341
  change management, 243–257
  competitor analysis, 39–52
  customer analysis, 225, 338
  industry analysis, 244–248
Business Expense template, 121, 124, 125
business insurance, 269
business finance. *See* finance, loans
business models. *See also* strategic
    advantage
  assessing, 4, 147, 160, 162
  cost-based pricing, 78
  defining, 15
  performance quiz, 249
  scoring, 25
  sparking inspiration, 323, 325
business names protecting, 265
business planning process. *See also*
    business plans
  different paths, 202
  doing a course, 11
  how much time required, 9
  how often to update, 15–18

information and resources, 11, 129, 164,
    270, 324
long-term vision, 201–218
planning cycle, 18
process of, 9–26
pulling together different elements,
    275–294
when to start, 10
business planning software
  benefits of, 12–13, 197
  versus templates, 13
business plans. *See also* business planning
    process
  avoiding jargon, 316, 324
  calendar for action, 292
  capability platform, 119–197, 219–241
  checklist for, 277–278
  completion checklist, 319–325
  cover sheets, 309
  different formats, 10
  elements of, 14, 275–294
  financial platform, 147–197
  formatting, 309–317
  interactive elements, 315
  length of, 9
  one-page plans, 22
  period for plan, 119, 161
  protecting confidentiality, 282
  sample, 327–347
  strategic platform, 27–55, 243–273
  structure of, 14–16, 275–293
  table of contents, 310
  templates, 12
  who they are for, 10–11, 23, 327
Business Plans Pro, 12
business scorecard, 25–26
business strategy. *See* strategy
business structure, choosing, 267
buzzwords, 316, 324

 • C •

calendar-based planning, 292
capability platform, 119–197, 219–241
capital contributions, 186
capital expenditure, 182

cash versus profit, 180, 263
cash balance, predicting, 190–191
cash break-even analysis, 170, 177
cash management
  risk of not managing, 262
  sustainable growth, 191–192
  things that eat up cash, 186
Cashflow Projections. *See also* financial
    projections
  analysing cash inflows, 184
  analysing cash outflows, 186
  creating, 179–192
  example of, 335
  how often to update, 16
  showing supplier payments, 189
  versus Balance Sheet Projections, 197
  versus break-even, 176
  versus budgets, 127
  versus Profit & Loss Projections, 127,
    179, 182
  when to include, 284
cell references, 298
cells (in financial projections)
  formatting, 300
  merging, 301
  naming, 116, 151
change, preparing for, 243–257, 290
channel analysis, 226
charts
  copying into Word, 313
  inserting in your plan, 306
checklists
  business plan elements, 278
  Gross Profit Projection, 159
  start-up expenses, 62
  systems for growth, 211
  variable costs, 99
  what to include in your plan, 277–278,
    319–325
  where to find online, 3
circuit layout rights, 264
climate change, 243, 253
closing inventory, forecasting, 187
cloud-based software, 13
collateral (family home), 73, 74
columns (in Excel), freezing, 301

comfort zone, avoiding, 230
commissions, 99
company description, 279, 281, 330
company names, checking, 266
company structure
  directors salaries, 170
  explained, 267
  limited liability, 267
company tax, 134, 158, 188
comparing budgets against actuals, 20–21,
    195, 240, 273, 291
competitor-based pricing, 78
competitor analysis
  barriers to entry, 247
  checking quality of, 320
  example of, 46, 338
  future competitors, 41, 43, 251
  grouping, 41
  head-to-head, 41, 42–43, 47
  how to do it, 39–55
  importance of, 40
  industry trends, 42, 244
  online competitors, 44, 251
  summarising, 227
  where to include in your plan, 220, 278
  worksheet, 45, 47
competitors. *See also* competitor
    analysis
  differentiating yourself from, 27,
    209, 221
competitive advantage. *See also* strategic
    advantage
  summarising, 48–51, 53, 319
  understanding, 28
  versus risk, 52
  versus strategic advantage, 50
competitive-based pricing, 80
complaint procedures, 211
conditional formatting, 302
confidentiality agreements, 266
consistency, guaranteeing, 210–211
constraints to growth, 213
consultants
  as part of management team, 16, 215,
    249, 255
  as source of advice, 11

content management systems, 233
contingency planning, 74, 87, 260, 269
continuous improvement, 18, 20
contractors
  as a variable cost, 98–99, 107
  versus employees, 216
conversion rates, measuring, 242
copyright, 264–265
corporate branding, 212, 222–223, 337
corporate speak, 53, 316, 327
cost leadership strategy, 48
cost of goods sold
  as a start-up cost, 61
  understanding, 61, 97–103
  versus inventory purchases, 187
cost-based pricing, 78, 80
costs. *See also* expenses
  calculating, 97–103
  for manufacturers, 102
  for products, 113, 148, 176
  for services provided, 99
  incoming versus outgoing, 100
  reducing, 68
  valuing labour, 103
  varying exchange rates, 101
  when importing, 101
  worksheets for calculating, 100
cover sheets, 309
creative business, limitations of, 214
credit. *See* customer credit
credit cards
  as a form of finance, 74
  dangers of, 137, 143
credit insurance, 262
credit limits, 261
crowdfunding, 75
custom manufacture, 104
customer credit
  cash management, 184
  how this affects cashflow, 180
  importance of credit checks, 261
customer service, 211, 220, 238
customers
  analysing growth, 244
  analysis, 225, 338
  defining your market, 223–224

importance of feedback, 227, 239
lapsed, 236
profiling customer needs, 225
purchase frequency, 224
template for analysis, 225

dashboard reporting, 23
debt collection, 184, 261, 262
debt finance, 73, 75
decimals, hiding, 300
delegating, how to do it well, 218
demand, being realistic about,
  37, 95
demographics
  customer analysis, 224–225
  impact of change, 251
designs, protecting, 265
difference, defining yours, 27, 209, 221
differential pricing, 83–84
differentiation strategy, 48
direct competitors, 41
direct costs. *See* fixed costs
director liability, 268
discounts
  prompt payment, 85
  using carefully, 85
  volume-based, 103
distribution and delivery
  costing imports, 101
  entry barriers, 43, 247
  pricing strategies, 81
  strategies for, 49
  summarising methods in your
    plan, 278
dollar signs, displaying, 300
domain names, 223, 265
dreams. *See also* business models,
  vision
  being realistic about, 95, 248, 320
  encouraging, 1, 26, 323, 325
  expressing as goals, 15, 159, 212
  realising, 159, 207
dummies.com, 4
Dunn & Bradstreet, 130

• E •

eBay, 233
eco-opportunities, 253
e-commerce shopping carts, 233
economies of scale, 34, 103
economy, analysing change in, 252
elevator speeches
  crafting, 52–55, 319
  versus strategic advantage statement, 35
email templates, 211
employees
  art of delegating, 218
  benefits of hiring, 205, 216
  calculating cost of, 217
  complying with legislation, 216, 270
  minimising risk, 271
  planning for, 215–218
  recruitment of, 216
  versus contractors, 216
entrepreneurialism
  as a role, 207
  cultivating, 1, 26, 205
entry barriers, 43, 247
environment
  analysing trends, 224, 244, 253, 290
  benefits of being green, 253
  competitive, 43, 50
  complying with legislation, 272
  pace of change, 21
equipment (new), 186
equity finance, 75
equity (on Balance Sheet), 197, 284
ethics and values statements, 282
Excel
  adding up figures, 122, 298
  AutoSum feature, 122, 298
  business plan templates, 12
  checking for accuracy, 305, 321
  conditional formatting, 302
  copying data, 299
  formatting tips, 300
  freezing data, 301
  graphs and charts, 306, 313
  hiding data, 303

  how-to tips, 297–307
  linking to Word, 311
  linking worksheets, 150, 154, 303
  merging cells, 301
  naming cells, 151
  naming worksheets, 148
  Paste Link command, 151
  relationships between expenses, 127
  using formulas, 304
exchange rates
  allowing for changes, 101
  modelling, 167, 244
exclusive distribution, 29
Executive Summary, 279, 281, 330
exit barriers, 43, 247, 341
exit plans, 213, 324
expansion. *See* growing your business
expenses
  10 per cent rule, 128
  being realistic about, 128
  budgeting for, 22, 119–144, 194, 260
  checking against goals, 322
  comparing to industry average, 131
  cutting back, 68, 144, 196
  forecasting, 119–144
  irregular, 128
  paid from personal funds, 63
  relationships between, 127
  start-up, 59–75
  versus assets, 61
export costs, 101
exposure (customer credit), 262

• F •

Facebook, 237, 315
family
  borrowing against home, 74
  borrowing from, 76
  commitments, 203
  importance of involving, 12
  looking after relationships, 52, 76
  offering home as equity, 74
feasibility studies, 33, 226, 340
Ferriss, Timothy, 213

figures, double-checking, 321
fill handle (Excel), 299
finance. *See also* loans
  applying for, 284
  comparing costs, 70
  crowdfunding, 75
  debt finance, 75
  equity finance, 75
  for cashflow difficulties, 192
  loans and leases, 73
financial planning cycle, 20, 162
financial projections. *See also* Cashflow
    Projections, Profit & Loss Projections
  checking, 321
  conditional formatting, 302
  how far to go, 18
  how long they take, 15
  inserting into Word doc, 310–311
  presentation of, 283, 300
  updating automatically, 148
  versus financial results, 17
  what to include, 15, 276–277
financial ratios. *See* ratios
financial risk
  bad debts, 261
  inventory management, 263
  low profitability, 260
  mitigating, 260–264
  poor cashflow, 262
fixed expenses
  defined, 98, 173
  per unit sold, 176
  personal, 142
  versus variable costs, 100, 121
fonts, choosing, 314
forecasting. *See* budgeting and forecasting
formatting
  as a PDF, 315
  financial projections, 300, 310
  your business plan, 309–317
formulas, copying, 299
franchise model
  as a goal, 202
  benefits of, 210
  creating your own, 206–207
  image management, 222

fraud, detecting, 117
freezing columns or rows, 301
future competitors, 43, 244
Future Competitor worksheet, 44

• *G* •

Gerber, Michael, 207
getting help
  business advisory centres, 11, 270, 324
  consultants, 11
  importance of, 324
  industry associations, 129, 164, 270, 272
  specialists, 11
globalisation, 245
goals. *See also* dreams
  checking against financials, 321
  examples of, 339, 346
  financial, 159
  how to set, 229, 291
  marketing, 228–230
  overall, 212, 332
  personal spending, 142
  SMART, 229, 291
  translating into action, 290
  versus objectives, 291
Goding, Seth, 49
Google Adwords, 233
Google Docs, 297
government legislation, 243, 245, 251
graphs
  copying into Word, 313
  inserting in your plan, 306
green trends, 253
gross profit
  calculating, 104–109
  defined, 160
  per hour, 110
  per unit, 113
gross profit margins
  adjusting, 260
  calculating, 105, 173
  understanding, 117
Gross Profit Projections
  checking, 159
  creating, 109–117

example of, 332
worksheets, 116, 153
growing your business
  building systems, 210
  by employing others, 205
  creating a vision, 206
  deciding not to, 203
  limitations, 204, 213
  perils of, 181, 192
  sustainable growth, 260
  techniques for growth, 201–218
GST
  in Cashflow Projections, 181
  in Profit & Loss Projections,
      134, 189
  in sales forecasts, 91, 92
  start-up expenses, 61

● *H* ●

habits, personal spending, 142
hats, wearing different ones, 209
head-to-head competitors, 47
hiding data on worksheets, 303
hire purchase, benefits of, 193
holidays, allowing for, 87, 128
home offices, 272
hourly charge-out rate, calculating, 107
how to use this book, 2
hybrid pricing, 80, 82

● *I* ●

Identifying Variable Costs checklist, 99
image of business
  building, 212, 222
  franchises, 222
Income Statement. *See* Profit & Loss
    reports
income. *See also* budgets, profit
  allowing for seasonal changes, 140
  benchmarking, 131–132
  defining how much is enough, 136,
      170–171, 203
  estimating, 86–92, 159, 164

from employment, 136
from loans, 185
goals, 212
identifying sources, 136–137
measuring, 213
versus cash, 180
versus profit, 66
income-protection insurance, 269
incoming costs, 100
Indiegogo, 75
indirect costs. *See* fixed expenses
industrial relations, 216, 270
industry analysis
  as a means of backing up
      assumptions, 324
  declining industries, 248
  example of, 340
  future competitors, 44
  how often, 17
  how to do it, 244–248
  trends, 247
  worksheet, 245
industry associations, 129, 164, 270, 272
industry benchmarking. *See* benchmarking
injury, guarding against, 270
insolvency, 268
inspiration, 23, 26, 40, 212, 279, 280,
      323, 325
insurance, 268–269
intellectual property
  protecting, 259, 264–267
  strategic advantage, 29
interest expense
  calculating, 72
  sensitivity of target market, 225
  showing on financial projections, 72
  showing on Profit & Loss Projections,
      135
inventions, protecting, 265
inventory
  at start-up, 60
  forecasting, 187
  managing quantities held, 263
  on financial projections, 187
  turnover ratio, 287
  versus cost of sales, 187

investment capital
  angel investors, 75
  attracting, 5
  bank loans, 75
  comparing costs, 70
  crowdfunding, 75
  from family, 76
  leases, 73
  personal assets as, 74
  tailoring your plan for, 10, 327
irregular payments, 128

• *J* •

jargon, 316, 324
job costings
  for big projects, 109
  for custom jobs, 104
  for manufacturers, 102–103
  importance of consistency, 212
  linking between worksheets, 113, 148
Jobs, Steve, 34

• *K* •

keywords, 235, 241
Kickstarter, 75
KPIs, sales, 228

• *L* •

labour
  allocating to roles, 207–210
  budgeting for, 95
  calculating cost of, 217
  valuing, 103
language
  avoiding jargon, 316, 324
  checking for clarity, 316
  choosing words, 53
laws, complying with, 270–272
leases (on property), 269
leasing
  as a form of finance, 73
  benefits of, 193
  versus buying outright, 68, 193

legal advice, 11, 265, 267
legal structures, 267
liabilities (on Balance Sheet), 197
liability (personal), limiting, 267–272
licence requirements, 270, 272
life cycle of a business, 44
lifestyle issues, 202–203, 214, 252
limit of sustainable growth, 192
limitations to growth, 213
limiting liability, 267–272
line of credit finance, 74
LinkedIn, 237
linking worksheets, 150, 154, 303
litigation, protecting yourself against, 268
LivePlan.com, 13
living expenses. *See* personal expenses
Loan Calculator template, 72
loan repayments. *See also* loans
  affordability of, 68
  calculating, 70
  how they affect cashflow, 180
  including on financial projections, 72, 135, 182, 189, 285
  schedules, 70
loans. *See also* finance, loan repayments
  borrowing from family, 76
  security against, 74
  showing on financial projections, 185
loyalty schemes, 83, 241

• *M* •

management and leadership
  analysing capabilities, 249–253
  financial, 169–195, 262
  managing change, 243–248
  managing risk, 259–274
  operations, 289
  people and roles, 201–215, 288, 336
  playing to your strengths, 322
  risk management, 259–273
manufacturers
  costings, 102, 113, 148, 176
  custom products, 104
  gross margins, 108
  Gross Profit Projections, 112

pricing strategies, 81
procedures, 211
start-up budget, 60
variable costs, 98
margins. *See* gross profit margins, net
    profit margins
market (for products or services)
    analysing, 338
    forecasting sales for, 89
    researching, 33, 226, 340
    testing, 95
    understanding, 41
market segments, 89
marketing budgets
    allocating, 231
    matching with financials, 289
marketing plan
    creating, 219–242
    competitive analysis, 227
    example of, 337
    market research, 226
    sales strategies, 230–238
    structure of, 220
    what to include, 289
marketing plan cycle, 21
marketing strategies, 230
MAUS MasterPlan, 12, 23
mission statements, 15, 277, 279–280, 331
monthly expenses, 122, 124, 128
moving annual turnover analysis,
    277, 285
multi-level pricing, 84

• *N* •

negative amounts, highlighting, 302
net profit
    benchmarking, 131
    calculating, 72, 105, 134, 158
    deciding what's reasonable,
        159, 160–162
net profit margins, calculating, 160
networking with others, 130, 236–238
new equipment, 180
Nice Classification System, 265
niche businesses, 25–26, 31, 46, 49, 321

no-frills pricing, 81
non-competition provisions, 267
non-disclosure agreements, 282
non-financial performance measures
    conversion rates, 234, 242
    one-page dashboard, 23
    referral tracking, 234, 241
    sales goals, 228
    website performance, 233, 241–242
    work/life balance, 202–203

• *O* •

objectives. *See also* goals
    costing, 321
    setting, 229
    summarising, 278
    versus goals, 291
Occupational Health & Safety. *See*
    Workplace Health & Safety
offshoring of labour, 44
one-off expenses. *See* start-up expenses
one-page business plans, 22
online resources, 12
online success, analysing, 233, 241–242
OpenOffice, 297
operating expense versus start-up
    expense, 64–68
operational plans
    distribution, 43, 49, 81, 101, 247
    people and roles, 215
    plan structure, 278
    what to include, 288–289
opportunities
    analysing, 251–253
    exploiting, 255
outgoing costs, 100
overheads. *See* fixed expenses
owner-operator businesses
    assessing net profit, 160–162
    benefits of 202–203
    budgeting for owner salaries,
        63, 135–144
    budgeting for tax, 158, 188
    costing services, 107
    different roles within, 207–209

owner-operator businesses *(continued)*
  difficulty expanding from, 213–214
  factoring owner salaries into
    break-even, 170
  legal structures, 267
  managing personal expenses, 135–141,
    171
  people plans, 215–217

• *p* •

package pricing, 82
partnership structure, 267
Paste Link command, 151, 154, 304, 311
Paste Special command, 150, 304
patents, 265
PDF format, saving your plan as, 315
Peerbackers, 75
people plan
  example of, 336
  employee hiring decisions,
    216–217
  Task Allocation template, 216
  what to include in your plan,
    16, 215–218, 288
percentages, formatting, 301
performance measures
  benchmarking, 128–132, 227, 283
  conversion rates, 234, 242
  gross profit margins, 105, 173, 260
  net profit margins, 72, 105, 134,
    160–162
  one-page dashboard, 23
  referral tracking, 234, 241
  reviewing, 23
  sales goals, 228
  website performance, 233, 241–242
permit requirements, 270
personal liability, 268
personal break-even point, 170
personal expenses
  break-even point, 171
  budgeting for, 59, 63, 119, 135–144
  different kinds, 143
  managing, 264
  showing on projections, 182, 191

Personal Expenses Worksheet, 139
personal funds used for start-up, 63
personal guarantees, 268
personal tax. *See* tax
phone scripts, 211
plain English tips, 316
plan of action. *See* action plan
planhq.com, 13
planning regulations, 272
point of difference
  articulating, 221
  as a strategy, 48
  example of, 330
positioning statement, 50–51, 53, 79,
    227, 337
Pozible, 75
premium pricing, 80
presenting your plan well, 309–317
press releases, 235
pricing strategies
  cost-based, 78
  cost leadership, 48
  differential pricing, 83
  hybrid pricing, 80–83
  monitoring, 85
  no-frills pricing, 81
  overview of your choices, 77–85
  package pricing, 82
  positioning against competitors, 40, 78–79
  quantity-break pricing, 83
  standardised, 212
  strategic advantage, 34
  value-based pricing, 79–80
principal (on loans), explained, 72
procedures, importance of, 211
product branding, 222
product costings, 101, 102, 113, 148, 176
production labour, 98, 108
production plan, 289
profit. *See also* gross profit, net profit
  versus cash, 180, 263
Profit & Loss reports, 17
Profit & Loss Projections. *See also*
    financial projections
  calculating, 147–167
  checking, 159, 321

example of, 333
forecasting sales, 153
format of, 156
how often to update, 16
linking to budgets, 304
showing start-up expense, 67
testing how robust it is, 165
variable costs, 154
versus budgets, 127, 193
versus Cashflow Projections,
    179, 182
what-if scenarios, 206
what expenses to include, 121
profitability. *See also* break-even
    point
  analysing, 67, 107, 160, 162, 240
  maintaining, 260
projects, costing, 109
psychographics, analysing, 225
psychology of budgets, 22, 194
public liability insurance, 269
public relations, 235

• *Q* •

quality assurance, 270
quantity-break pricing, 83

• *R* •

ranking (search engines), 233, 241
rate of return, 162
ratios
  accounts receivable, 286
  in your plan, 285
  moving annual turnover analysis, 285
  stock turnover, 287
raw materials, 61, 98, 99
REDgroup, 261
referral sources, tracking, 241
registered designs, 265
relationships, 52, 76
rental property income, 136
renting versus buying equipment, 69
repairs and maintenance, 65
repayments. *See* loan repayments

resource requirements
  equipment, 73, 193
  finance, 59–76
  people, 11, 201–218
restricting employees, 266
retailers
  start-up budget, 60
  variable costs, 98
return on investment, 162–163
risk management
  assessing risks, 52, 161, 163
  creating plan for, 259–274, 278, 290
  example of plan, 345
  mitigating risks, 271
  risks versus gain, 31
  strategies for, 17
  template for plan, 273
ROI, 162–163
roles
  debt collection, 262
  defining in your business, 207, 215, 288
  example of role planning, 336
  task allocation template, 215
  within a business, 207
rows, freezing (Excel), 301

• *S* •

salaries (owners), 63, 135–144, 170
sales. *See also* sales targets
  budgeting for, 194
  forecasting, 89–95, 115
  managing collections, 185
  setting goals, 228–230
sales strategies
  advertising, 234–235
  brainstorming, 231
  different kinds, 230
  establishing, 228
  evaluating, 234, 239–242
  marketing materials, 232–234
  networking, 236–238
  public relations, 235–236
  ranking, 231–232
  social media, 236–238
  websites, 232–234

sales targets. *See also* sales
adjusting, 260
breaking into detail, 228
online performance, 233
setting, 227, 232
versus actuals, 240
sales templates, 91, 92, 114
sales tax
in Cashflow Projections, 181
in Profit & Loss Projections, 134, 189
in sales forecasts, 91, 92
start-up expenses, 61
savings, protecting, 259
scenario analysis
break-even point, 175
example of, 333
how to do it, 164–167
how-to video, 164
long-term growth, 206
manipulating, 10
using Excel, 305
variable costs, 117
versus projections, 194
when to include, 284
Scenario Analysis Worksheet, 164
scoring your business model, 25–26, 32–35
search engine optimisation, 233
seasonal variations
budgeting for expenses, 128
cash management, 184
sales forecasts, 91
security (on loans), 73–74
self-employment, benefits of, 203
selling your business, 324
service businesses
costing your services, 99
Gross Profit Projection, 110
pricing your services, 82
template for income forecast, 112
variable costs, 98, 107
shareholders, 267
shipping costs, 99
situational analysis. *See* SWOT analysis
skills, rating your own, 249
SMART goals, 229, 239
SME benchmarking tool, 130

social media, 236, 237
social responsibility, 282
sole trader structure, 267
specialist advice
importance of, 261, 271
industry associations, 272
reviewing your plan, 324
spell-checking tips, 315
sponsored advertising, 233
sponsorships, 236, 238
spreadsheets. *See* Excel
staffing requirements. *See* people plan
stakeholders
customising your plan for, 285, 327
finance options, 73
start-up expenses
budgeting for, 59–76
defined, 65
on financial projections, 186
reducing, 68
versus operating expense, 64–68, 120
worksheet, 61
stock. *See* inventory
stock turnover ratio, 287
strategic advantage
customer demand, 37
examples of, 28, 30, 330
growing over time, 36
identifying, 28, 32
key attributes, 33
measured against risk, 31, 52
pricing, 34
retailers, 29
scorecard, 30, 34
statement, 35
summarising, 277, 319
versus competitive advantage, 50
versus unique selling point, 221
strategic alliances, 238
strategic planning
change management, 243–257
example of, 340, 344
identifying strategic advantage, 27–38

risk management, 259–274
sales, 230–238
SWOT analysis, 253–256
strengths
  analysing, 248–250, 254
  exploiting yours, 322
structure of written plan, 276–291
subcontract labour, 98, 99, 107
success. *See* performance measures
supplier credit, 189
sustainable growth, 69, 192
SWOT analysis
  creating, 253–256
  example of, 342
  template, 254
  translating into goals, 290
synergy, example of, 36
systems, 218, 239–242

table of contents, 310
target market
  channel analysis, 226
  defining, 220, 223–224
  reviewing, 338
targets. *See* goals
task allocation template, 215
tax. *See also* GST, sales tax, VAT
  budgeting for, 134, 144
  for partnerships, 188
  for sole traders, 188
  how tax payments affect cashflow, 180
  on financial projections, 158, 188
  planning for, 68, 134, 158, 180, 188
technician role, 207
technological change, 44, 245, 251
templates
  Bplans, 12
  break-even analysis, 177
  business expenses, 121
  Cashflow Projections, 190
  customer analysis, 225
  for emails, 211
  labour costs, 217
  loan calculator, 70

non-disclosure agreements, 282
people and roles, 215
personal expenses, 139
risk action plan, 273
Sales Forecast worksheet, 92
scenario analysis, 164
SWOT analysis, 254
true cost of labour, 217
versus business planning
    software, 13
  where to find, 4, 12
The E-Myth, 207
threats, guarding against, 255
time frames, managing, 14, 229, 257, 273,
    291, 321
top ten sales strategies,
    230–232
trade secrets, 265
trademarks, 265
trading while insolvent, 268
trends
  demographics, 330
  economy, 43
  environmental, 341
  industry analysis, 15, 247, 290, 330
  sales, 91, 323, 335
true cost of labour template, 217
Twitter, 237

under-capitalisation, 64, 143
Unique Selling Proposition
  articulating, 221
  example of, 337
  versus strategic advantage, 221
unit costings. *See* product costings
URLs, choosing, 223

value-based pricing, 79, 80
values statement, 277, 282, 331
variable costs
  explained, 97–99, 172
  identifying, 99

variable costs *(continued)*
  modelling, 117
  percentage of sales, 114
  personal, 142
  Profit & Loss Projection, 154
  service businesses, 100, 107
  versus fixed expenses, 100, 121
variances, analysing, 21, 195, 240, 273, 291
VAT
  in Cashflow Projections, 181
  in Profit & Loss Projections, 134, 189
  in sales forecasts, 91, 92
  start-up expenses, 61
veechicurtis.com.au, 4
video content in your plan, 315
videos
  cashflow projection, 190
  creating formulas, 117
  Excel tips, 297–307
  naming cells, 152
vision
  building, 201–208
  creating a franchise, 207
  nurturing, 1, 26, 205, 323, 325
vision statements, 281

wages
  budgeting for, 128, 132
  company directors, 333
  on Profit & Loss Projections, 161
  oncosts, 127

Watson, Don, 280
weaknesses, analysing, 248–250
websites
  analysing traffic, 242
  branding, 223
  backing up, 233
  choosing an address, 265
  for this book, 4
  planning for, 232
wholesale price versus retail price, 81
wholesalers, start-up budget, 60
work/lifestyle balance, 163, 202–203, 214, 252
workbook, definition of, 149
working capital, 73
  ensuring you have enough, 64
  getting a loan for, 73
  monitoring, 179–193
  preserving, 68, 69, 72, 83, 192
working week. *See* billable hours
Workplace Health & Safety, 270–272
worksheets
  business performance, 249
  Cashflow Projections, 190
  Industry Analysis, 245
  linking, 150, 154, 303
  naming, 148
Wozniak, Steve, 34

your time, allowing for, 160, 163
YouTube, 237, 315

About the Author

Veechi Curtis is passionate about business and the potential that people have to achieve financial independence and realise their dreams.

Born in Scotland, Veechi attended university in Bathurst, New South Wales, where she completed her degree in accountancy and business management. She has been a small-business consultant for more than 15 years, working with hundreds of businesses over this time.

Running a business in theory is very different from running a business in practice. In *Creating a Business Plan For Dummies*, Veechi draws from the experience of running her own businesses, mentoring dozens of start-ups, and many years working as a director for a local non-profit organisation.

Veechi is also the author of *MYOB Software For Dummies*, *QuickBooks For Dummies* and *Bookkeeping For Dummies*.

Veechi has three children and lives with her husband in the beautiful Blue Mountains of New South Wales. Feel free to send Veechi a message, or ask a question about this book, via her website at www.veechicurtis.com.au.

Author's Acknowledgements

Thanks to the John Wiley editorial team, particularly my beady-eyed editor Charlotte Duff, acquisitions editor extraordinaire Clare Dowdell, and 'it-has-to-be-on-time' project manager Dani Karvess.

Many thanks also to Rob Ashley from PwC Private Clients for his expert and thoughtful technical review, as well as Aja Stuart and Abby Veitch for their 'on-road testing' of the manuscript during development.

Thanks also to Robin Jaworski for her assistance in researching international differences.

Publisher's Acknowledgements

We're proud of this book; please send us your comments through our online registration form located at dummies.custhelp.com.

Some of the people who helped bring this book to market include the following:

Acquisitions, Editorial and Media Development

Project Editor: Charlotte Duff

Acquisitions Editor: Clare Dowdell

Editorial Manager: Dani Karvess

Production

Graphics: diacriTech

Technical Reviewer: Rob Ashley

Proofreader: Catherine Spedding, Jenny Scepanovic

Indexer: Veechi Curtis

The author and publisher would like to thank the following copyright holders, organisations and individuals for their permission to reproduce copyright material in this book:

- **Cover image:** © iStockphoto.com/alphaspirit.
- Screenshots reprinted by permission from Microsoft Corporation.
- **Figure 1-3:** © MAUS Business Systems, Maus Masterplan is produced by MAUS Business Systems. MAUS Masterplan is the premier business planning software solution.
- **Table 7-1:** © MAUS Business Systems, Maus Masterplan is produced by MAUS Business Systems. MAUS Masterplan is the premier business planning software solution.
- **Figures 10-4 and 12-2:** © MYOB Australia.
- **Appendix image of watercolour circles:** © iStockphoto.com/crisserbug.
- **Appendix image of balloons:** © iStockphoto.com/MariaPavlova.

Every effort has been made to trace the ownership of copyright material. Information that enables the publisher to rectify any error or omission in subsequent editions is welcome. In such cases, please contact the Legal Services section of John Wiley & Sons Australia, Ltd.

Notes

Notes

Notes

Made in the USA
Middletown, DE
20 April 2021